GLASTONBURY

BISHOPAUCKLANDCOLLEGE
LIBRARY

ACCESSION 212290
DEWEY 781.66
AUB

GLASTONBURY
AN ORAL HISTORY OF THE MUSIC, MUD AND MAGIC

Crispin Aubrey & John Shearlaw
Foreword by Michael Eavis

EBURY
PRESS

In the spirit of Glastonbury Festival's support for good causes, a donation from the proceeds of this book will be given to a charity nominated by the festival organisers.

This edition published in 2005 by Ebury Press.
First published in 2004 by Ebury Press.

10 9 8 7 6 5 4 3

Text copyright © Crispin Aubrey and John Shearlaw, 2004
Foreword copyright © Michael Eavis, 2004

Crispin Aubrey and John Shearlaw have asserted their moral right to be identified as the authors of this work in accordance with the Copyright, Design and Patents Act 1988.

All rights reserved. No part of this publication may be reproduced, stored in a retrieval system, or transmitted in any form by means, electronic, mechanical, photocopying, recording or otherwise, without the prior permission of the copyright owner.

First published in the United Kingdom in 2004 by
Ebury Press
Random House UK Ltd
Random House
20 Vauxhall Bridge Road London SW1V 2SA

Random House Australia (Pty) Limited
20 Alfred Street, Milsons Point, Sydney,
New South Wales 2061, Australia

Random House New Zealand Limited
18 Poland Road, Glenfield,
Auckland 10, New Zealand

Random House (Pty) Limited
Endulini, 5A Jubilee Road, Parktown 2193, South Africa

Random House UK Limited Reg. No. 954009
www.randomhouse.co.uk

A CIP catalogue record is available for this book from the British Library.

ISBN: 978 0 091 897 635
ISBN: 0 091 897 637

Printed and bound in Great Britain by Bookmarque Ltd, Croydon

CONTENTS

CAST OF CHARACTERS

Richard Abel, festival site manager from 1989 to 2000, now runs a major marquee hire company

Stephen Abrahall, involved in 1981 as local CND activist, has run the festival information service ever since. Known to most people as 'Infoman'

Sheelagh Allen, Pilton resident for nearly fifty years. Michael Eavis's 'gatekeeper' and personal assistant since late 1980s.

Tony Andrews, main stage soundman for well over a decade from 1971 and ran Experimental Sound Field on his last appearance in 1992. Currently runs Funktion One

Rachel Austin, grew up in Pilton and graduated from making hippy hats to a senior management position. Now works with a leading children's charity

Bob St Barbe, recruited from Wells concrete works in 1993 and now runs festival 'infrastructure', including supplying 2,500 toilets. Keeps his own boat on the farm's sewage lake

Melvin Benn, London-based trade unionist who first came to the festival with the Workers Beer Company during the 1980s. Later joined Mean Fiddler Organisation. Glastonbury Festival Operational Director and Licensee since 2002

Tim Booth, musician and songwriter, formerly with Manchester-based band James

David Bowie, debut performance at dawn in 1971, when a relative unknown. Returned in 2000 wearing a replica of the same beautifully decorated coat he'd worn then

Polly Bradford, first came as an eight-year-old in 1983, then nearly every year since.

Billy Bragg, has played at least 15 times, and every year since 1992. Flag bearer for the festival's radical, independent spirit

Mark Cann, local teacher, first involved as CND activist in 1981, then took over management of main stage production. Lives at Worthy Farm

Julie Christie, much awarded British actor. Came in 1971 with Nicolas Roeg, director of the movie Glastonbury Fayre

Arabella Churchill, grand-daughter of Sir Winston, 'dropped out' to help run 1971 festival. Started running theatre events in 1981 and ever present since. Founded the charity Children's World

Norman Cook, first appeared as a Housemartin in 1986, then in every musical guise since, including four consecutive years as Fatboy Slim. One of the Festival's biggest supporters

Thomas Crimble, bass player with Hawkwind, helped organise 1971 festival. Subsequently worked at Pilton every year until 1998

Jeff Dexter, London-based DJ and promoter who put the bill together for Glastonbury Fayre. Returned with David Bowie in 2000

Emily Eavis, Michael's youngest daughter, brought up on the farm, surrounded by the festival. Now runs her own company, Bottle, in London

Michael Eavis, took over Worthy Farm at 19 after his father died suddenly. Inspired by 1970 Shepton Mallet Blues Festival to run his own event that September. Has been the main organiser and inspiration ever since. A Methodist, he also stood for parliament in 1997 as a Labour candidate for Wells

Martin Elborne, co-founder of WOMAD world music festival, his involvement spans 25 years. Now Programme Director for the Festival

Liz Eliot, part of the core festival team, has kept alive the spiritual heart of the festival in the Green Fields since 1990

Roy Gurvitz, originally came as traveller, involved during the heavy conflict years, later incorporated into the event as founder and inspiration for Lost Vagueness

Louise Harding, promoter and events organiser. First came as a parent volunteer with a local school

Bill Harkin, designed original Pyramid stage after visualising it in a dream. Now runs successful staging design business.

Malcolm Haynes, Bristol-based promoter and DJ, regularly involved since the late 1980s. Now runs Dance and One World stages

Peter Hook, musician. First appeared at Glastonbury with New Order and an inspiration ever since

Chris Howes, local GP, has run festival medical service since 1981. Now oversees team of 500 medical staff

Crispin Hunt, grew up in Somerset as a festival regular, then played as frontman of The Longpigs.

Ian Japp, the creator of some of Glastonbury Markets' most inspirational experiences, from Mussa to Maximum Funky Intentions

Robert Kearle, lives in Pilton, defends festival against local opponents, has worked at Worthy Farm since mid-1980s. Recruits post-festival army of litter pickers.

Andrew Kerr, leading light in group of so-called 'aristocratic hippies' who decamped to Somerset and fired up the festival's original 1971 spirit. Site manager in early 1980s before Richard Abel

Linda Lewis, London-based musician. Appeared as a teen protégé in 1971, jamming with Terry Reid. Returned to One World stage in 2003 with her own band

Chris Martin, musician, contributing here on behalf of Coldplay

Bill Mackay, Mendip District Councillor, solidly opposed to festival for many years, always voted against the licence being granted

Ralph Oswick, founder member of the Natural Theatre Company, who've been suprising festival-goers with their mad street theatre antics since 1971

Robert Plant, musician. Achieved worldwide fame with Led Zeppelin before embarking on a solo career. A festival regular (though never with Zep)

Dan Plesch, former CND organiser in Bristol during the 1980s, mainstay of the legendary 1980s 'gate and traffic' team

Simon Roiser, festival press officer from 1985 to 1995, learnt how to handle the national media 'on the job'

Tom Rowlands, one half of the Chemical Brothers (see also Ed Simons)

John Sauven, first came in 1979, closely involved on behalf of CND in 1980s, then with Greenpeace in 1990s. Helped facilitate the 1994 wind turbine

Brian Schofield, commanded Avon & Somerset Police units at Glastonbury during 1990s, now in charge of festival's own security arrangements

Ed Simons, one half of the Chemical Brothers (see also Tom Rowlands)

Michael Stipe, musician with REM, headliners in 1997 and 2003. A master of disguise …

John Tiberi, managed Joe Strummer's 101-ers before becoming tour manager for the Sex Pistols

Nik Turner, originally saxophonist with the ultimate free festival band, Hawkwind. Has probably played at Glastonbury more times and with more different bands than anyone else

Dick Vernon, one of the few 'full timers', responsible for booking all the market stalls from the early 1990s to the present

Angie Watts, accountant and Site Office stalwart throughout the 1990s, currently occupying the nearest house to the Tor

Bob Young, musician, songwriter and industry consultant. Status Quo's tour manager in the 1980s, now looks after Paul Oakenfold and Lemon Jelly

FOREWORD
BY MICHAEL EAVIS

This book is a series of tales by people who have many experiences and stories to tell about the Glastonbury Festival. I hope it will give you something of an insight into why so much energy and time are put into making it work so well. I am also pleased that some of the proceeds from this book will be going to a good cause nominated by the festival.

For myself, I just started something 34 years ago as a result of watching bands at the Bath Blues Festival. I had a farm of dairy cows and an excellent site, I thought, for what could be an extraordinary event. Little did I know then that it would succeed on such a grand scale!

It took many trials and tribulations over the years, and there were so many times when we almost gave up. I pushed the grace of fate beyond all reason, but somehow I had a deep conviction that if we were doing it right and for the best of motives then it would have to succeed. There were bank loans that put Worthy Farm on the brink of disaster, and New Age travellers hell-bent on free entry and claiming ownership of the land. There was rain that fell non-stop for days on end and the almost impossible task of producing a suitable infrastructure for such a huge crowd of people. Then licensing, which came into force in 1982, meant we had to convince a majority at the council that what we were doing was good and in some way beneficial to the community. When we failed at that task we then had to appeal to the magistrate's court – fortunately we usually managed to win these cases. Little wonder then that one could be led to believe that lady fate had dealt us a very good hand of cards – but in reality we've all worked at it every inch of the way. We fought hammer and tongs whenever conflict arose and somehow or other always made it happen.

Okay, I took chances and risks, but all the time we were gaining popularity. More and more bands were wanting to play at reasonable fees, and the public were always eager to buy tickets. Glastonbury was becoming more than just a name. It was an idea of how life could be for an idyllic midsummer weekend in the Somerset pasturelands, with music, theatre, dance and poetry as well as 'way out' stalls and eccentricity beyond what you could expect probably anywhere else in the world. Green politics and youth fashion all have a huge part to play in what we call our youth culture of today. There will always be something new and unique that can be found in these fields – beautiful things, challenging art and incredible music.

Long may the expression of free-thinking people reign over this land!

Michael Eavis

GENESIS
1970–1979

'Oh, I was so much older then
I'm younger than that now'
Bob Dylan (*My Back Pages*)

1970
THE FIRST FESTIVAL

Inspired by watching Led Zeppelin at a nearby Blues Festival, Somerset dairy farmer Michael Eavis organised his own event in the hope of paying off his mortgage. This hope wasn't realised, but 2,000 people came to hear Marc Bolan and T Rex. Held on the day after Jimi Hendrix died, it cost just £1 to get in and there was free milk from the Worthy Farm cows.

Bands in 1970: Al Stewart, Keith Christmas, T Rex, Stackridge.

Michael Eavis, farmer and festival organiser

I was only 19 and I had to leave the sea because my father had terminal cancer. I was trained for the Merchant Navy, but I realised that the farm was really important. It had to be saved. So although I wasn't really a farmer, I had to get stuck in at a very early age. All the other children were younger than me, my second brother down was academic, so he wasn't interested, the third and fourth ones were too young and my little sister was only just six. But my mother was quite supportive of me to carry on with it.

The trouble was I'd been born and bred and weaned on the farm, so I always thought I didn't want to be a farmer. I wanted to do something more exciting. Hence the festival I suppose. Even so, we were so short of money that eventually I had to work in a coalfield in order to make up my income. I did a day shift in the coal mine – I worked in the morning on the farm and then in the evening when I got back. I ran the farm like that really. That £25 a week was a fortune to me and helped to make the farm work.

I was always very keen on pop music and I knew what was what. I used to listen to Radio 1 all the time when I was a kid and I knew a lot about the pop industry. I was very keen on Elvis Presley and all that early stuff, so while my brother was playing the violin and classical music and the little ones were playing their recorders I was into serious pop music. I was the eldest and I was wearing the tartan shirt and the jeans. My favourite then was Peewee Hunt and the Twelfth Street Rag – that was number one for weeks – and then The Beatles came in and the Stones, and I was just totally immersed in it. I still am. When I wake up in the morning I put on Radio 1, and alternate with Radio 4. So by the time I leave the house at nine o'clock I've had a good fill of pop music and I know what's going on.

I even really wanted to be a pop star, as well as everything else. So I went down to Bournemouth one day and found a recording studio, said I wanted to make a record, have you got a pianist, I've got the songs. I knew the songs I wanted to sing, which were 'Around the World' and 'True Love'. But I still had to pay a fiver to have a 78 record made, which was quite a lot then. The kids listened to it the other day and said 'Fantastic, Dad'.

Then in 1970 I went with Jean, who was then my girlfriend, to the Blues Festival held at the Bath and West Showground. I thought 'This is great, this is wonderful.' I'd been working hard to keep the farm going and I thought maybe we could do this as a diversion, or as well as the farming, to help deal with the overdraft, which even then was £5,000. So I came back, got on the phone the next morning, phoned some bands and got some agents' numbers from the phone book. I was really keen on it, I thought this is terrific. So we got the show going in the autumn.

Marc Bolan was offered to me instead of The Kinks, who cried off at the last minute. The Kinks would have been great, but then Marc Bolan was even better. He was very fashionable. He'd had a hit song with 'Ride A White Swan' when his band was called Tyrannosaurus Rex. I remember meeting him halfway down Muddy Lane and he didn't look too pleased at going down this bumpy track in his big American car. So he wound down the window and said, 'Which way's the stage man?' The car was covered in some sort of suede material and, to be friendly, I put out my hand to stroke it. Then Marc jumped out and said, 'Don't touch my car, man!' It wasn't a good start, but then he went on to play one of the best sets we've ever had.

Financially it was a struggle. We eventually lost £1,500 on that first event, which I didn't really have, so to pay Marc Bolan I had to put aside so much a month from the milk cheque. He charged £500, which wasn't much compared with what he was worth at the time.

Ruth Garbett, teacher from Taunton

I was just 14 then and living in Chard. My mother was a slightly unusual lady in that she used to take us places that other people my age wouldn't go... So she found out about it and thought we all ought to go and have a look. We went late afternoon and spent a few hours there during the evening.

We drove there in an old Jowett Javelin with my mother, my older sister and my aunt. I think we just strolled through the gate, I don't remember paying. We must have looked very odd, like people on a day trip, I'm sure we didn't fit in with everybody else. It was mostly hippie-like people in their twenties, sitting about in groups, not necessarily facing the music. We walked right up to the front where there were quite a lot of people dancing about rather wildly and madly. It wasn't crowded or packed, they had plenty of room to run about. I think they were probably high on something and enjoying themselves.

In the middle of them was a lady, rather scantily dressed, and a man in white underpants, and he was crawling about on the ground with this dog's choke chain around his neck, and she was pulling him along. At that tender age I was rather taken by this. I was quite fascinated by them, which is why I don't remember what the music was.

Terry Hann, book dealer and Glastonbury resident

I remember the first one, which was a free event, and going up there for a look see. It's a lovely little village, Pilton, although I'd have to win the Lottery to live there these days. There weren't hundreds of thousands there, like there are now. It was just a day out with bands. Can't even remember the name of any of them now. And donations by coins tossed into a milk churn tied to a jeep, that's how you paid. We drove up to Pilton, Kevin and me, in that bloody old Austin Cambridge we had and just wandered around taking in the crowd and all the different people. A few people having a smoke and drinking a bit of cider, we were taking it all in. That's the entertainment really, the crowd and the people, the atmosphere, and I wish they'd show more of that on the TV now.

Clive Price, cheese manufacturer, Wells

I was living over at Frome at the time and everybody was on about the shindig, so we mosied on over and ended up working all through the night. It was big local news that there was something going on.

In those days a lot of people just went out of curiosity. It was the hippie times, all that stuff Timothy Leary started, everything was free, or supposed to be. We turned up with a cement mixer on the back of a pick-up because that's what I was using for work at the time. We came to a bit of a queue outside and it was: 'Straight on through for you' because they must have thought we were contracted. And we did ask about work too.

Some Hell's Angels pointed out a tent down the hill and said they needed people, so the next thing we were bunging bits of cheese on bread and sausages on rolls and heating up soup powder on a big old burner. Kept that up the whole night, smoking the old pot to keep us going. And this girl working with us, I'll always remember, she says: 'I'll have you – if you've got a skin.' What she meant was the old johnny, but it threw me, I'd never heard the expression before.

•••

1971
GLASTONBURY FAYRE

Disapproving of the blatant commercialism of most pop festivals, Andrew Kerr helped organise a free event at Pilton. Christened Glastonbury Fayre, it was held at the summer solstice. 12,000 people saw David Bowie, Hawkwind and Traffic play on a pyramid-shaped stage made from scaffolding covered with expanded metal and plastic sheeting. In the mystical spirit of the times the stage was located on a ley line identified by dowsing. A now rare album was recorded to help make up a loss and a Woodstock-style film shot by Nic Roeg and David Puttnam.

Bands in 1971: Arthur Brown, B.B. Blunder, Brinsley Schwarz, Bronco, Daevid Allen and Gong, David Bowie, Edgar Broughton Band, Fairport Convention, Flash Gordon, Gentle Fire, Gilberto Gil, Hawkwind, Help Yourself, Henry Cow, Linda Lewis, Magic Michael, Magic Muscle, Melanie, Million, Quintessence, Quiver, Sattva, Skin Alley, Terry Reid, The Illusions, The Pink Fairies, Traffic, Uncle Dog, Worthy Farm Windfuckers.

Glastonbury Fayre Manifesto, 1971

Glastonbury Fair [sic] will be held at Worthy Farm, Pilton, near Shepton Mallet, Somerset, from Sunday June 20 to Thursday June 24, encompassing Midsummer's Day. It will be a fair in the medieval tradition, embodying the legends of the area, with music, dance, poetry, theatre, lights and the opportunity for spontaneous entertainments. There will be no monetary profit – it will be free.

Man is fast ruining his environment. He is suffering from the effects of pollution; from the neurosis brought about by a basically urban industrial society; from a lack of spirituality in his life. The aims of Glastonbury Fair are, therefore: the conservation of our natural resources; a respect for nature and life; and a spiritual awakening.

Glastonbury is rich in legends. It was here St Joseph of Arimathea is said to have brought his young nephew, Jesus, and later to have returned with sacred relics to found the early Christian Church in Britain. It was here that King Arthur and the Knights of the Round Table are said to have carried out their quest for the Holy Grail. It was here that the ancient Druids are said to have been initiated into the secrets of the Universe. It is a magical place.

Worthy Farm lies in the Vale of Avalon some seven miles from Glastonbury. Pilton was once a port (although it is now 20 miles from the sea). Legend says that St Joseph of Arimathea and his nephew Jesus once visited the village on their way to the tin and lead mines nearby. The farm is 110 acres of pastureland (with another 50 available) forming a natural amphitheatre facing the proposed site for the stage. Glastonbury Tor stands at the end of the valley and is clearly visible from all parts of the farm. The ley line between Glastonbury and Stonehenge runs a few yards from the stage site. The hills on the opposite side of the valley go to make up the sign of Sagittarius in the zodiacal plan; the country which lies between the farm and Glastonbury is Capricornus, and the Tor itself is Aquarius. The site lies on the solstice axis of the Zodiac.

Michael Eavis

Then came Andrew Kerr and Arabella Churchill with plans for a bigger festival in 1971 to be called 'Glastonbury Fayre', which could, among other things, possibly recoup some loss. The *Guardian* once described Andrew Kerr as 'charismatic'. It must surely be praise, and with a name and, as it turned out, a personality like Arabella, I felt we could not go wrong …

('"Cows always calve over a blind spring", Waifs and heretics at Worthy Farm', in *Glastonbury Fayre*, 1979)

David Bowie, performer

It was 1971 and I was bottom of the bill. I remember my going onstage time being shoved later and later (I was originally scheduled to go on around midnight or so) but things got so delayed that I didn't make it onstage till around 5 in the morning. So, what better than to spend the intervening hours ensconced in the farmhouse, along with a crew of latter-day hippies, singer Terry Reid and all kinds of mushrooms. By the time I was due to perform I was flying and could hardly see my little electric keyboard or my guitar. I have no recollection of the show itself, although I seem to recall a strange girl getting up onstage and whirling away, mostly without any music playing, while the audience cheerfully awoke from its slumbers.

Linda Lewis, singer

I was so young, like a little girl really. But we all lived in this communal house in Hampstead, Ian (Samwell), my boyfriend at the time; Toad (Toni Attelle), she was a mime artist; Jeff Dexter, he was helping set up the bands, and others, and Jeff asked me if I wanted to go there and live in a tent, whatever. We ended up hanging out and staying up all night with David Bowie and all the other cast who'd ended up down in Somerset. Bowie didn't mean anything to me then, but they were lovely people. I was there, didn't really know how I got there, and it was one big party in an amazing place.

The little village was so quaint, so tiny, with lots of little old people walking around, then there were these fields where everyone was so high. My whole life was like that then, one big party, and God, I wish I could still think like that now. I remember the farmhouse being really magical, old and kind of spooky. I liked it when I was tucked up in bed with my Wincyette nightie, yes it's true. I was so young and naive I wasn't really part of the goings-on.

The tent wasn't ready, surprise, so we stayed in one of the little cottages near the farmhouse and got a bath there occasionally. It was just a time for getting high and playing music. Terry Reid was there but I didn't know I was going to be performing. We were floating around with the hippies, the bubbles and the flowers – and there was a bit of mud too, like you'd expect on a farm, even though I'd never been away anywhere except a caravan site before. It was a great time. I took some natural acid – mescalin – and at some point I was dancing with a tree. I thought I was Guinevere and the tree was Sir Lancelot, so the whole legend of Avalon had taken over. Then, right at the peak of the trip, in the middle of the night, I was watching Arthur Brown and it was like entering the gates of hell. Then from dancing in a field, it was 'Oh right, I'm on!' and I was up there jamming with Terry Reid, asking the audience to play along with me, still out of my head. You lived moment by moment, and that was one of them. Except that I did keep on singing when the band were trying to stop, and I still curl up when I see that on film now: stop Linda, stop, I'll be saying...

I remember thinking Michael [Eavis] was ever so posh. He certainly seemed to be a farmer-type person, from what little I knew about them. I was from the East End, I'd just left school, I hadn't been hanging out with gentry people, so I didn't join in the conversation. I didn't know the grown-up games and things people do to each other. Andrew [Kerr] and Arabella [Churchill] were all very sweet but I think maybe they thought I was a bit rough. Even in the house in London, I was the youngest, like a little puppy dog hanging around. And I used to come out with malapropisms – I still do! – and have people all laughing at me for saying the wrong thing. The result was I didn't really know they were putting all this on, this Fayre thing; it just seemed to be days and days of drinking tea with nobody actually doing anything. But then there it was, something that felt like another land altogether. No rules, no offending, people rolling about filthy dirty with their hair matted, no separation. And music everywhere, day and night. It all seemed so easy, so natural. For me who was a hippie 24/7, all love and peace and big hair, floaty dresses and no bras, it was the total trip, completely everything I believed in and wanted to do. I think I've still got that with me, even today.

Andrew Kerr, organiser, Glastonbury Fayre

I was in my early thirties and I had been Randolph Churchill's literary assistant for ten years, mainly working on his father's official biography, when he died in 1968. I was completely devastated because Randolph had become, although he was a dreadful person to work for, a surrogate father to me (my own father died when I was very young) and he taught me all I knew about journalism. And after he died – it's a strange thing to say – Jonathan Aitken (Lord Beaverbrook's nephew and then a journalist) came round to my flat and said 'What are you going to do?' and I hadn't got the slightest idea.

I remember driving back up from the Isle of Wight with a car full of outrageous people and saying: 'We've got to have a proper festival, it's got to have at least some cosmic significance,' and I decided that Stonehenge was the place. But having come from a farming background, I went and did a bit of research and it was surrounded by arable fields and I thought it wasn't suitable to have a lot of hippies rampaging around.

Then about three different people rang me, knowing I was interested in putting on a festival, and all suggested Michael Eavis's farm. So I went to meet him in Pilton (in late September 1970). I said I wanted to do this festival, and he said 'yes'. It was unbelievable – he didn't know anything about me – and in October I moved into the farmhouse (where Michael now lives). I even sometimes milked the cows.

The extraordinary thing about this festival was that nobody got paid for anything. The whole thing was absolutely free. I put all the money I had into it, which wasn't very much. But one of the people who came down to see me was Arabella Churchill, because I'd known her since she was eight years old. She got enthused by it, moved into the farmhouse and helped financially, and we put in equal amounts of cash to pay for things like lavatories and scaffolding. The name of the company which put on the festival was officially Solstice Capers Ltd – this was set up to avoid problems with liability.

I think the only person who made any money out of the festival was Sid Rawle (later nicknamed King of the Hippies). He invaded the farmhouse and started assembling all the plates in the kitchen ready to feed people. He said it was a revolution and the rich should give to the poor. There was a bit of an argument and he left.

Sid had a huge cauldron and he would go off to Bristol market to collect unwanted vegetables and make food for everybody working on site. The model, Jean Shrimpton, paid for the kitchen. When the festival started Sid and his friends would go round the site collecting money, saying 'pay now, eat later'. All sorts of things went in the hat – world coins, bits of dope and so on. There was other food at the festival supplied by Craig and Greg Sams, who started Ceres bakery in Portobello Road and then Whole Earth foods. There was a tent with bowls full of food and it was 1/6d a bowl. And now he (Craig) is President of the Soil Association.

The lavatories were holes in the ground with a scaffolding framework, and each compartment was divided off in a zigzag way, shielded by long strips of hessian sacking. People had to rest their bottoms on scaffold poles – it was pretty basic. They were all dug by hand, quite deep, with lots of people down there covered in alluvial jelly, and the sides kept on falling in.

For the siting of the main stage I actually dowsed the area with a divining rod. There's a straight line that goes from Glastonbury Abbey to within about a hundred yards of the main stage at Worthy Farm and then on to Stonehenge. I knew there was a ley line but then there are spirals that go off it. So I found it and marked it out. What you are tapping into is the planet's life force. So the apex of that first Pyramid stage was over the spot I had found.

Thomas Crimble, co-organiser, Glastonbury Fayre

Andrew asked me if I wanted to help organise this festival, which was going to be the exact opposite of the Isle of Wight. I thought that was a really nice idea. It also coincided with my being sacked from Hawkwind. I was 20 at the time.

There were a lot of people around at first, all going for this idea, although Andrew was one of the main leaders. At one stage we had to make a choice between Andrew and a chap called James, who was a DJ from Radio Caroline. It came to a point where we had to shape up or ship out. It's like with Michael, really, it's a benign dictatorship – you need someone who'll say let's do this. The trouble was that everyone was talking about it, but no-one was taking any action. We had a vote, and James left.

So we kicked everyone out who wasn't actually doing anything and it was just the core of four or five of us. We used to see Bill Harkin once a week; he'd drop by with a van, delivering foodstuff for the company he was working for, and he always managed to leave some oat cakes or something. Although Michael has called us 'rich hippies' we had little money of our own and were mostly on the dole.

That winter we spent most of the time clearing out Brimley Lane, and used the wood to fire the Raeburn. And we just contacted people, put the vibe out that something was happening, and people just used to turn up – anyone who was doing anything weird and wonderful. It really was an education, I didn't realise that half of these things existed. But we had Reiki healers and foot massagers using the meridian points on the body, and others into ghosts, spirits, UFOs, environmentalists – all serious people. Every evening we'd have someone new sitting round the kitchen table who would give us the latest on some new type of meditation or something bizarre. I'd heard a few things when I was in Hawkwind, but this was full on. The availability of what you could get into just amazed me. We tried to watch the sunset every evening over the Tor. That was always nice, it centred us and calmed us down.

The ethos was, if there's a problem, sort it out yourself, don't expect anyone else to do it, it's your festival. That's where the magic came from, and that's all from Andrew's inspiration. And that magic has gone on even to this day, although people are a bit lost now; they don't quite understand it.

People started arriving a few months before the festival, there weren't fences or anything, a lot of people just turned up, knocked on the door and said they wanted to help. We were all vegetarian, we didn't have meat in the house. We had Maran chickens and our own eggs, although during the festival someone moved into the hen house, which was a bit of a cheek!

Michael Eavis spent all of his time farming. He came round for his rent and milked his cows and that was about it. He had a Morris Minor 1000 van with a hooped canvas back. He says that I offered it to someone to take off and sleep under, although I don't remember. He says it was the first 'bender'.

Arabella Churchill, co-organiser, Glastonbury Fayre

I was 15 when my grandfather, Sir Winston Churchill, died at the age of 91. I wish in many ways that I had been born earlier so that I could have known him during his prime, but I have lots of happy memories of him both at Chartwell and in London. We shared a hatred of Latin! One of my last memories of him is sitting with him holding his hand at Hyde Park Gate while we watched a film about the war and his leadership, and when Hitler's face came on the screen he gripped my hand and muttered ferociously, 'Bloody Nazis'.

So with that background – my father was Randolph Churchill – I went through all the debutante stuff, and then I worked as a researcher in the public affairs department of London Weekend Television. I organised the Biafra Ball, because the Biafra crisis was going on then, and then I went and worked for Lepra, the British Leprosy Relief Association, as their public relations officer. I went out to Tanzania and Zambia with them.

It was while I was working for Lepra that I was invited to be the Azalea Queen at a festival to be held at NATO headquarters in the

United States. Tricia Nixon, daughter of President Nixon, had done it the year before. But partly encouraged by some more radical friends, including Andrew Kerr, I decided to reject the invitation and to write a letter with an anti-aggression message, especially with the Vietnam War going on. For me with my family background that was a big step, and when it was leaked to *Rolling Stone* magazine there was an inevitable furore.

Suddenly all the world and his wife wanted to get at me, the press were ringing all the time, so I had to leave London very fast. My mother suggested I should tell them I'd had a nervous breakdown, that would be less shaming on the family, and my brother was furious. So I literally ran down to Worthy Farm, where Andrew had been since late summer and I'd been going down at weekends. So I moved into the farmhouse in the late autumn of 1970 and basically that was the end of my straight life.

It was very strange living there. I was then a very young 21, I'd never really lived anywhere else before, I'd always lived at home with my mother. And then endless weird people would just arrive, like Mick Farren from IT [*International Times*, alternative magazine] – I remember seeing him get out of his black limousine; he had this really tiny little cloak which he kept on trying to flick round himself, and high-heeled shoes – and an extraordinary religious type figure called Zee and his girlfriend Heila, and little Linda Lewis, who is still doing gigs, and she brought a lovely American girl called Toad, who was in *Hair*. Melanie came, and I had no idea who she was at the time. And then there were Seventh Day Israelites, there was Leonard O'Houlaghan with his domes. Literally everybody came, and we'd have them all to dinner and then send them on their way.

I remember at some stage being asked to open West Pennard village fête. How they got me to do that I don't know. There was this amazing photo of me in my flowery kaftan and flowers all over my hat. I don't know what they thought they were getting. I suppose they probably saw me as an aristocratic hippie, which is how Michael always described me.

Nobody had formal roles; Andrew was the only person doing anything much at all really, and he was just getting the message out that there was going to be this wonderful free festival. Plus he was very into the ley lines and all that. And I do remember that quite a large part of the festival site was to be set aside for the flying saucers to land. How serious he was about that I don't know. For money he [Andrew] put in all he had and I suddenly had £4,000 come free from a family trust. I was going to buy an old chapel in the village, which was then for sale for the same amount, but I put the money into the stage instead – and got a lot of good karma out of it. I also paid most of the household bills. I supported it financially partly because nobody else had any money.

Michael Eavis

After 1970 I couldn't really afford to get out. I was thinking of a way to recoup the £1,500 loss when all these rather glamorous hippies turned up and said, hey, we want to do a festival next year. So I said, pay off my losses and I'll let you have the site. So we agreed a rent for the farm, which would cover it. In fact, they lost even more, so I ended up being even worse off.

I was just an ordinary farmer, enjoyed hard work, got up about five in the morning. I enjoyed music and I enjoyed singing, but I didn't really understand what they were on about. At one point I went into their upstairs office and asked what I thought were some pertinent questions. I was being a bit impatient at their lackadaisical ways, and said, come on let's get things moving. And at that point a chap called Rollo threw some tarot cards on the table, and Andrew asked, what does it say? And Rollo said, it says that no-one with the name of Michael should be involved with this event. So that was like they'd given me the sack at that point, although I thought this simply proves they're just a load of dreamers. After that I just got on with what I was doing, my farm work, which was a lot more uplifting and a lot more fulfilling.

But in the end I thought oh well, it's all rather fun, it's all rather romantic, there's no harm done. So I began to be more sympathetic to their ideas of dowsing and that sort of thing, looking for the ley lines. And I got more involved later because they kept running to me – they wanted this, they wanted that, they wanted lorries, they wanted tractors – so in the end I did my bit, they did their bit and it all came on quite strong. I remember all these hippies with jugs queuing up for milk, which I sold to them at cost price, probably about three pence a pint. Apart from that it was a free festival, there were people wandering everywhere. It was a bit weird, but it was OK.

Jeff Dexter, Glastonbury Fayre DJ

The original Glastonbury connection came through my ex-girlfriend Jean Bradbery, who was responsible for killing off the Night Assemblies Bill. After the first Isle of Wight festival MP Mark Woodnut introduced this legislation that was going to stop rock festivals ever happening again. Many people claim to have stopped it but it was Jean's tireless efforts and organisation that helped kill off a ridiculous Tory bill. She had been to Glastonbury and met up with Arabella and Andrew; like many young 'nobs' they had become very groovy.

They wanted to do a free festival similar to the free concerts in Hyde Park, but in the Vale of Avalon in summer solstice week. A groovy, cool idea, man. I was volunteered into the project by Jean, so I went down to Worthy Farm early in the year to start arranging bands. Basically I asked all the bands who played at the Roundhouse to play at the Fayre. Top of the list were Pink Floyd and The Grateful Dead, the most famous underground bands, the ones doing the most to promote the new dawn. And as soon as I arrived I came down with flu; a temperature of 103°F stuck in a room at the left up the stairs in the farmhouse, looking out to where the Fayre was supposed to be and seemingly surrounded by toffs. Rather than stay in bed I dropped a tab of acid and I ended up in Wells Cathedral for the whole afternoon with Floyd's manager Steve O'Rourke and the Dead's manager, who at that time was Mickey Hart's father. In the end the Dead didn't come but they sent a donation, some recordings we could use.

As the festival approached I was getting busier and busier with a band called America, so I went to *Frendz*, the underground paper, and handed over the whole shooting match to John Coleman, who did music. I passed him the whole list of bands, with all the contacts and phone numbers, many of whom he was interviewing for the magazine at that time. He carried on while I was on the road with America; I was also still running the Sunday night Implosion shows at the Roundhouse. John was the liaison point for Worthy; meanwhile Implosion started putting money in to get the bands there and make sure the scaffolding was erected. Basically all the little bits and pieces that needed to be paid for and couldn't be acquired for free. We gave them money three times in all.

Most of the film crew were working for free, apart from the people who ran the catering trucks. Sandy Lieberson and Nic Roeg wanted to be involved, as well as Alfie Benge, a talent co-ordinator lady whose real Christian name was Alfreda. In reality, the talent was all co-ordinated by me and John Coleman and they just happened to film it while they were awake, or when they had power in their generator. I've still got the list of names in my diary for '71, with little Xs marked against The Who and the Dead, who didn't play, and a late addition of David Bowie, who did. The only band I can't remember anything at all about were the Downhome Rhythm Kings – does anyone know who they were? Or what happened to them? Lord Jellicoe and Viscount Brocks [sic] are in there, I said we were surrounded by toffs, and I've made myself a note to ring the police on the Monday. Very organised!

Thomas Crimble

The event itself was basically a tribal meeting of minds. The whole thing was about, look, we're going to set up a situation and we just want you to come and do what you do best. So if you're a musician, do your music, if you're a religious leader, come and do your leading. There was a man called Greg who came and built a maze, spent a month or so making the shape, and other people came and performed healing in their tents or whatever. And on that level, there were people who came along with their own spades to dig in other people's turds where people had been shitting in the hedge. We didn't ask them to do that.

There was music on the stage, but everyone made their own entertainment. There were the Rainbow Gypsies who came over from America and they were doing all this crazy naked dancing in front of the stage, dancing in the mud. They were very colourful, loads of beads and bangles.

The sound was produced by Tony Andrews, who had created this 'turbo sound' system. It was the first prototype, which Tony designed. We set it up first on the lawn outside the farmhouse and then drove round to the far side of the valley and listened to the Steve Miller Band, Neil Young and The Grateful Dead.

I did play with Hawkwind in the end that year but I also played with my own band, which was called The Worthy Farm Windfuckers. The windfucker is a bird of prey, like a kestrel, and it flies, hovering, for ever. We'd played a lot in the lead-up to the festival, round the table in the farmhouse. I played 12-string guitar and sang about the whole ethos of the event, about love and peace. And we did the last gig on the Sunday night, we closed the show down. Everyone got up on stage, it was very freeform.

Bill Harkin, stage designer

It wasn't just the stage, it was what was happening around it. There were so many structures, from benders to geodesic domes to high-tech inflatables. Two guys built a half-acre inflatable dome in what was then a mustard field. It was a place where people without tents could crash. There were even people building Savonius (wind-powered) rotors out of 45-gallon oil drums. It was an opportunity to do anything you wanted.

Later in the festival I had done mescalin, I think, when I had a call from John Coleman to say the stage was falling down. When I went down I found that what had happened was that the scaffolding wedges had got loose. On the stage there were all these people from Quintessence in outrageous big hats and boa feathers and make-up. There were so many of them, so I went round asking whether they were all necessary to the performance. If they said no, they were off. And when I climbed underneath, all these loose wedges were rattling around. It wasn't dangerous, but it made a lot of noise.

Arabella Churchill

I remember walking up the hill the night before the festival with Bill Harkin. He made me turn round and look back down the valley – the film crew had just turned on their huge lights and the stage looked like a wonderful shining diamond. The festival had a really magic feel to it. I know I was dancing on the stage to Fairport Convention, because I've seen it on the film. I'm looking staggeringly pretty, very blonde, and I had this extremely attractive black kaftan on which had a fantastic border down each side. I was looking at my best, very thin because we'd been eating brown rice and veg. I remember being interviewed for the film, but I was so desperate not to say anything that might upset my family that it was the most boring interview ever and it wasn't used. However, both the Somerset Fire Officers and I get special credits at the end. I'm not quite sure why.

There were drugs at the festival, but mostly dope. Some people got strongly into the free festival spirit. I remember this dope dealer, who found me up at the house, and he said 'I've got all this acid and I was going to sell it, but no, man, you give it away to people for free.' So I had this briefcase full of tabs of acid, which I put under a bed. I wasn't going to distribute it, and I can't remember what happened to it in the end.

I remember that my mother came during the festival. She was directed straight to my tent – nobody had thought to come and check first – and of course I was in bed with my boyfriend! He was called English John and had very very long hair. Apart from that, I think she thought the festival was rather wonderful, although she thought

I should have been dressed up all the time, rather than in jeans and a jumper.

I have no idea what happened afterwards with sorting out the money and so on. I went off to Morocco and then got involved in other adventures.

Jeff Dexter

America were supposed to play, but the night before I had Al Kooper at Implosion. I drove out to Glastonbury first thing on Monday morning with America, in two vehicles, one with my DJ gear and another with their gear. The sad thing was that getting there spooked them. The boys could not handle all these really freaky people. They had seen all the freaks at the Roundhouse and at other gigs but this was the beginning of a new age. America arrived and saw the audience and ran away. They couldn't handle the idea of going on stage to play with this audience!

The biggest act we had were Traffic, who were just magical...and then David Bowie, who got on stage at daybreak on the morning of the 22nd to be confronted with an audience of 5,000 people, all lying in their sleeping bags in front of the stage.

Nik Turner, saxophonist and singer

I've played at Glastonbury and Stonehenge loads of times. I just generally enjoy playing music and getting people to enjoy themselves if I can, because I see music as a healing force and a means of communication. And when I'm not playing gigs I'm busking on the streets of Cardiff or somewhere else in the world.

Hawkwind started in 1969 as Group X. We were playing electronic music, but very orientated towards people having drug experiences – LSD and hallucinogenic drugs. It appealed to people who were taking drugs because it was very easy to identify with. It was a mind trip really. Each piece was really long, with long solos, a bit like John Coltrane, who I used to listen to. I was playing free jazz, expressionist music in a rock band.

We were invited to play at the Isle of Wight Festival in 1970. The Pink Fairies had got something going with Gerry Fitzgerald and a guy called Vince, who were involved in organising. They had an inflatable dome which they set up outside as a side event. We thought the main festival was a bit of a cattle market, with high prices and fascist organisation. This inflatable was called Canvas City, and we just moved in and played and played for hours.

Thomas Crimble, who played with us at the Isle of Wight, had moved to Glastonbury to help organise the first big festival. That's how we got involved. We'd been to rehearse at the farm a few times. Hawkwind then featured myself, Dave Anderson, Dik Mik, Del Dettmar, Dave Brock, Terry Ollis and Robert Calvert. But the day before we had to play Dave Brock got really ill, some sort of bug, so we asked Thomas to play bass and Dave Anderson played guitar, Robert Calvert did some vocals, and I think I did some of the singing. I stayed there for a week or so, and I remember meeting other bands – Gong and The Pink Fairies, a lot of the Notting Hill bands – Help Yourself, Mighty Baby. And a lot of people got into Guru Maharaji and some of the crowd threw scaffold clips at him. But generally people were having a good time and being positive about it.

Thomas Crimble

I was up on the Pyramid, and Brinsley Schwarz were playing, when this boy Guru Maharaji, who was only 13 years old and supposedly the Lord of the Universe, arrived to speak at the festival. He drove up in a Rolls Royce, which was rented for the day, and everybody started jumping up and down and chanting. It was so distracting that Brinsley Schwarz stopped playing in the middle of their number, turned round and said what the fuck is that. The energy just went from them. They gave up.

I'd brought a chair up from my room in the farmhouse and Maharaji was going to sit on it, but suddenly the vibe went round the Pyramid that he wasn't going to speak unless the whole area was cleared. I could see there would be a riot if all these stoned hippies were told to leave. The whole ethos of the original Glastonbury was that everyone is welcome to come and do their thing, but no one person is any more equal than anyone else.

So I went and talked to him. But he said it was alright, and he did then get to speak for about 20 minutes. He talked about revealing the peace inside of oneself and the evils of taking drugs, but the thing that freaked everyone out was when he said there would be no more 'sex' in this world. His English wasn't quite perfect and what he meant to say was that there would be no more 'sects'.

Andrew Kerr

When the thing actually happened, I turned over the farmhouse to the Red Cross, so when all these people came down from London looking for me, the door was opened by a nurse in a starched apron.

During the festival I was living in a field with my girlfriend, Jytte, and a couple of dogs and a brilliant view of the film screen put up to show the Jimi Hendrix film, *Rainbow Bridge*. His manager, Mike Jeffries (at Electric Ladyland studios in New York), had rung me up and said we've got this film and we'd like to put it on at your festival as a world premiere. But I never saw it because I was so exhausted that I went to sleep in the tent.

Then there were the Brazilians, who just arrived, and they had a huge amount of drums, and The Pink Fairies, who had two drummers, and used to play naked. Pink Floyd couldn't get there because they were stuck in Milan. Melanie flew over from the States at her own expense. David Bowie says he stayed in the farmhouse, but I don't remember that.

A film was made by Nic Roeg with David Puttnam as cameraman. A guy called Si Litvinoff, a US producer, had got involved through Willow Morrell, a friend from London. I took him [Roeg] round the site and I really enthused him about it because I was absolutely fired up about the whole thing. They shot 72 hours of film – 35mm and 16mm cameras – and they had two big arc lights on either side of the Pyramid that illuminated the surface, which had been covered with expanded metal. It looked rather tatty during the day but at night it sparkled like a diamond.

Although we stopped the music at midnight, it was quite noisy. I went up into the village, and my God it was loud – the acoustics of that place were extraordinary, and dumped a huge amount of noise there. Michael said at one point that the music had to stop. He was worried about what was going to happen in terms of general ill feeling in the area. And I could see him chasing this guy, who he thought was in charge of the sound, right around the Pyramid. But the guy was wearing a baseball hat and a wig, and he just took all this off and suddenly turned and walked back past Michael, quite slowly, who didn't recognise him at all.

In terms of what the village would find dreadful, there was a huge amount of drug-taking going on – mostly dope and acid. Release [London-based drugs advice centre] had a geodesic dome behind the farmhouse, a chill-out place, and a Christian set-up.

We were told that a young officious policeman said, when they were all hanging around in the station at Wells, 'Let's go and bust Worthy Farm,' and their boss, who was an older and wiser officer, said: 'Don't worry. Leave them alone. They don't mean any harm.' During the festival the police were stationed in the Pilton village playing fields. They couldn't come on to private property, but I did walk round the site with a policeman who turned out to be the head of the drugs squad in Frome. He said they realised that a lot of people were smoking drugs, but he was only interested in dealers. And as he was talking we went past this guy who was rolling up an enormous spliff. I was later told by the police that there were only three arrests for drugs.

There was one absolutely appalling incident when I was talking to the people from the Milk Marketing Board – there was a plan to have milk bars all over the place but Michael couldn't officially supply all the milk – and they were suited, standing outside the farmhouse, and to my horror, Jip, who was a stunning looking bloke with long curly hair, arrived. He had a top hat on and a cloak and high boots and a ruff at his neck and he walked straight up to us and opened the cloak and said: 'Do you like my lovely clothes.' And he was bollock naked, and high on acid as well of course. They didn't know where to look.

And later that day, he went up into the village and picked all these gladioli out of a garden and then rang the bell and said: 'I've brought these beautiful flowers for you.' Unfortunately, it was one of Michael's cousins.

Nik Turner

What was sad was that there was a lot of organisation, but there seemed to be rather too many chiefs and not enough Indians at one point, although it sorted itself out. They ended up losing a lot of money – one of the reasons was that they didn't get it together. They had these etchings of John Lennon's which were going to be raffled but they forgot to sell any tickets.

Andrew Kerr

Afterwards The Grateful Dead put down a whole side for the benefit album – they didn't play at the festival itself because their management wouldn't agree. We had to find some money at the end to pay off some of the doctors who didn't want to do it for free and things like that. In the end everything was paid, but it was a bit awkward, and the album helped pay for it. I think they [the record company] sent us £1,000, but by that time I was a crofter in the Highlands. We also had a benefit concert at the Rainbow Theatre in Finsbury Park. I hitched down from Scotland to go to it.

Julie Christie, actress

I went with Nic Roeg, who was making a film, Alfie Benge [painter and poet now married to Robert Wyatt, the musician] who was my pal and festival-buddy, and a bunch of other friends. We went to festivals at that time – that's what we did! – and the word was that this was going to be amazing and different.

What we did was try and catch the bands we particularly liked. We tried not to eat too much so as to avoid having to sit on the very public toilet trench. The rest of the time we wandered around what was like a huge exotic town out of a science-fiction story that had suddenly mushroomed up in this field. There was always something new to see, glorious sights, you could wander into anyone's tent and be welcomed on floors covered with kilims and walls hung with tapestries.

Everyone talked to everyone else and the air was vibrating with sexuality. People seemed to be so beautiful in their breathtaking finery – or indeed without it! Two images that stay with me are of a big carthorse – the kind you hardly ever see nowadays – with a whole naked family sitting on its back and of a naked motorcyclist, his penis laid tidily out in front of him. There was dancing, of course, and the nights were full of adventure and music. I don't think the music ever stopped.

I remember David Bowie because his music was wonderful and, like so many of the boys, he looked like a girl. I remember the Guru Maharaji because he arrived in a limousine and he had these terribly posh shiny shoes on – no-one else had shoes so they stood out. I remember that Release was there, very busy and very active which seemed like a good thing, that people were being cared for. It seemed part of the generosity and the goodness.

I have not been back – I left England for a while after that and the music had changed when I came back to live in England again and somehow I never got round to it, although people I know who have been say it is just as wonderful as it was.

Dee Palmer, then fashion model,
now partner in stage design company

It was a life-changing experience for me, and for everybody that I knew who went there. Nobody was ever quite the same again. It just opened one's mind. I was very pregnant at the time, I'd been left behind because my then husband fancied getting away from the prospects of being a father, and went off [to the festival] without me. He was Nic Roeg's stills photographer, so he had a route down there, but I heard about it and had such a gut feeling that this was something I had to be involved in. I went down with a girlfriend and ended up staying in the same van that all the camera crews were using. We all piled in together – Jean Shrimpton, Julie Christie, a whole bunch of us.

I also found it quite frightening as well, because I'd never experienced anything so different. So I felt very insecure, but that was part of the draw, exploring all that, people who were so able to express themselves, running around naked in the mud. I found that quite terrifying, in case someone asked me to do it. But that breaking through inhibitions was very interesting.

The festival changed all my ideas. I'd been a fashion model until then. I was already questioning the materialistic world I'd been involved in, and this kind of clinched it. I dropped my profession completely after that, which wasn't necessarily a good thing, but that's what happened.

1971: The Original Pyramid Stage

Bill Harkin

At the time I was doing two things in my spare time – climbing, and reading Jung. One weekend a friend of mine asked me to move all his possessions from his little flat in Soho to the South coast, Swanage in Dorset, where there are awesome cliffs that look like cream cheese. And sitting in the car looking out at the stars I got this extraordinary feeling. So I turned the car round, started to drive north and the first sign that caught my attention was Glastonbury.

I drove up to below the Tor, brewed up a cup of tea, when all of a sudden all these outrageous people appeared from the hill – Andrew Kerr, Tony Andrews, Bella, Nik Turner, loads of folk. I invited them for tea and oat cakes – they had dope, I had the goodies. They said they'd come down to do a free festival on a local farm. I said I'd had a good vibe to come here and it was my intention to sit on top of the Tor and meditate. Which I did, for about 18 hours.

One day I had a vivid dream of a stage and an audience and two beams of light forming a pyramid, and beyond that a hillside and a building. Because of Jung, I made some notes and sketches from the dream. The next morning I made a cardboard pyramid in my studio. When I helped move the others down to Worthy Farm in my van I took the model with me.

Andrew said he had the perfect spot for the stage, he'd dowsed it, so we walked down and found the spike they'd driven in, and looking back towards the farmhouse I saw the landscape from my dream. I talked to John Michell, who'd just written *The View Over Atlantis*, and he said it should be based on the dimensions of Stonehenge. This was interesting because I'd been looking at sacred geometries as part of the whole Jungian thing. So eventually we had a design that had pretty accurate dimensions to a hundredth part of the Great Pyramid.

To build it, we looked at the latest modular scaffolding systems made by a company called Kwik Stage. It was the first time their system had been used for a proper stage. It cost £1,100 altogether, about £430 for the scaffolding and £480 for the expanded metal (used as partial cladding). So many people say they built the Pyramid, which is true. The expanded metal didn't arrive until a few days before, so we co-opted a horde of people. They were coming up like ants carrying leaves – the metal sheets to be wired on to the framework.

And at the very top of the stage there was a pyramid-shaped stone which somebody had found on Glastonbury Tor, and in a depression in it, as we were watching David Bowie at dawn, we placed a grass seed, an offering to the early morning mists.

•••

1978
TURN UP AND DROP OUT

Nearly every year during the mid- to late 1970s informal events were held at Worthy Farm with Michael Eavis's (sometimes reluctant) agreement. The most organised was in 1978, when a convoy of travelling people looking for a festival site ended up at Glastonbury.

Michael Eavis

After 1971 Jean and I decided to abandon the whole thing. It was all a bit too much, there were too many hippies and too many drugs and all in all we thought, let's leave it. But of course it wasn't as easy as that.

One year I went out with the kids for the evening and when I got back there was a police car parked outside. I said, what's wrong, and they said you've got some visitors. I said what do you mean, so they said there's a few people and vehicles, and I could see already it was a lot of people. The police had obviously led them all to the site in a convoy, although they wouldn't admit it to me. I think they thought it would get them out of the way.

So that year we had a free one, even though all the 'visitors' knew it was a farm not a festival site. I couldn't really do anything about it, I couldn't move them off, so I kind of joined in, I thought oh well, it's a party. I phoned Andrew [Kerr] and asked him to come down and give me a hand, show people how to make loos and so on. There was nothing here except the fields, so they just dug holes in the ground. They stayed for a few weeks in the end, but it did rain like hell. It rained and rained and rained, which was probably a good thing because it got rid of them. They were in the way.

Andrew Kerr

I ended up living back at Worthy Farm in 1978. I'd been away for the weekend and I came back and saw these tipis over the hedge near the farmhouse, and there was Michael on his tractor with a couple of milk churns on the back. I said what's going on and he said with a broad grin on his face, we've got a festival on our hands.

He told me that – I think it was something to do with Sid [Rawle] – all the people from Stonehenge had been chucked off and Michael was driving back from Glastonbury and there was this convoy of vans and he was stopped by the policeman who was escorting them and the conversation went:

'Where are you going with this lot?'

'We're going down your farm.'

'You can't do that, we haven't got any facilities.'

'You still haven't got that van taxed and insured, have you?'

'OK, just for the night.'

That's how the 1978 festival happened.

Word got round that something was happening and there were maybe a couple of thousand people in the end. I did all the lavatories and the litter picking afterwards.

Thomas Crimble

In the mid-1970s, from about 1974 onwards, I started getting phone calls every year or so from Andrew, who was then living at the farm again, saying there's a whole bunch of hippies looking for a festival. Do you want to come down and help? They never had a name, they were just the 'solstice weekend', a load of people who wound up at Worthy Farm. I played at a number of those, with the Windfuckers or whoever else happened to have turned up. The whole point was it wasn't organised, it just organically came together.

In 1978 I helped to escort a group of people who had been camping on the common next to [the local MP] Heathcote-Amory's back garden. The police had asked Michael if they could bring them to Worthy Farm. It was like that for nearly every solstice during the Seventies. That was the year we had Nik [Turner's] Pyramid stage. That was also the one where we ran a 13 amp cable out of Andrew's caravan to the stage and there was someone there with a whole bag of coins feeding a meter. So whenever they got spaced out or forgot, the music would stop.

At that festival on the solstice there was a fantastic double rainbow over the valley.

Nik Turner

In 1977 there was a festival at Butleigh Wood, which is just up the road from Glastonbury. Then there was all this clever tensile staging floating around, and some of it got used at these free festivals. Some of it came through Bill Harkin, who was the designer of the original

Glastonbury stage, and was then doing stage design for The Rolling Stones. There was a thing called the magician's hat, which I think was the section of the staging that had been used as a mixing desk by the Stones on one of their tours. The magician's hat was used at Butleigh Wood that particular year.

We had our own stage constructed out of aluminium and canvas, which was a scale model of the Great Pyramid. It had a base 35 feet square and was about 35 feet high, and it folded out from a trailer. It was like an orgone accumulator, based on the theories of Wilhelm Reich. Orgone accumulators are structures made from alternating organic and inorganic materials which generate a life-force energy. They form an order out of random energy, so they were seen as a cure for cancer.

So in 1978 I had a call from Harry [Williamson] saying there's a festival going on at Glastonbury – bring the stage. So I piled the part I had on to my VW van and took it down and set it up on Worthy Farm. What had apparently happened was that these people who were at Butleigh Wood the previous year had tried to go there again but the police had road-blocked it, so there was this long convoy of traffic looking for a site. Michael Eavis got caught up in the middle of it, so being a nice guy he agreed that they could pull off the road for a couple of days.

With the album I had done about Egyptology, we had done a big free concert at the Roundhouse, which Barney Bubbles had choreographed, financed by Charisma Records, which was my label at the time. So we had all these professional dancers re-enacting The Egyptian Book of the Dead in a science-fictional context with two-dimensional hieroglyphic mime. That was the story I had thought about in the Great Pyramid in Egypt personified on stage. So we did that performance at Glastonbury.

•••

1979
THE YEAR
OF THE CHILD

Michael Eavis secured a bank loan enabling Arabella Churchill and others to organise a festival in aid of the United Nations Year of the Child. The Children's World and Theatre Tent were initiated, with fringe theatre groups including Footsbarn Theatre and the Natural Theatre Company. On the main stage music was provided by Peter Gabriel, Steve Hillage and Sky. The ticket price rose to £5 for the 12,000 strong crowd.

Bands in 1979: Genesis, Nona Hendryx, Peter Gabriel, Sky, Steve Hillage, The Only Ones, The Sensational Alex Harvey Band, Tom Robinson, UK Subs.

Bill Harkin

When the [UN] Year of the Child came up, and Arabella had this idea of staging an event, we already had a resource of people who had been working with Revelation Staging. I was designing tensile lightweight stage systems in the mid-1970s, although when the bands stopped touring for a while, the company went bankrupt and we had to sell the stages.

We had the idea of doing this festival for as low a ticket price as possible and with very few financial resources. Michael came in on it, so there was Michael, myself, Arabella, John Coleman and Emily Young. As we'd done a favour for Peter Gabriel a few months before, he agreed to perform for free. All the bands performed for free in fact, just expenses. Freddy Bannister lent us the inflatable roof he'd bought from Revelation, so all we had to pay for was the scaffolding deck and the towers that carried the roof. But we didn't have the money for the four searchlights which should have been at the corners producing a pyramid of light, with the inflatable at its eye.

Arabella Churchill

It was my idea to do it for the Year of the Child. I said if we're going to do it let's do it for charity. There was Steve Hillage and Miquette, Bill Harkin, John Coleman, Tim Davis, that was the core group, and it was run out of my flat in London, in Elgin Crescent. I was pretty much co-ordinating the whole thing, and then it all got too much, and I remember giving the theatre side to Frances Salter, and she actually managed to get Footsbarn Theatre doing King Arthur, and very nice it was too.

John Coleman did bands, Bill did the staging, Tim was more the money man. The trouble was we didn't charge enough. No wonder we lost money. I think it was about £5, plus I think the people who did the gate may have been a bit dodgy as well. I remember we ended up £49,000 down, which was then an awful lot. There were a lot of people who didn't get paid. We called a creditors' meeting on the Monday after the festival, and I remember sitting in this big circle on the grass, and there were people really hating us, saying things like you've got a house, I'll burn your house down. But we just didn't have the money.

Michael Eavis

In 1979 we decided – Arabella, Bill Harkin and me – to have another proper festival. I thought this sounds a good idea, Arabella's got a lot of energy, so they fired away. Bill had a stage and they had a lot of the infrastructure, nuts and bolts. So they were trying to get it off the ground, but it didn't really go, and then Bill came round about six weeks before the event and said we're going to cancel. I said, surely you can't do that, with all the press and publicity and all the work that's been done.

The problem was they didn't have any money, so I said I'll go to the bank, and Barclays actually lent me fifteen grand, which was a lot then, but they said will you make sure that you write all the cheques yourself? Don't let anyone else write them. The manager was a lovely bloke, really, he was ever so brave. So I got much more involved, because I'd put the farm on the line to get the loan, and if I lost fifteen grand I'd have to sell it for sure.

In the end we just managed to pull the thing off. It was really, really good. There was Sky and Peter Gabriel, it was a really fantastic event and the sun shone. We had about 12,000 people. The John Williams set with Sky was amazing actually and with Tim Blake we got lasers over from France.

Dee Palmer, markets manager

I had a baby strapped to my front in a carrier, and I had to go round collecting money for the stalls, mainly craft and food. I'm not very good at that sort of stuff because a lot of those really wild people just wanted to tell me to clear off, and a lot of them did. I met some wonderful people doing it, and some absolutely terrifying nightmares. It rained, which never helps, there was no money to pay for anything, and that formed our belief that in order to go forward with the festival it had to be charged for – as little as possible, but in order that the people who'd organised it didn't lose out.

It took me months to recover – I was very, very tired – but people told me afterwards it was the only part of the festival that made any money.

Chris Howes, local GP

I'm a local GP in Shepton Mallet, Pilton's in our practice area, and I first got involved in 1979. We had a huge marquee that year with a registration desk, Red Cross nurses and first aiders, but hardly any patients.

John Sauven, London

I ran a café for the Central American Human Rights organisation. This was at a time when Central America was in flames – Guatemala, El Salvador, Nicaragua. The Sandinistas were in power, there was a civil war in El Salvador, and lots of human rights abuses because of the death squads.

We had no experience of running a café, we'd probably never cooked anything but baked beans on toast, but we just thought, it's Glastonbury, let's run a café and make money for the campaign. So we hired a refrigerated truck, hired a marquee, got all the cooking stuff together and went down there – it was just unbelievably hard work, 24/7. And of course it was difficult communicating with the punters because they were not always that coherent, even in terms of being able to order food. So it was quite amusing. It was quite a big investment to organise all that, but I remember we made £2,000.

Dan Plesch, CND organiser, Bristol

I first stumbled there in 1979 as a mid-twentysomething. I was just moving to Bristol from Nottingham, and I was training as a social worker. It had the impact on me that it has on so many people. It wasn't so much the music as that something on that scale was such fun and yet had no visible evidence of orthodox officialdom. Here was something that even at the time was quite large but where all sorts of wild, wonderful and slightly scary things were going on. It was off in some other realm. There's always been the immense attraction of the buzz for me, as for so many people.

I remember camping opposite the second stage, which was then a tent, and some punk band from Edinburgh arrived at about 4 o'clock in the morning and started tuning up at full blast. And when people started saying that they wanted to be asleep at that time, they were quietly told to shut up and 'get with the programme', whatever that was.

I'd recently shorn my shoulder-length hair after leaving university and was looking remarkably straight, and I heard someone say that since I was wandering around aimlessly I must be from the drugs squad. And when I went to the information stall and enquired about the weather forecast I was lectured that I should be enjoying the festival regardless.

Then we were sitting round our camp fire when some youth turned up in an obviously stolen Austin Maxi that he'd driven right across the campsite. He came and joined us carrying a lady's handbag that had clearly been in the car and contained a remarkable variety of prescription drugs. He then proceeded to munch his way through them, with a little help from some of us, and several hours later, as the camp fire dimmed, he got back in the car and drove off across the festival, crunching over tents as he went. That was my earliest exposure to drug culture. I think I was gobsmacked at the time.

Nik Turner

I've been referred to as the keeper of the flame, the spirit of Hawkwind. I always had these principles about peace and love and stuff like that, which was how Barney Bubbles got involved, and *Frendz* magazine and Michael Moorcock [fantasy writer] saw the band as something with principles. Michael Moorcock featured the band in his books.

I'd been taking the Sphynx show on the road round free festivals, starting off with this brilliant mime show, and in 1979 I was commissioned by the BBC to perform the Egyptian show on my stage at Glastonbury…it came out of a series of articles that Jeremy Sandford was writing for the *Sun* about reincarnation. They filmed it and interviewed me and a girl called Karina, who was singing with us.

The Sphynx band wasn't very commercial, it was very spiritual, a bit too soft, so by then I'd formed a new band called Inner City Unit. So we performed this Egyptian show and then at one o'clock in the morning, with the proper Inner City Unit band, we started playing some loud, hard-edged almost punk music. Then we incurred the wrath of Michael Eavis and Tony Andrews, who came down and said we were spoiling the festival for everybody. I supposed we'd broken the curfew, although we were right down the bottom. It wasn't as if there were a lot of people living round there. It was a bit anarchic, I suppose, we weren't trying to get up people's noses, we were just a bit bored with the sort of airy-fairiness of everything, and the lack of anything happening.

Thomas Crimble

The 1979 festival was organised from London, which was a big mistake because there seemed to be a lack of co-ordination somewhere. Lots of shuffling of paper, but there didn't seem much reality. I actually went to see Guru Maharaji for the first two days of the festival, he was appearing in London, and when I got down on the Sunday night everyone was in floods of tears. It had all gone horribly wrong. We had this country–town thing going on, but it proved a failure. You've got to organise a festival from where it happens. It was after that that Michael took hold of the reins.

Michael Eavis

There were funny people that dealt with the money, they were kind of gangster types. One of them was called Straight Mick, I don't know where they found him, who seemed a bit dodgy. But eventually we got enough in cash from the gate takings to pay off the £15,000 bank loan, so I took that back to Barclays in Wells, and Straight Mick came with me and a nasty-looking security bloke with a baseball bat and baggy shorts and hairy legs. So I said don't let him get out of the car for heaven's sake. They were all really weird.

The whole company we'd formed was folded up in the end. But I suddenly realised at that point that I didn't get scared, I didn't get sleepless nights and I enjoyed the challenge. I was actually enjoying myself, which was extraordinary really because it wasn't in my background. And I realised then that I had skills that I hadn't seen before. I get on with people quite well, I can manage them, I can persuade them to do things, I can get them to put in their time and effort and energy for a reasonable rate or even voluntarily in some cases. It still lost a lot of money, but it was laying the seeds for future festivals.

•••

PEACE, POLITICS AND THE POLICE
1980–1990

'I saw a crescent
You saw the whole of the moon'
The Waterboys (*The Whole of the Moon*)

With the election of Margaret Thatcher in 1979, the alternative culture of the Seventies began to be brutally assaulted by middle England Conservatism. The hippie dream went underground. Thatcher espoused defence of the Empire, nuclear weapons, stronger police powers and pushing back the boundaries of the welfare state. There was no such thing as society, she roared.

Glastonbury Festival, meanwhile, changed in two important ways. First, Michael Eavis took more direct control of its finances and organisation. Secondly, he decided to hitch its fortunes to the political movement with which an increasing number of young people were identifying – the Campaign for Nuclear Disarmament. It proved an inspired move.

From politically committed performers like The Poison Girls and Paul Weller, the festival spread out to encompass favourites like Madness, Ian Dury, Elvis Costello, New Order, Sinead O'Connor, Echo and the Bunnymen and The Cure. And apart from the music there were whole new areas opening up in the Worthy Farm fields, with theatre performances, a children's field, a classical music tent, world music arena and, on the calmer upper slopes of the site, the spiritual core of the festival was kept alive in what became known as the Green Fields. Through the 1980s, Glastonbury grew from a small gathering of 18,000 to become a major event in the alternative summer calendar, with numbers pushing towards 100,000.

1981
THE FIRST CND FESTIVAL

Undeterred by the losses made at all the previous festivals, Michael Eavis decided to organise a large-scale event to raise money for the peace movement – the first Glastonbury CND Festival. It took two months to build a permanent Pyramid stage out of telegraph poles and ex-Ministry of Defence metal sheeting; it doubled up as Worthy Farm's winter feed store. From it, the crowd was addressed by historian E.P. Thompson and CND chairman Bruce Kent. Entertainers included Ginger Baker, New Order, Aswad and Taj Mahal. 18,000 people came, and enough profit was made to give CND £20,000.

Bands in 1981: Aswad, Ginger Baker, Gong, Hawkwind, John Cooper Clarke, Judy Tzuke, Matumbi, New Order, Rab Noakes, Roy Harper, Supercharge, Taj Mahal, The Jazz Sluts, The Sound.

Andrew Kerr

During 1980 we did monthly gigs in the wagon shed (next to the farmhouse). It could take 350 people, but when Ginger Baker played with Airplane there were over 1,000.

We also had Jajouka, which was a Moroccan band that Brian Jones of The Rolling Stones had found. They came and took over the wagon shed and lived in it. They were musicians that went from village to village in Morocco and were doing the same sort of thing here. While they were staying they invited us (myself, Michael and Jean) to dinner. They'd bought a sheep from Harold Butt, the next door farmer, and slaughtered it in hallal fashion and cooked it, and there was this huge brass plate full of meat. It was absolutely delicious. Michael said: 'I never thought I'd be eating one of Harold Butt's sheep on the stage of the wagon shed.'

Then Michael suddenly made this tie-up with CND – an absolute masterstroke. But he didn't like to tell me about it because he thought, because I was a bit of a toff, I might not approve. But it was really wonderful.

Michael Eavis

After 1979 was all folded up (Bill Harkin had left and taken his funny stage away with him), we took a year off. But the following year I thought I would try and do it all myself, especially since I'd virtually come in at the end of the last one to make it happen. So I started all over again on my own.

At that time there were cruise missiles coming into Newbury, we were involved with the formation of the Shepton Mallet CND group, all our friends were involved, so we were sucked into it. Jean and I and the children went off to the CND marches and listened to E.P. Thompson in Trafalgar Square. Emily was born in 1979 so I took her on my back. And the fact that we had a baby around, and other children in their teens, made me think even more about the horrors of nuclear war. You get a lot more passionate about it when you've got a little baby.

So we were treading it out, marching through the streets of London, hundreds of thousands of people, and I thought at that point I would go into the CND offices, see Bruce Kent (CND general secretary), and see if he was interested in being involved with a festival. I was very apologetic at first. I said to him we're not very tidy round the edges, the image may not be perfect, maybe it's not the sort of thing you want to be associated with. But he said, that sounds absolutely ideal, a great way to get people on board. I was being most apologetic but he was very keen.

So once I had his support and all the officers of CND's support, we were able to use the mailing addresses of all the members. We printed a festival poster and sent it out, and the CND supporters loved it, they worked at the festival and got bands to play. There was no licensing legislation then, we just did what we wanted, so it was all income. And we made £20,000 for them in the first year. That was an absolute fortune.

Mark Cann, main stage production

I was a teacher at a local comprehensive in Wells when I first got involved in 1981. I'd already been to a few gigs in the wagon shed during the late Seventies, but never really met Michael properly. Then he phoned up just before the festival and said could we [mid-Somerset CND] supply an information service. That was a table at the end of a marquee with a couple of bus timetables and a few maps.

The following year we did it more professionally, but about halfway through the Saturday night someone said that a band needed paying – nobody seemed to be organising money from the farmhouse to go to the stage for them to be paid – so I got deputed to do a couple of journeys with money through the fields. I think Randy California was one of the acts. Then on Saturday night everything came to a grinding halt because they ran out of diesel for the generator. There was this hiatus for about three-quarters of an hour until people realised that the fuel had run out.

Arabella Churchill

In 1981, after Michael took it under his control and made it a CND event, I suppose we were all summoned back. By then I had set up the Children's World charity, and I'd already got involved in running the Glastonbury Children's Festival, so I decided that since my main work was with children, I would take on theatre, although I didn't know much about the theatrical side in those days.

That first year I had one marquee right over towards the main stage, not a proper field. I tried to cordon off an outside area as well, but that soon disappeared entirely under people's tents.

Ian McAllister, *Sanity* (CND magazine, 1981)

With just under 20,000 people, hundreds of stalls, health food till it came out of your ears, secondhand clothes, books, Zen Buddhists and others, the festival got under way on Friday, 19th June.

Bruce Kent gave a rousing speech. On Trident: Do you want to spend £6,000 million to kill people in other lands? 'No!' came the reply. Do you hate Russians? 'No!' Do you hate the Chinese? 'No!' We are the ones here today who will stop the nuclear arms race!

We slumbered out of our tents on Saturday morning, screwed our eyes back in and then gathered for breakfast – Reggae soup *Matumbi* – conclusive proof that 'skank' before lunch does not seriously damage youth health.

The Sound, a new-wave group from London were on. Looking lost on the massive Pyramid stage they powered their way through the relaxed atmosphere of the festival: 'What are you going to do, whilst you've still got the strength to move?'

Really though there was more fun to be had in the small theatre and children's area. I saw some singers, theatre groups (watch out for the excellent European Theatre of War), mime artists and Ekome – an African dance troupe with drummers and singers. I even got to play along.

Billy Jenkins, musician

Not many people remember Ginger Baker's Nutters, maybe it was too long ago, but we were headlining. The stage was the cows' winter quarters and the whole place smelled of shit. Roy Harper was on before us, droning on, way over his allotted time, and we were running into the midnight curfew. We were worrying we might not get paid. So Ginger got on stage and started dismantling the other drummer's kit, and ended up having a punch up with Harper before we got on.

When we did start playing there were missiles flying about everywhere; maybe after half a day of Peace and Love the audience needed something different. Ginger stopped when he got a big rock in the face. He had blood running down his face and he was pleading with them. Then we played 'Wheelchair Dance Festival', which the crowd took as an even bigger insult, and we were stoned off for good. As soon as I got off stage I fell into a two-foot deep running sewer. I've never been back again.

Peter Hook, musician with New Order

I'm having difficulty remembering anything but the first one we did. We'd played the gig, great show, and we're on our way back to the hotel, about half past one in the morning. And Bernard sees a UFO. Really clearly. And we're all talking about this and thinking it's great. Until we realise that probably everyone sees UFOs at Glastonbury all the time. Because they're all so twatted...

The Second Pyramid

Dan Plesch

CND had a marquee allocated in 1981, we ran an information stand and we showed *The War Game* [classic film attacking concept of civil defence against nuclear attack, then banned by the BBC] on an endless loop – that got quite a lot of people coming in. About halfway through the festival someone came in and said they needed help taking the tickets, so I found myself in Muddy Lane with a group of people including Michael Eavis and some kids from Millfield School.

We were soon dealing with up to 2,000 volunteers each year, many of whom wouldn't have come to the festival if it hadn't been a fundraiser for a particular cause. Michael's always had a very good approach, that if people want to benefit from the festival they should contribute in some way. I think it's a very sound principle.

Of course the CND involvement was also massively controversial, both within the festival and with the local community. It was quite a high risk stance. Within the festival there was a sense that CND was certainly not New Age, more like Old Age, very hard left politics and frankly a lot of very unpleasant varieties of arrogant communism within its ranks. Some people even objected to the CND symbol going up above the Pyramid, and preferred a sun.

Bill Harkin

For 1981 Michael asked me to design another Pyramid stage for the site, but to do it using telegraph poles. I wasn't that happy with the idea, but I then spent a little time looking at the feasibility of how to get the structural calculations right. I came up with a way it could be done, but then Michael couldn't get enough telegraph poles, and could only get hold of newly cut pine thinnings. At that point I said I'd love to work with you on this, but if I used the wrong wood it could ruin my reputation. Tony Andrews took over at that point and saw the thing through to completion.

Michael Eavis

It was a good focal point because I got all the local unemployed people involved with building the Pyramid. We bought up all the old telegraph poles from all over the south west of England and we found a way of bolting them together. It was a good thing to get people off the streets, it gave them something to go to work for, they were excited about it. People that weren't any good we didn't keep, we were quite tough on that, but they were mostly quite talented builder, carpenter types, although we didn't pay them a lot. There's one guy who remembers to this day that I paid him £7 a week, and we have a laugh about it.

The only problem was that I had no idea what we would cover the framework with. I just told everybody that something would happen, something would turn up. Then I went down to Taunton cattle market one Saturday to buy some cows, and there was a lorryload of sheet metal there, a huge artic trailerload of it. So I asked about it and they said it was reinforcing sheets for Ministry of Defence ammunition dumps. It was really well-made stuff, the sheets all interlocked, and it looked just the job. So we put some sheets on the ground and all the farmers came to have a look. The guy wanted £10 a sheet, but I got them for £6 and he drove them all back to Pilton for me.

All the people there – Roger, Ian and Tony (Andrews) – were very sceptical, but I said, this is absolutely perfect. So we started to put them up, and as they went on, one by one, even Roger agreed it was fantastic. So then I had to get special bolts to fix them on to the wooden beams, and ironically they cost more than the sheets did. The amazing thing is that I have never seen anything like that in the market either before or since. Isn't that weird?

Tony Andrews, creator of Funktion One

I've got the top of the original Pyramid right here in my house. Found it lying round in the general rubble around the stage and rescued it. It was part of the work, and it means a lot to me, and to a lot of people who were there. Glastonbury is a very spiritual place…and we definitely had something at the beginning. I was starting out in sound and we needed a gathering. We'd meet up at Andrew's [Kerr] house at Strand-on-the-Green, Twink from The Pink Fairies was involved, Mick Farren from IT and The Deviants…

There's been a window open for great work only a few times in the last thirty years – in the late Sixties, and Glastonbury Fayre was part of that really, and then again probably in the mid to late Eighties, the beginning of the house thing. There certainly isn't a window open now. Music has no juice in it any more; it's like toothpaste coming out of a tube.

My main thing was the spiritual purpose of all these people coming together…it was for something greater. As an example, why do people go to churches and pray? Glastonbury to me wasn't ever about politics, it was the people. It did attract the underground avant garde, that's who put the energy into it from the start.

Michael got me to go to a meeting and we sat up all night talking about a new stage. I persuaded him to put in a permanent structure and he was adamant it had to be a pyramid. Something that was built for reasons of love, for the greater good.

The seeds of division were there early and it did start to get a bit strange. We put a huge sun on the Pyramid, on top, and it was taken off, and this great heavy CND symbol went on. So I rolled that off… it was literally crushing the stage. Then this doctor running the medical staff said he would pull out if we didn't have CND.

Michael and Jean had only just had Emily and they were worrying about nuclear weapons, fair enough, but in a nutshell my view of Michael is he tries to bring it down to his own level. His land, his festival; he was very earthbound.

Then they had a peace march, torch-lit down through the site, and it looked like the Ku Klux Klan – to me it was wrong. There were so many metaphysical demonstrations arising from the Pyramid – there was stone in each corner which I'd gathered from the genuine Great Pyramid in Eygpt. I think he got fed up with us lot having minds of our own. Because we weren't aiming for a million pounds for charity, we were aiming for something higher, a global solution, a critical mass.

And Glastonbury was a big name, it didn't need 'big names' to come and play there, but all of a sudden Michael started talking to promoters, and we had this band and that band that had to play with them. I think he got starstruck.

Dan Plesch

Taj Mahal played a couple of times. 1981 was a slightly damp festival and the electric power was provided by surplus Royal Engineers generators on trucks and the weather got into them and there was hardly any power. Other bands didn't want to risk their reputations but Taj and his band had just got in from Heathrow, having fought their way through our traffic, and for several hours, without any ado at all, he just came out on to the stage, with several tens of thousands of people in a bad mood, and started singing solo, with a guitar and spot, African-American field songs. And within a few minutes he had everybody roaring and singing along and then started into a broader repertoire and then, when they got the rest of the band on stage and got the power sorted out, they played a full set. It was absolutely stunning music.

•••

1982
FLYING PROTEST

The festival was becoming established, with a supporting casbah of market stalls selling everything from jewellery to scrumpy cider. When a low-flying aircraft towing an anti-CND slogan buzzed the site, two rockets bought as celebratory fireworks were fired off in its direction. The Bishop of Bath and Wells spoke from the main stage and artists included Van Morrison, Steel Pulse, Jackson Browne, Richie Havens and John Cooper Clarke. Lasers pierced the sky in a spectacular finale. This was also the first muddy year, with the highest rainfall in 45 years recorded on the Friday of the three-day event. CND and local charities benefited to the tune of £25,000.

Bands in 1982: A Certain Ratio, Aswad, Black Uhuru, Climax Blues Band, Jackson Browne, John Cooper Clarke, Judy Tzuke, Richie Havens, Roy Harper, Steel Pulse, Talisman, The Blues Band, The Chieftains, Thompson Twins, U2, Van Morrison.

Mark Cann

It was a very tiny backstage area then, the dressing room area was very small, everybody just mucked in together. So the bands turned up in cars and minibuses, vans, trucks – there weren't many big tour coaches then – we'd find them somewhere to park and then there were portacabins for dressing rooms. That hasn't changed that much. There was a catering tent, or we'd take food and drink into the dressing rooms. It was all very informal. When Bananarama came, with three quite smartly dressed girls, they asked for somewhere to wash and one of the people doing the dressing rooms said, here's a bowl of water. They looked rather askance. But when they were told this is the middle of a field in Somerset, this is the best we do for running water, they just got on with it.

In a sense Michael didn't see why he had to spend the money on providing lavish facilities. It had always been part of the philosophy that you did Glastonbury almost on the same terms as the punters.

Sometimes it's been difficult. Van Morrison, for instance, has always been a very private person in terms of not wanting to be seen backstage. That was difficult, trying to keep people away as he walked from dressing room to stage. It became a bit of a saga for half an hour. But the vast majority have accepted that Glastonbury is different. Even if the band haven't done it before, the tour managers and the crews have, so they know what to expect. They enter into the spirit of it.

Sheelagh Allen, personal assistant to Michael Eavis

Van Morrison was a regular, and very much appreciated. But his appearances had to be carefully co-ordinated. Michael had to arrange to pick him up at his hotel personally and drive him into the backstage area. The timing had to be spot on, literally, so that he would just arrive in time to go on stage. I think he got very nervous before the performance and it was cut very fine, but we always got him there.

John 'Rhino' Edwards, bass player, Status Quo

Can I claim a record for playing the main stage twice on the same day? I was on with the Climax Blues Band, then I was back on with Judy

Tzuke. Can't remember if I changed my shirt. I've never played there with Status Quo, though, we've never been on the bill…

Mark Cann

It was always something of a drama getting the lasers going because they would require large amounts of cooling water to make them operate. They generate a lot of heat so there needs to be a constant flow of water. So we had these great big plastic barrels on the corner of the stage, which was always a struggle to organise. But when they worked they were amazing, especially when there was a bit of mist late at night.

Dick Vernon, markets manager

The early organisation of trading at the festival looks rather random in retrospect – with a few invited traders, lots of gatecrashers and hundreds of 'fly pitchers'. The markets people were just let in at a certain time and it was like the Klondyke gold rush as they charged down, trying to get the best pitches. It was on a first come, first served basis and fairly chaotic.

Dick Jones, stallholder

In the beginning it was a free for all, you'd go and see Mike Eavis beforehand and then turn up on the delegated day. It was like a Le Mans start, you just drove around and claimed your pitch. It was complete anarchy, no policing, and you never knew who your neighbours were. Even when we pitched up next to the ex-services CND stall, a guy came over brandishing a bread knife, thinking we'd taken his cool box. It took my wife, who was about four foot nothing, to rugby tackle this bloke before he legged it.

The CND Backlash

Stephen Abrahall, local CND activist

I first got involved with the festival through CND. We were invited by Michael to run an information stall. The idea of getting a donation of £500, as it was then, was worth an awful lot of jumble sales.

There have always been other music festivals, of course. But the difference with Glastonbury, and with the peace movement as well, is the spread of people that they attract. So we didn't just get young things, we had stalls from ex-services CND selling tea and cakes. There was just a really good cross-section of ages. I think that spread has a mellowing effect, it tones down the more boisterous element in the crowd.

That political dimension has always been an undercurrent of the festival. Maybe it's a very subtle one, a bit like eating in a vegetarian restaurant and you don't realise until you've left that you haven't actually consumed any meat. Similarly with the festival you were taking on the ethos of an alternative society that had a socialist element to it, without realising it, because it wasn't thrust down your throat.

Of course there was a backlash. There was a time when an aeroplane flew over the site with a banner floating out at the back saying something like 'Support CND, Back the Russians'. And somebody symbolically sent a rocket off in its direction.

Michael Eavis

The plane flying over was obviously timed to coincide with Bruce Kent speaking on the main stage on the Sunday afternoon. So as it went round and round it drowned him out, you couldn't hear him speaking – the PA wasn't that good in those days. It was really noisy and he was almost dive-bombing us with this slogan.

Someone was going to do a firework show at the end of the evening with some huge rockets – they cost about £70 each – so I got on the radio to him and said, 'The next time he comes round can you let one off?' So the rocket went off and it just exploded in thousands of particles all round the plane. It was really brilliant, he got it spot on, and everybody cheered like mad. It was a marvellous moment. The plane never came back again. After that, there was a court case and the pilot was fined £400 for flying over a crowded area without a licence. And during the case the pilot pointed at me and accused me of firing a rocket at him, which he said was really dangerous.

•••

1983
LONG ARM OF THE LICENCE

The Local Government (Miscellaneous Provisions) Act was introduced, requiring the festival to have a licence for the first time. This set a crowd limit as well as a long list of requirements for access roads, water supply and hygiene. The festival's own radio station, Radio Avalon, broadcast for the first time. 30,000 people came to laugh at Rik Mayall, Nigel Planer and Alexei Sayle, and to listen to Marillion, Aswad, The Beat, UB40, The Chieftains, Fun Boy Three and King Sunny Ade. £45,000 went to CND and local charities.

Bands in 1983: A Certain Ratio, Aswad, Curtis Mayfield, Fun Boy Three, Incantation, King Sunny Ade, Marillion, Melanie, The Beat, The Chieftains, UB40.

Mark Cann

Organisationally, the Pyramid hadn't been that wonderful as there was nobody co-ordinating the production. It had just been a group of friends who took it on. So by the end of 1982 it was decided that they needed someone to do all that. That's how I ended up as production manager. From 1983 onwards I was managing the main stage, and eventually that grew to the second stage as well. It was a matter of co-ordinating everybody – making sure the services were supplied, making the arrangements for the acts, looking after them while they were on site, paying them and so on. Even though my role has changed, I've continued doing bits of that job right up till now.

Arabella Churchill

One memorable performance was the Greatest Show on Legs. I remember sitting on the edge of the stage when they did their balloon dance. What happens, to a soundtrack of cha cha music, is that three apparently naked blokes move these balloons round really quickly between each other, but always managing to keep their private parts covered. But then for one reason or another they start to burst them one by one. So at the end they're completely naked, and then this girl in the audience took her clothes off too and I had to persuade her to put them on again. I wasn't expecting any of that at all.

We moved quite soon up to where the children's area is now, which was great except it had a slope. So when it was wet, all our outside performers would just be sliding down the hill. There was a lot of sliding in the wet years.

In the Eighties we had European Theatre of War, who included David Rappaport, the dwarf, who was great fun. It was one of the most moving shows I've ever seen, and one of the few times I've seen nudity work. Robert Stredder said: 'I go naked into the council chamber', and nobody laughed, it was brilliant, it worked. Then they acted out what the government suggested you should do in the case of a nuclear attack – all get under the kitchen table.

Then there was Rik Mayall with his character Kevin Turvey, Jools the poet came every year and a group called Incubus did walkabout turns looking like leprous fifteenth-century people. One of them had this awful habit of coming and embracing me whilst he'd got this pustulous thing on.

And Jonathan Kay's a very good mime artist, but more than that he's sort of like a schoolmaster in that he can get his audience to do anything. So he tends to start in the Cabaret Marquee and then he takes the audience out and does extraordinary things with them, like they'll serenade the police with Yellow Submarine. One year he was making a member of the audience pretend he was Jesus, and this guy then had to convince the multitude that he really was. 'Show us a sign, Lord', they shouted at the top of their voices, and just at that moment the Red Arrows appeared flying low over the field. It was one of those extraordinary things where people come running in and say, 'You'll never believe what's happened, but…'

Ralph Oswick, founder member, Natural Theatre Company

We've come every year since 1971, when we did Beau Nosh, a theatricalised food outlet. We've always done things that are a bit smart, that look completely wrong because everyone else is covered with mud, for instance. In one of the muddy years we dressed in really smart evening dress but with Bolloms see-through plastic dry cleaners' bags right over us. We just made our way right across the site, treading very carefully, and then getting stuck with our bottles of champagne dangerously near the toilet trench.

Then there's National Silence Day, where we have cotton wool in our ears and we walk about at noisy places trying to make everyone be quiet. And No Smiling, where everybody watching tries to make us laugh, which of course they never can because it's our job not to. It's peer pressure, really, the others get annoyed if you start laughing. You also get very spiteful in those characters – you don't find the audience very funny.

Sometimes we've been taken more seriously than we expected. In the 1980s we did a CIA-type security thing, pretending that a helicopter was about to land and running right through the crowd in grey suits and mirror shades. We had walkie-talkies made out of American cigarette packets. But then the real security came and rugby-tackled us, got us up against the wall until suddenly one of them recognised one of the actors and let us go.

Dan Plesch

King Sunny Ade was quite phenomenal, not least because the sound and light show was extraordinary, including the summer lightning which accompanied it. He had a large Nigerian troupe, an enormous amount of power and energy that blasted round the whole site, and giant searchlights that carried out into the surrounding hillside.

Polly Bradford, Nether Stowey, Somerset

I was about eight in 1983 when I first came. A friend of mine's mother had a jewellery stall. We came on to the site down a track near the farmhouse. That's when it started getting exciting because you could see all the vans and old ambulances coming down in front of you – that's when they used to let travellers in.

We used to camp those first years behind the row of market stalls and if it wasn't raining we spent nearly all the time in the children's field. We spent a lot of time there doing circus skills – acrobatics and stilt walking – and queuing up to get our faces painted. I've got a photo of myself with a night sky and a rainbow on one side and a moon on the other. And watching loads of shows of course. The good thing was you didn't need to have an adult there because it was safe.

Next to the children's area there was a gulley between two fields with a hedge and trees that had been turned into a grotto, with lights and decorations, bits of painted wood. It was like a maze, with weird things to explore. It was magical, especially at night, although it wasn't obvious who had done it.

One year, after the local carnival in our village, we went to the festival in an old Austin van with horsehair seats which had been painted up specially for our village carnival in blue and white and 'The Snow Queen' on the side. One bloke came up to us and asked if we were selling coke.

And once we camped round the side of the farmhouse. That was when the cows escaped from their field. They were just walking right through the tents.

Robert Kearle, festival worker

The cows used to run round the whole site until quite close to the festival, literally the day before the punters came in – so they could walk in all the cow pats – which with e-coli and things nowadays you're not allowed to do. So we'd spend time getting the cows out of the big top tents and from behind stalls – it was a bit of a mammoth effort. I think Michael used to like that really, the cows causing mayhem around the site.

It was Taff, Hank the Bin's mate, who used to watch the cows when they were in their own separate field during the festival, and famously one day he didn't keep an eye on them. He was watching one gate and they got out from a gate at the other end of the field and then proceeded to run amok around the site. It was just before the festival and it took a few hours to get them back in again. And then Michael came along, wound down the window of his Land Rover and said, with a bit of a smile: 'Ten thousand years of evolution have just passed you by, haven't they Taff?' And Taff's response, which was just as good, went: 'You don't pay me enough to keep me in dope all day long, let alone to make sure I do the job properly.'

Ian Japp, proprietor, Maximum Funky Intentions

My first attendance was in a minivan which we parked illegally in a field, before walking all the way in. I must have been there all of four hours. To me, going there as a punter wasn't so nice. I'm a guard animal by nature, I wanted to work on a stall, really dig in for the duration. I'd been at college with Brian Ebor Hardy, the boss of Mussa, who imported Moroccan pottery, and I came back employed by him. He thought I'd be pretty good on security, or maybe he just fancied my beautiful girlfriend Sarah.

The old market strip was up on the hill near the farmhouse, and it was a tiny little reggae sound system we were near – just two guys and a portable boom box – that gave me the idea of installing entertainments. Only we didn't get to use them at first. Right up next to us was Fort Apache from Manchester, manned by six lads who really didn't particularly want me to take their photos, although they did ask to borrow our speakers. There was nothing we could do about their noise level either. They were, to put it mildly, a lot more streetwise than we were.

•••

1984
THE GREEN FIELDS

The festival went ahead after Michael Eavis successfully defended himself at Shepton Mallet magistrates' court against five charges of breaching the site licence. Specific parking areas were designated for the first time, with stewards employed to direct traffic. The Green Fields started up as a separate area to celebrate traditional skills, pleasures and rituals. Speakers included Bruce Kent and local MP Paddy Ashdown. Main bands were The Smiths, Fairport Convention, Billy Bragg, Ian Dury, and Elvis Costello as surprise guest. £60,000 was raised for CND and local charities.

Bands in 1984: Billy Bragg, Black Uhuru, Elvis Costello, Fairport Convention, Fela Kuti, Howard Jones, Ian Dury, Joan Baez, The Smiths, The Waterboys, Weather Report.

Ann Waterhouse, original member of the Green Collective

The roots of Glastonbury's first Green Field go back to 1980, when activists from the Ecology Party held a summer gathering – a conference in a field – on this site. It was a very ad hoc event, a mixture of green events under canvas, a few stalls, some entertainment, tipis and a sweat lodge. There was a wonderful co-operative spirit and all of us involved were determined to do it again.

By 1982, the perspective had broadened from the party political to the wider Green movement. The sunflower logo of Die Grünen, the German Green Party, was adopted and its leader Petra Kelly sent representatives to the gathering: she attended in person a few years later. In 1983 the gathering had moved to Lambert's Hill and it became clear the area could not sustain two events – the gathering and the festival – so we agreed with Michael to use Norman's Close for our own show. By 1985 this had become like a festival within a festival, a village to the main event's city.

Liz Eliot, Green Fields co-ordinator

I suppose that kind of rebellious streak first turned up in the Fifties when we were anti-this and anti-that and angry young people, and then the hippies came along, which was a completely different scene. I loved that belief that everything was possible, providing everyone saw it our way. Our way was caring for the planet and not being hugely consumeristic, against chemicals and antibiotics unless they were absolutely essential, very reasonable really.

Then in the Seventies I joined Friends of the Earth to campaign against the sewage going into the sea. I was living in Kent then, with three small children, and lived the hippie ideal in a big farmhouse with goats and chickens and growing vegetables.

I came to the festival in the early Eighties for pure hedonistic pleasure. I was helped by a few little bits of psilocybin – at that time magic mushrooms were completely legal. I spent several wonderful festivals on mushrooms. I came with my children and a crowd from around Crickhowell in Wales, where I was then living, and as the decade progressed, we had a large CND group with us. We camped within a stone's throw of the Pyramid, so close to the whole thing. You could see everything, including the faces on the stage. I remember Judy Tzuke being astonishingly colourful. She played very wild rock music. That was the first time I saw lasers. They just seemed to be everywhere, up and down trees, bouncing back off the clouds. They were spectacular.

I camped with the Crickhowell 'greens' in the first Green Field in 1984. We made a big circle of tents with a huge sunflower in the middle. We were all members of Green CND, which was a bit more anarchic than the main campaign. Our house in Wales was the centre of that group and we had a food-sharing cooperative. The whole belief underpinning that was self-empowerment, and that people in authority weren't necessarily the ones that knew everything, or had necessarily got it right, and the Earth was obviously fundamental – one Earth, one people and living in harmony with each other. That was the year that the totem was carved and erected in the middle of what is now the acoustic field.

The essence of the Green Fields was always about personal growth and self-discovery and empowerment. There was a belief that everybody has a place, a value and worth. That to me was wonderful because part of the workshops that were going on was about how to enjoy yourself all over again if you missed out in childhood. So they did all sorts of crazy games which helped you connect with other people, like turning into a big tank wheel with people lying down and rolling over one another. It's breaking down barriers all the time. It was huge fun.

Michael Eavis

We were building up areas all the time, roughly a new one every two years, so there was a whole galaxy of stuff to organise. I get the people who are skilled in their particular area, like Arabella in the theatre area, Liz Eliot in the Green Fields, and so on. I've tried to recognise people out there who can do things. If people have a flair for it I give them more responsibility.

And they always come to me if there's a serious problem. They know I'm always here, I'm not going to be away on a world cruise, so they can phone me up any time or knock on the door. They know it's my job to sort it out. They know that I'll care and I'll act. That's a great thing, I feel, it's very reassuring. In the Green Fields, for example, we had a sauna that was slightly unsavoury – the women who were working in that area said the chap who was running it had a problem with the ladies. So I went down there and interviewed this bloke and I could see he was a bit dodgy. There were obviously things going on that weren't right. So I said, OK, let's just take the thing down. So we closed it down, sacked him and burned it to the ground. End of story really. I have to do things like that sometimes.

I don't sit on everything, I just do the money and the general policy. My job is to fire people up and get them interested. Without that it wouldn't work. They put so much time in, and they don't get a normal wage or anything. But they know they can call on me, that's my job. They wouldn't want to do it any other way. They wouldn't do it at all.

Enter the Angels

Mark Cann

There was no professional security then, just a bunch of friends checking passes into the backstage area. There was no pit in front of the stage, the barrier was just constructed by us. So one day, twenty or so Hell's Angels from the Windsor chapter turned up with motor bikes, a car and a van. They'd obviously crashed into the site from the perimeter and just driven all the way through. So they said, we're coming in. We took the view that if no-one could stop them from coming on site, there was very little we could do, so they came in to the backstage area and set up camp.

This was a group who had a reputation – they'd had run-ins with the police, been arrested, a couple of them had been shot. They were serious. I think they might have thought they were going to run the stage security, as they had at other big concerts, but it didn't quite work out that way. In the end, a guy called Peewee from Trowbridge, who used to run one of the bars, took them under his wing and they went out on forays into the site to clamp down on illegal beer sellers. They used to confiscate the stuff and return from these trips with stacks of beer and anything else that was contraband. There may have been a few incidents when they were outside, I'm not sure, but when they came back they had this stash of stuff and didn't know quite what to do with it. They got rather bored, they were much happier out on site doing something, so one year they had got hold of a lot of food, cans and so on – it must have been one of the wet years – and they begged, borrowed or stole some cooking equipment, started cooking up some soup, with cans of this and cans of that, felt-tipped a sign and then tried to sell it over the fence to punters in front of the main stage. We just let them get on with it.

There was one incident when they said they were going on stage, and the stage crew had to diplomatically suggest that this wasn't a good idea. Then they went on to Madness's bus, saying they wanted to say hello to Suggs. That was probably the most difficult time we had – the potential for it all going wrong made me feel uncomfortable. But we struck up something of a rapport with their 'leader', for want of a better word, and they were reasonably good after that. It became a bit of a ritual – they came for three or four years in succession until the end of the Eighties.

•••

1985

Worthy Farm had become too small to accommodate the festival so the neighbouring Cockmill Farm land was purchased to enlarge the site by 100 acres. This was also the second year of the mud, and at the end of three days not a blade of grass was to be seen. An army of tractors was commandeered to tow away stranded vehicles. Nonetheless, 40,000 people enjoyed the music of The Pogues, The Boomtown Rats, Joe Cocker, Echo and the Bunnymen and The Style Council. Michael Eavis said, 'We have had the mud bath and proved we can still cope with the conditions.' CND and local charities received £100,000 from the proceeds.

Bands in 1985: Aswad, Billy Bragg, Clannad, Doctor and the Medics, Echo and the Bunnymen, Hugh Masekela, Ian Dury and the Blockheads, James, Joe Cocker, Jonathan Richman and the Modern Lovers, Microdisney, New Model Army, Roger Chapman, The Albion Band, The Boomtown Rats, The Colourfield, The Men They Couldn't Hang, The Pogues, The Poison Girls, The Style Council, Third World, The Untouchables, Working Week.

Emily Eavis, Michael and Jean Eavis's daughter

We're all a bit mad, otherwise we wouldn't have been doing it so long. But we're not a 'mad' family, we're quite a conventional family really. Particularly my dad. People perceive him to be the head of this off-the-wall, hippie family but the irony is actually that Glastonbury, the hedonist Glastonbury that everyone experiences, has been born from a pretty straight bunch.

My mum and dad were nonconformists, but in a subtle way. They didn't run around naked or barefooted in the fields or anything, but there were things verging on rebellion – their own form of rebellion. As Michael says now, he would never stop the festival as long as there was an element of struggle. He would never give up if the council, or anyone else, was being really difficult, and that's an interesting form of rebellion. I was brought up with that – there's a fighter thing I have. Witnessing the struggles they had when I was a child obviously had quite an impact.

I did have mixed feelings quite a lot of the time. There were some incredible, life-affirming moments just through seeing and being surrounded by all those people, in my space, having an amazing time; that's imprinted on my whole being. But there were moments when it freaked me out, too, when I wanted to be like everyone else, in a normal childlike way.

It was also frightening sometimes. Nobody ever actually sat me down and explained what it was about. To me it seemed every year people would just turn up, and they had a look of ownership in their eye. Like, this is our house now, our land, we'll live here for a few weeks and just go for it…it was quite an invasion.

But it quickly became a huge bonus, and the great thing in my life, to the extent that I can't imagine being without it, it's my whole focus. I'm the youngest, of course, I was born in 1979, and that's a significant thing, perhaps why I have the relationship I do with the festival. It was the year Thatcher came in, the year the festival changed, when it developed a political drive, and CND came on board. Thatcher was there bellowing, and the focus was firmly against. We used to go to 'Maggie Out' marches a lot when I was little. And my relationship with the festival's ideals has stayed the same since.

Patrick, my brother, was 14 when I was born. He grew up when Glastonbury was a very different event. It was a huge risk at that time. It then took on a new meaning because of Thatcher. And of course I was dragged around with my parents everywhere, either on my dad's shoulders, or in my mum's arms, but I wasn't a tantrum-y spoilt child, I was quite shy really.

Rachel Austin, Pilton village childhood

We'd waited until the Sunday and headed for the Children's Field, where there were all these ginormous inflatables that made a big impression.

We always went down as a family. The first year Mum and Dad let us go on our own it was really exciting. Rebecca says she went when she was 11. I'd have been more like 18. And my friend's mum wouldn't let us go on our own either. Our parents were seen as stricter than others, but at festival time they were really quite lenient. Mum has loved the festival from the year dot and they were great for helping people where they could. Some villagers would be saying we don't want them in the shop or in our pub, while Mum and Dad would be very accepting of all races and levels. Mum would quite often pick up the hitchhikers, give them lifts or a bed or a mattress for the night. She loved the stories they had to tell.

Our first camp actually at the festival wasn't until we were at university. Which is also about the time we were both made to realise where we lived was actually 'cool'. 'You live in Pilton and you actually know Michael Eavis?' Well, yes we do. We were quite obedient…and yes it was good to be able to go home and have a nice bed. It was the lazy way to do it, knowing you didn't have to experience the toilets, though in later years I've never minded, as long as they're open air.

We called it the Pilton Pop Festival, we didn't have a clue how big it was till much later. It was like Michael Eavis, he's not special, he's not famous – which he obviously is. I still think of him like that now. Our parents went to church every weekend, and though Michael's a Methodist there were quite strong communal services. His first wife, Ruth, was the infant help at our primary school and she was the loveliest person you could meet. And Mum used to enjoy it so much, she was a fiend, desperate to get down there.

It's quite amazing that this little city grows from nothing and then goes back to nothing. The rest of the time it's a great place to go and walk, ride horses. Michael's always really good about that. He'd always welcome people enjoying the beauty of the farm. And we'd take people to see the dragon field and the stone circle. Michael's attitude has also always been quite open about people coming along. Mum came across this poor lady struggling one time and gave her a leg up over the fence. She went down the other side, straight into the police compound, and nobody stopped her.

Emily Eavis

From a child's point of view, witnessing it from quite a short height, it was the whole year, every year and it had the same rhythm. First all the stress with the licence and the booking. It would start to get a bit warmer, and the first people move on site, familiar faces. After that it would get quite a lot warmer and everyone would arrive. Then the whole summer was clearing up and winding down, before I was back at school for winter term, and by the end of that it was the licence application again.

Another year of festival!

Simon Roiser, press officer

I first started doing press, for want of a better phrase, in 1985. It was really basic stuff. I'd done a bit of writing, put roofs on people's houses, taught English in Cornwall but as far as 'public relations' went I was green really. I learnt on the job, came up with some brilliant inventions, especially with the fax machine (there was just one, in the farmhouse), and made sure that people really were who they said they were, and were doing it for the right reasons. That was the big challenge and that took up most of the time.

It was Michael's idea to contact the local papers. Not local as in Somerset, but local as in Aberdeen or Ipswich or somewhere in Kent. We'd do a deal with them. 'Give us a preview', we'd say, and you can have a ticket. Then people would read about it, and they'd turn up, having travelled from all sorts of unlikely places. We had people from Eastern Europe, Russia and Japan as well, a fascinating mixture of foreign journalists, with the same tactic. Then it all got too big and we stopped. But we definitely had to sell it at the beginning.

But the nationals were only interested in the bands, nothing else at all. All they wanted to do was hang around backstage talking to each other. It's probably not much different now. The festival was also a massive freebie for the *NME*, who'd have something like a hundred tickets; but I do remember that the second stage, which was their stage, was fantastic.

I think we got two front-page photographs in the national press my first year, which we all thought was pretty remarkable. It didn't happen again for years and by then the stories were completely different. It wasn't 'Hippies In Drug Riots' or anything sensational then – one of them was just a picture of people baking bread in a mud oven. Then the next year somebody tried to shoot Princess Anne and that wiped us off the front pages for good, really. Until the convoy came along.

Twinkle, Twinkle

Emily Eavis

Out of my two appearances on the main stage, I probably remember more about the first one, even though I was only six years old. It was actually my friend's mum's idea. I was playing my violin in the house, in the kitchen…then within ten minutes I was on the stage. I was wearing my favourite party dress that I was really proud of, lacy with a pink ribbon, pretty unbelievable, with all these stage people shouting: 'Dim the lights.' There was one man with a luminous coat right down at the front I focused on, until I had to turn to Jean and tell her my legs felt like jelly and it was time to take me home. My dad missed it because he was sectioning a madman on the other side of the fence at the time. But I did get a Valentine card from someone in the audience every year until I was about 15.

Thomas Crimble

There was one time when Emily and Jean asked me to take them down, with a friend, to the main stage because she wanted to play her violin. So we went backstage and arranged it. Then we discovered, horror of horror, that her violin was violently out of tune. So I thought, here we are, backstage at Glastonbury, apparently surrounded by musicians in a large guests' tent. So I shouted out – was there a musician there, we need some help tuning up – and the whole place shut up and looked round at me and Emily, but there were no musicians, just 150 hangers on. Then we met Taj Mahal outside and he helped us tune up the violin. Emily played 'Twinkle Twinkle Little Star' and it went down a storm.

Dan Plesch

In 1985 it rained all the way up to the festival, and drizzled during it. It was a swamp. But Michael, to his eternal credit, had a commitment that hard-working people who couldn't get on site until Friday night should not lose all the best camping spots. So he put steel stakes in to protect the prime fields and special gates, which were sunk in concrete. But being wide farm gates, when they opened, they also closed the road ahead. So every time we opened this gate to let one person in, the road was closed, and behind this, in the pouring rain, for several days, we had seven or eight miles of traffic. So on the Thursday, at about midnight, we got a very large tractor and pulled these concrete blocks with the gates on them out of the ground, leaving a sheet of mud and a six foot hole underneath. Andrew (Kerr) stood for at least an hour with a parasol, a torch and a stick, shouting 'hole' loudly, to stop people falling into it.

At the other end, coming up the hill out of the village, we had to spot any vehicle which might have a problem and explain to the probably totally stoned driver who'd been waiting in traffic for six hours how they needed to get into first gear, put their headlights on, use lots of horn and basically rush the hill, with paying customers scattering into the hedges.

Meanwhile in Cockmill Lane, at the exit from the site, we had to commandeer a helicopter to investigate what the blockage was two miles away, and then have several tractors assigned to it. At one level, this sort of festival work is utterly ludicrous, but at another level it's a massive adrenaline buzz.

Mark Cann

In 1985 Paul Weller turned up absolutely immaculate in his white suit to sing with The Style Council. The contrast with the mud was extraordinary. We put down pallets everywhere and somehow he must have managed to pick his way through to the stage.

Liz Eliot

Living in Wales, I used to do food support things during the miners' strike. In 1985 I wore this huge black plastic mac that one of the striking miners had given me at Greenham Common. It came down to the ground on me, and I fell in the mud on my back. It formed a kind of suction pad and I just couldn't get up. It was in the dark, I had to yell, with my feet in the air, and somebody came and hauled me out.

Polly Bradford

I remember the feeling of it as a child. I know it rained a few years. One year we spent a lot of time on the trampoline because it was the only dry place in a sea of mud. It was that kind of mud, not the really stodgy kind, but when it's really slippery on the top. But most of the time I remember it being really hot and nice and dry on the grass. It was better in the evening because you had these really massive piles of wood that you could just take to burn, and everybody had a fire when it got dark. So you could just see lots of fires dotted around the whole festival, lots of lights in the distance and smoke from the fires and lots of shouting and calling as people tried to find each other.

•••

1986
THE 'CONVOY' ARRIVES

Increasingly bigger festivals demanded expansion of the relatively minimal infrastructure, including the farm office, communications, welfare and medical teams. The theatre and children's areas moved to new homes. A temporary refuge was provided for homeless 'convoy' travellers escorted to Glastonbury by the police. For the first time there was a classical music marquee under the auspices of guitarist John Williams. On the Pyramid stage were Black Uhuru, The Psychedelic Furs, Level 42, Simply Red, The Housemartins, The Cure and Madness. German peace activist Petra Kelly gave an address. About £130,000 was raised for CND and local charities, but the Eavis mortgage still hadn't been paid off!

Bands in 1986: Billy Bragg, Black Uhuru, Fuzzbox, Half Man Half Biscuit, Level 42, Madness, Microdisney, Ozric Tentacles, Ruby Turner, Simply Red, Ted Chippington, The Cure, The Dream Syndicate, The Go-Betweens, The Housemartins, The June Brides, The Nightingales, The Pogues, The Psychedelic Furs, The Waterboys, The Woodentops.

Bob Young, music industry consultant and songwriter, London

It was the mad old, bad old Eighties – the year after Live Aid, and two years after Status Quo did their first End of the Road gig at Milton Keynes Bowl when I was playing harmonica with them – and Glastonbury stood, still stands, for everything bands wanted to do. It was the cool festival to play, the only one left standing, and playing on the Pyramid was the absolute pinnacle.

I was managing Buddy Curtess and the Grasshoppers and we played the gig, then partied seriously after that. No hotels and definitely no camping, Glastonbury wouldn't have been Glastonbury then if you didn't just fall out of it at the end. It's just one of those festivals that should always be there, the fact that it's still on is enough. In terms of rock and roll as it was at the time it was chaos, absolute madness. Backstage and front of stage everything happened just the way it shouldn't have happened, but, by God, what an end result – it was chaos that worked really well. I've had artists I look after down there since, Paul Oakenfold, and Lemon Jelly a couple of years ago. But I don't think I'll go back until they get Status Quo down there, and then I'll definitely pack my harmonica. It must be about time Quo got a look in after all these years. After all, if Metallica like them, why can't Michael Eavis?

Norman Cook aka Fatboy Slim, DJ/producer

I must confess I've never actually been to Glastonbury as a punter. I wouldn't have gone there as punter, no, no, no! It was just a lot of hippies in a field; I had a preconception of what it was, and I made my choice. I did all my roughing it as a Forest School Camper when I was younger. I like my creature comforts, so now I only go when I'm working.

But the first time I played, the first time I actually went, was with The Housemartins in 1986. I was dragged there kicking and screaming. It was pretty much in and out. We were really, really nervous and I think the result of that was our introduction from the stage was: 'Fuck off, you hippy twats!' We called the crowd bearded hippies and encouraged them to throw objects at us, which they did. That was our warm introduction to Glastonbury, kind of half ironic and half not knowing what to do. And we got away with it! I would like to apologise for this; we were young, impressionable and short-sighted at the time and totally gauged the audience wrongly. I would also like to sincerely thank anyone who *didn't* throw anything!

Roy Gurvitz, founder, Lost Vagueness

The first time I ever went to Glastonbury Festival was in 1986. I went there with a rucksack, I hitched a lift from Yate (near Bristol). There was a travellers site up there and I knew a couple of people. I got to Glastonbury quite late in the day, I remember it being dark; it was much more open then, the fence only went half way round so it gave the illusion of being a fenced off festival but if you didn't want to pay you just came in round the back. I remember somebody, maybe Michael, showing us which fields we were allowed to go into. There were lots of groups of people who had already arrived.

The first thing that actually happened, which was quite instrumental in things afterwards, was that as I got out of this bus, an FG truck [a horsebox] pulled up next to me, dropped the side down and they started building this little stage. That was the Wango Riley travelling stage – the first time they'd ever put it up. I helped them piece it together but they had no intention of running it as a proper stage. So when it was all erected a chap called Scouse said to me, do you want to run a stage for the weekend? I didn't have a clue but I said yes because it sounded like quite an interesting thing to get involved with.

I remember running around quite a lot at the beginning trying to find all the necessary things that were required, like a generator and a PA and a drum kit. It was live music, we had lots of bands playing, but it was never part of the official programme. I came every year after that. I'd become addicted.

Cash and Carry

Michael Eavis

We ran the festival in aid of CND for quite a few years, and in fact we took cash up on some occasions to pay for the trains to bring people down to demonstrations in London. We even took £5,000 in cash up to Barrow in Cumbria for a demonstration there.

Then some time later the accountant said one day that the Inland Revenue had been on the phone and wanted to know about the festival's profits. I said, there aren't any profits, because we gave it all away. But they said you can't just give it away, you've got to pay tax on it first, so in the end there was a big inquiry and they wanted £7,000, which I didn't have. But by then we were on a roll, so as money came in I just paid the tax off. We got square in the end.

Janet Convery, CND head office

Looking back on it now you can't quite believe it, but throughout the 1980s CND was selling all the tickets for the festival. They were doing all the mail order and they were the key London outlet for personal sales. So staff were employed just to work as a ticket agency.

We were responsible for counting all the ticket money. We used to be in these horrible little caravans stuck at various points behind the gates, with all the windows sealed. It was really the most disgusting working conditions, really hot, and then people would walk in with thousands of pounds. You'd have a table with it all spread out and we'd be counting all through the night. And then these guys would turn up with tool boxes, like they were mechanics working on the site, and we'd put the money in them. It was all very hush hush so that people didn't know there were large amounts being carried around. Then they'd go up to the farmhouse where there was this elderly accountant sitting in Michael's living room who was bagging and banking all the cash.

John Sauven

We had a very good relationship with Michael and he obviously trusted us a lot in terms of what we were doing for the festival. In a way nobody knew that CND was doing this, because it was a relatively secret operation, but the underpinning of the festival was really important in terms of it working efficiently, both before and during the event. The whole thing relied on a relatively small number of personal relationships like that which made quite a complex operation work. I always laughed at the thought of the festival being run from an outhouse next to the farmhouse, where Sheelagh [Allen] worked. For a long time that was the festival office – no computer, one phone, a fax machine and a lot of box files. You just couldn't believe that out of there this amazing organisation spread out. But then you realised that the infrastructure of the festival was actually happening on lots of different levels, a lot of which weren't obvious, were delegated out, and that Michael knew exactly who was responsible for what.

Glastonbury Soukhs

Dick Vernon

Due to licensing issues, health and safety legislation and the increase in crowds, the markets changed shape, with stalls sited close together and in a circle so security could be tightened. It was likened to wagon trains in the American West forming a circle when attacked!

Ian Japp

It wasn't long before Glastonbury started to organise the markets on the 'wagon train' principle. A circular market is more efficient and secure than a market laid out in a line. When I was first there with Moussa, we were incredibly vulnerable. When widespread organised crime arrived in 1986 we were up a hill somewhere (near the farmhouse) in a line of stalls requiring two market gates. The 'impossibly impenetrable' hedge guarding our behind was only impossibly impenetrable to someone lacking (a) a bit of purpose and (b) a small amount of determination. That is, not at all. Other festivals seemed to be obsessed with lines of stalls, but the circle is much better: one market gate and office, the 'wagon train' formed into a protective corral. The logic is that it is easier to defend and to sell at the same time. This was in the days before 'Herras' fencing and everyone had to help each other.

My first impressions back in the 1980s were that the festival was chaotic, anarchic and potentially very challenging. Then you dealt with those challenges, large and small, and you enjoyed it. The environment at the festival can never be totally controlled, which is very exciting – and a little frightening too.

The so-called rastas in their yellow jackets and carrying pickaxe handles were a familiar, boring sight.

I always thought it was really important to find out which stalls had which resources as soon as we arrived. Who had the drill, or was good with lighting? Who had wood? Where could you get hold of a second genny [generator] in the middle of the night? In India, when you're travelling, in every city, or even small town, there's always 'a man in the alley' who'll fix something or sort something out, create miracles out of a bit of wire and a fuse, or something lying around. And we all need a man in the alley at Glastonbury. You need to know what to do and where to go when the environment suddenly changes, and it certainly proved capable of changing very quickly at the festival.

Dick Jones, stallholder

I remember we pulled up next to a guy selling cakes – proper cakes, not wacky baccy ones – and when someone tried to rob him, which did happen occasionally, I looked up and there he was running down the road with a shotgun. Whether it was loaded I don't know, but that's how much anarchy there was at the time. It certainly put the wind up everybody. That was bad boys time, people waiting on every corner to mug you. You had to be streetwise.

So it was good business, but it was risky as hell. And with thousands of pounds in your purses you can't be too careful – people rob post offices for less. So in the early days, when you couldn't get out to bank it, everybody would be out there with a spade secretly digging a hole in the ground to bury it. Then of course you had to find it afterwards. When we did drive out one day in a van with a lot of money from several stalls we ran out of petrol just as we were going up a hill, and with all these rastafarians at the top looking really dodgy. Fortunately, they came down, pushed us up the hill and gave us some petrol. That put my humanity back together.

•••

1987
TWO WEDDINGS
AND A FESTIVAL

The council's decision to refuse a licence was overturned in court in May, only just before the festival. Elvis Costello, New Order and Robert Cray played to 60,000 people. The WOMAD world music stage was inaugurated and the Mutoid Waste Company built their legendary 'carhenge' from upturned wrecked vehicles. Then, after the biggest and busiest festival ever, it was decided to have a fallow year in order to regroup and review the problems associated with the increase in size.

Bands in 1987: Billy Bragg, Courtney Pine, Elvis Costello, Felt, Gaye Bykers on Acid, Green on Red, Hüsker Dü, Julian Cope, New Order, Pop Will Eat Itself, Robert Cray, That Petrol Emotion, The Communards, The Soup Dragons, The Triffids, The Weather Prophets, The Woodentops, Trouble Funk, Van Morrison.

Chris Tofu, director of Continental Drifts, Hackney

I've sweated my arse off for Glastonbury over the years: playing, getting bands on, bringing the spirit of the underground down to the festival. It's a unique event, I love it. There's never been any money in it, but it's something you have to do. It's the only place, out on the fringes, where that line between the audience and the bands can be invisible, where you can be feeding off each other, it's incredible. When I started it was up in Avalon, in the Greenpeace fields, up on the edges where the travellers were involved. Incredible excitement, and a lot of shit.

I first went there at the tender age of 15, believe it or not on a school outing organised by the religious teachers, which I think they later bitterly regretted. I became a Glastonbury junkie almost immediately, I was hooked. My band, The Tofu Love Frogs, dare I say it, the legendary Tofu Love Frogs, first played there in 1993...we were Celtic punk, very loud, lots of swearing. We were playing big stages almost too soon, it was like that in the 1980s down there, you could get on before you could even play as long as you weren't chasing money. And I loved it so much that I almost became a lightning conductor for other underground bands who were involved in the same scene. The Tofus had their roots in the Hackney squatter set-up I was involved in, and we were also organising other really big underground festivals; there were plenty of bands around who just wanted to play.

The Tragic Roundabout were my all-time favourite, kleizmer insanity I called it, and one year they must have done about 15 gigs in five days. The Headmix Collective, now sadly no longer operative, were also the unsung heroes who filled the vibe everywhere they appeared. But there was this kind of glass ceiling – for all their underground appeal the bands, and I must have brought about forty of them in over the years, could never break out. Yet they *were* the festival, they *were* the bands who were keeping it going all night, who were providing that really special atmosphere.

Andy Hope, partner,
Croissant-Neuf Circus and Green Roadshow

We were on the road from 1979, travelling round with what was known as the peace convoy, in various trucks and trailers, originally working at free festivals, fruit picking, doing scrap metal and whatever else we could to get by. At one point we were with the Tibetan Ukrainian Mountain Troupe, who were travelling performers.

Then six of us got together at a farm in East Anglia we were staying in over the winter, bought a £200 ex-hire tent and started playing music and became entertainers and eventually a travelling circus. We travelled in the summer, holed up in the winter, getting by however you can. Sally used to make candles, I used to make gypsy baskets.

We first went to Glastonbury in 1987 with a band that played Irish and bluegrass music and a tiny 20 foot by 30 foot tent. It was a cabaret venue at the top of the Green Fields, with coffee and cakes and straw bales for seats, a very laid-back, semi-acoustic thing. There were no proper roads then, just tracks disappearing off into interesting corners.

One year when we did the clowning thing it was so hot my make-up ran all down my face. And we've been there ever since, we've never missed one.

Chris Sutton, runs computer graphics company, London

I was a student in 1987 and everybody said you could get into Glastonbury for free by jumping the fence. But I'd never been before and didn't have much idea what the set-up was. Two of us drove down with our girlfriends in a clapped-out car. They'd been far more sensible and got tickets, but me and my friend weren't up for that at all, we thought we knew much better.

The first mistake we made was to think we were nearly there. In fact, having jumped out of the car it took us about two hours to walk to the site. Then we started heading cross-country because we'd heard all these stories about Hell's Angels and bouncers, so we were quite anxious that we'd get beaten up. It was dark by now and a bit of paranoia set in.

At one stage we decided we'd been spotted, so we started running across this cabbage field, which was really muddy and wet. It was a quagmire everywhere we went. I had just basic decking shoes on, which were the fashion then, and they got completely ripped apart. After that there was a lot of scrabbling through hedges and I think we crawled under the fence in the end where somebody had dug a hole.

So by this time I was absolutely covered from head to foot in mud, with no shoes and not much money. We didn't even have a tent. Then it started to rain and it dawned on me the sheer madness of saying I'd meet the girls inside. With 50,000 people that was crazy. We spent the next day and a half looking for them. But it ended happily with us all sitting on top of a hill watching New Order.

Polly Bradford

When you're a teenager you have to go to the front to see the people you want to see properly. At 13 or 14 it was incredibly exciting to go and see your favourite bands so close. But even if you're right amongst the crowd in front of the Pyramid stage, people will still look after you, make sure you've got enough space. I never saw any trouble. People would just come up to you and talk. And by the Sunday that area in front of the stage was like a solid mass of cans.

When we watched a punk band, I think Gaye Bykers on Acid, on one of the smaller stages, they were a bit mental, the singer was quite nice looking, and people were throwing knickers at the band and the band were throwing things like cans back at the audience.

Arabella Churchill

I had an old car, which looked a bit rough, something had gone wrong with it and I took it to the mechanics, which we then had at what was called Gate 3. Then I forgot about it over the weekend. And it wasn't until the Monday after the festival that I went up through the Green Fields, saw this fantastic stonehenge construction made by the Mutoid Waste Company, and to my amazement, my VW car was on the top.

Picking Up the Pieces

Janet Alti, Green Party litter-picker

I'm in my sixties now and I came several years in the 1980s. I got involved with the Green Party crew doing the litter picking. Up to then litter was knee-deep all over by the end of the festival, absolutely disgusting. Eventually I had forty somewhat unwilling litter-pickers to get up at five in the morning. We got free food and a free pass but doing four hours litter picking every morning felt like jolly hard work.

There were some dividends, though. My very first year, when we were doing the final clear-up, I found an antique eighteenth-century silver spoon in very beautiful condition. I still have it and use it daily.

The first year it was a bit shambolic but after that I was given responsibility for the markets area, where a lot of the rubbish is generated. At the end of the festival I had to award a wooden spoon to the worst and a prize to the best stall for rubbish handling. I gave the wooden spoon to the cider bus, which was one of the most popular stalls. That wasn't considered very diplomatic, but it worked because the next year they had paper cups instead of plastic and they offered the litter pickers extra cider.

Liz Eliot

Those days were full of people coming to offer their wares, their skills, their entertainments. They'd bring samosas to sell in their handbags or whatever. The sound of 'hot knives' and 'sensimilia' was every-where, all this smoke and little lights and people shouting – it was so open, and in a way more fun because people weren't having to make their living, they came to pay for their expenses or just for the fun of it.

People would just turn up and do their thing. In 1987, when the Mutoid Waste Company came with their stonehenge of cars, they treated it rather like the Stonehenge free festival. You could wander around and find the most magical things, little fires with the person you'd just seen on the Pyramid stage coming round and playing guitar. Without the bright lights it was flares and candles and paraffin lamps on posts, all slightly suspect these days because of the fire risk, but it all added to this wonderful feeling of complete separateness.

In those days you just had to let all your defences go and just trust that everything was going to be fabulous, and it generally was. The kids were completely safe – I've never heard of any children being molested, and children ran wild. When they were teenagers I remember seeing this big black man climbing out of my daughter's tent at four o'clock in the afternoon, and she was so relaxed, she said he was really nice. Oh really, what was he doing? He just came for a chat. And I think he probably had. I used to think it was all a great initiation into being a member of the one world thing because you could go anywhere after being at Glastonbury without suffering any kind of culture shock.

Maybe you had to be a certain type of person to enjoy it as much as I did, but I loved it.

Double Wedding

Arabella Churchill

I never really met Haggis, my husband, through Glastonbury, because it was nearly always his juggling partner Charles who arranged the bookings and came to be paid. But at the 1987 Glastonbury Children's Festival he [Haggis] came early with Zippo the Clown to put up their tent and I got to know him then. And I got pregnant just like that; it could have been a disaster. I had to write to my family explaining that he was 13 years younger than me and he was a juggler and had an unusual name. It was all quite a lot for them to take on board. And we weren't going to get married actually, I didn't want to push him, but then Michael and Jean were having lunch here one day and he [Michael] said you really should get married. And Haggis said I'll marry Bella if you'll marry Jean. So we did.

We wanted to keep it terribly quiet because everyone thought that Michael and Jean were married, and had been for years, and I did because I was then very pregnant with my daughter Jess. So we only told Brian Walker, a local photographer, and he was allowed to come and take discreet photographs of me from the neck up. That was at Shepton registry office, and I remember that there was a Mendip District Council meeting going on just through the wicker fence where we were at one stage, and Michael was peering through to try to catch what they might be saying about the festival. Then we had a big party to celebrate both our weddings out at the farm on 1 July, the day we christened Jess.

Cash and Carry

Thomas Crimble

I worked for the festival right through the Eighties. I used to come down about two months before, at first living in the farmhouse with Michael and Jean, ordering things on the phone, day-to-day organising, fielding people who arrived. I was quite responsible, I issued passes, did the money, helped in the site office and did access control on the gates before the festival, although we never had any specific roles or titles.

From 1987 to 1990 I was responsible for picking the money up during the show – hundreds of thousands of pounds, and then going round paying all the bands at the back of the main stage. I had to make sure that nobody would follow me, or find me in the same place twice. I was doing that all the way through the travellers' period, collecting money from the pay lanes and running it to the house, literally sackloads of it. The CND people would roughly count it, give it to me in black rubbish bags and stuff it in the back of the Land Rover, and I'd drive through all the car parks, all the mud, all the travellers, all the drug dealer gangs eyeing you up, and then you'd get stuck in the crowd all walking at three miles an hour. In those days you only had to nudge a punter with a side mirror and they'd turn on you, they'd have you for breakfast. Most people would be paranoid in that situation. I dealt with it by winding the windows down and swearing a lot. They'd think, oh great he's one of us, leave that boy alone. But I had to blag it every day.

It was a big responsibility. If somebody had known I had that kind of money on board they wouldn't have fucked around. I would have been looking down the barrel of a shotgun or hit over the head with an iron bar.

At night I was sleeping in a room (in the farmhouse) surrounded by all this money. There was a safe up there but we didn't bother to use it because I couldn't get half of it in. So it was all under the bed, on top of the dresser. The Securicor van would come the next morning and we'd get rid of it, or we'd use it to pay the bands. It was a cash economy, but very dangerous.

I've still got records of all the payments I made. I think the most any one band got (up to 1990) was £55,000, but usually it was closer to £20,000 on the main stage. In the early CND days people used to play for a lot less than they would everywhere else. But the one person who was a real star, the only person who ever did this, was Jimmy Somerville (then with The Communards). He came round, and we said how much do you want, and he said I'm playing for free. So we said, when people say that it usually means a few thousand quid for expenses, and he said, no, I'll play for free, that means no money – give it to CND. He's the only musician that I know of who's done that.

Sheelagh Allen

I was working at the shop in Pilton when I was first offered a job. That was in 1987. I thought I was coming down to answer phones, but like Topsy it grew and grew. Everything was done from the farmhouse then, so I started doing paperwork for the market traders, then I took on the VAT returns, and eventually I was full time, handling all the phone calls and enquiries. I had no training for anything like that, no secretarial skills, just common sense. I became the last port of call before Michael.

It's a tiny office, very basic, but I've never wanted to move. Even in the late Eighties any faxes from agents for the bands used to go to an office in Shepton Mallet and they'd post them on. When we finally got a fax machine here, the very first one we received said 'Congratulations, welcome to the real world'.

•••

1988
CONFLICT, COPS AND CLASHES

The Thatcher governments of the 1980s could hardly be called festival-friendly and many Tories considered informal music festivals such as Glastonbury to be an anathema. The idea that they could be held anywhere, at any time and without regulation became unacceptable to the political establishment. In 1982, the Local Government (Miscellaneous Provisions) Act was passed, giving local authorities the power to regulate such events. That was the beginning of an annual battle in which the festival's organisers pitched their reputation against an expanding cordon of red tape. But the problems didn't just come from central government or local bureaucracy. There were mounting clashes involving not only the police and local councillors but a growing number of warring factions – drug dealers and security guards, local farmers and landowners, festival-goers and travellers.

Bill Mackay, Mendip District Councillor

Pilton has always been a divided village as far as the festival is concerned. You get one half who say we don't mind, we like it, we think it's good, we go to it, and the other half who don't want to know. And of course it's the other half where usually the problem arises. We've had all sorts of cases of trespass, fences and garden gates being broken down, houses being broken into…Some people decided to go away whilst the festival was on and then realised that was probably a worse mistake than staying, because it left their house completely vulnerable – people complaining bitterly that their gardens were being used as toilets, stones being thrown through windows. People who are prepared to engage in that sort of thing always seem to manage to find out who the objectors to the festival are, and target them accordingly. Maybe they read letters in local newspapers. Some of them have just had enough a long time ago, they've got totally fed up and demanded that action be taken.

Rachel Austin

Weeks before you'd get this influx of weird and wonderful characters that the pub wouldn't let in. But at least you had to respect Mr Hargraves, the landlord, for not jumping on the bandwagon like so many other people did. They'd open up fields, run stalls, charge cars for parking. There aren't many rogue traders now, but back then it was: 'Oh, look, there's a villager selling cans from a box saying "Sandwiches".' A lot of people made their own enterprise out of it, while some of them were speaking out against the festival at the same time.

Neil Macdonald, local farmer

I have in-laws who live in Pilton and it's absolute murder for three or four days. We've had people around at all times of the day and night, even walking through the house, vehicles dumped on the land. A lot of the older generation just find it completely and utterly intolerable. And the money that's paid to the church and so on is quite often felt to be bribery. Why should we have a week of hounding by these sometimes pretty miserable people just so somebody can earn some money out of it? There's a lot of ill feeling there still. You won't get rid of that.

Michael Eavis

The licence requirement came in in 1982 as a result of a bill promoted by our local MP, Robert Boscawen, but fortunately when the bill went to the House of Lords, Lord Melchett, who later became head of Greenpeace, introduced a 'best endeavours' clause. This meant that we couldn't be found guilty of breaking the law if we could show that we'd used our best endeavours to comply. That made a lot of difference.

So the long and the short of it was that every time I got done, there was always the best endeavours argument. So our solicitor, David Wood, would stand up and say that Michael has done his best, tried his hardest, so it was possible to get out of it. I was fined quite substantial amounts for some and not for others, but we used to win a few of those court cases. And we kept on getting licences again and again, which is surprising really because if they had really intended to stop me then, I think they could have done.

Thomas Crimble

It's not talked about very much but there were all the black drug gangs and it was all getting very grey, very dark. Everyone was looking at the ground as they walked around. We were being dragged down by the anarchist mentality. This was before the police came on site, and we were trying to police it ourselves.

One day some festival-goers came into the farmhouse and said there's a bloke down in Hawkwell Field with a gun, going round nicking people's stuff from their tents. So we went and crept up surreptitiously and caught him, with a few big lads. Then we bundled him into the back of a van and took him into the middle of Salisbury Plain and dropped him off with nothing. He was South African and he said he was very sorry. In fact it wasn't a real gun, although we didn't know it until afterwards, it was a starting pistol.

There was another time when one of the travellers shot at one of our site crew, the mechanic, with a shotgun. These were extreme cases and very rare, but they did happen.

Melvin Benn, Workers Beer Company

My memories of the late Eighties are of black gangs from Bristol effectively running parts of the site. And anarcho-travellers. Decent hippie travellers didn't get a look in. Muddy Lane was a 'no-go' area. Parts of the Green Fields even were no-go areas; some years the gates were barbaric, it was a free for all. But to my mind, it wasn't the festival, it was Thatcher. It was the culture and the times of 'grab, grab, grab'. And if on the one hand you got the yuppies, there was a low-life side as well. One lot breaking into the Bank of England from their desks, which seemed to be perfectly acceptable, and then the same culture carrying on down the chain. It was a sign of a community losing its values. And I've always considered Thatcherism to be to blame.

John Sauven

All the money from the programmes was collected and counted in the back of a van before we took it up to the farmhouse. One year [1987] we must have been watched by the police, because when we came off the site we were ushered into this field and surrounded by officers. We were all ordered out and all cautioned and then they took every single item out of the van. They went through all the CND badges, everything. I said we were all staff members of the campaign. And at the end they put it all back and said, we're sorry but we really thought you were running a huge drugs operation.

Brian Schofield, former officer, Avon & Somerset Police

I worked for the police for over thirty years, and I can recall policing the first big festival in 1971 as a young bobby. I'd only been in the job eighteen months or so. It was then just in Tom's Field with a small stage and about 1,500 people. It was on my local division, based in Yeovil, so it was our responsibility. We didn't go on site at all or in the field, it was just the surrounds. It was interesting to get away from where I was normally, working in Yeovil. We were just there monitoring people as they went in and went out. There were no big problems, certainly no public order problems, just a little bit of cannabis, a lot of nudity and a lot of cider.

After that I remember policing it a number of times during the early 1980s. Then we started getting complaints from parents whose children had gone, and others, that there was a lot of drug-taking going on, and a lot of individuals down there that were not as honest as they should be, thefts going on, robberies going on.

By the late Eighties, before the police were allowed on site, it could get quite ugly. Even our undercover boys were feeling threatened. They got exposed and had to leave on occasions. It got to the stage where, if you like, the criminal elements were taking over, and it was thought by both the police and festival-goers that we ought to have some level of policing on site as well as off. It was a big step. In fact my memory is that there were police on site and then they were taken off and then we were doing it again.

Simon Roiser

In the early days we didn't have much of a fence, yet as long as you sold all the tickets it didn't matter – you couldn't really control the extra people who turned up. Then the police came on site and there were more questions being asked, which led to me sometimes saying the wrong thing. One year the *Western Daily Press* were with me at the temporary prisons which had been set up at the Bath & West showground, and one of them asked me about someone who had been arrested with a sword at the festival. What did I think? A very silly thing to take to a festival, I said, especially as it was raining. And they always, always asked about the drugs. I was once quoted as saying that 'as far as I could see it was the perfect place to catch drug dealers'. Because where were they going to run to? Behind a tree? That was written up as 'Festival Accuses Police of Incompetence'.

John Sauven

A lot of people in the organisation were very unhappy about bringing the police on to the site. The whole essence of the festival was that people could go in there and express their freedom and creativity without any kind of authority. You left the police behind, you left the teachers behind, you left your parents behind.

Interestingly, what happened when the police did come on site is that they came in relatively small numbers. They weren't like the Metropolitan Police. We all had this idea of riot shields and vans racing through the site beating people up. In fact it was not like that at all, they weren't heavy and if anything they were somewhat shocked at seeing all these naked people and everything. But there was a definite difference from 1987. They just calmed the thing down. The drugs didn't go away, but they went underground into the back street. Nothing was so in your face, it had a marked effect on the whole atmosphere. I think everyone then realised it was the right decision.

Michael Eavis

When they closed down Stonehenge in 1985, we started picking those people up as well. So we became a Stonehenge festival as well as Glastonbury. They had a parson bloke, who was a Baptist minister, as their spokesman – he was looking after the children's area – and I had a meeting with him and some of the traveller leaders as well. 'Lost Vagueness' Roy was involved in that. And I decided to let them in. I was seen as being very benevolent and decent about it, I tried to accommodate them, but in fact it was very difficult to manage, and a lot of my staff left because they couldn't cope with it.

In 1987 we had a lot of convoy problems. We had all the travellers from what seemed like the whole of England arriving here. It was very difficult to control, and it got a bit dangerous. The mid-Eighties were a bit like that really. So I decided to knock it on the head and take a year off in 1988, mainly because of the problems of overcrowding and the travellers coming in without paying.

Jean was always a bit worried about that side of things. She thought it was very scary, and I don't blame her for that at all. She always thought it was too much of a risk. She would support me when I said I wanted to do the festival, but she was never 100 per cent on side. I would often say, maybe this will be the last one, and we always thought it might really be the last one. But then I said to Jean, we won't do it again unless you're really happy about it.

Then the phone went about Christmas time, and there was this girl at the other end asking if there was a festival the next year. At first Jean said it definitely wasn't going to happen, but after the girl had said in a lovely Liverpool accent that her mum had said she could go, she completely seduced Jean. And suddenly I heard Jean say that it was going to be at the end of June, and she gave her the dates. So that was that. She knew I wanted to do it, but she wouldn't relent until she had that phone call. I've never met that girl – we put a call out for her but I don't know who she was.

●●●

1989
ENTER THE POLICE

Once again there were complications with the local council over granting the licence. The police were brought into the organisation and planning for the first time. Heathcote Williams initiated the biggest ever poetry reading and Van Morrison and The Pixies performed before an audience of 50,000. Suzanne Vega appeared despite a death threat to her bass guitarist.

Bands in 1989: Black Uhuru, Elvis Costello, Fela Kuti, Suzanne Vega, The Bhundu Boys, The Pixies, The Waterboys, The Wonderstuff, Throwing Muses, Van Morrison, Youssou N'Dour.

Suzanne Vega, singer–songwriter

The big deal was the death threats – something to do with a girl and my bass player. She'd become infatuated with him and we were getting all these weird messages. The police advised us not to go on, but if I had backed down I felt I'd never be able to perform in England again. The whole thing seemed to go in slow motion. The minute I got onstage it occurred to me that anybody could put a bullet through my head. Every song seemed to last half an hour. Also, I was wearing a bullet-proof vest so I felt like a turtle. Ironically, we were dragged off not because of the death threat but because of the curfew.

Dan Plesch

My friend Martin Butcher was standing at Hiscock's Corner, at the top of Cockmill Lane, when a motorcycle policeman screeched to a halt, waved his arms and said get these people out of the way, we have a firearms incident. That was the first we knew that the police were sufficiently convinced that there was going to be an assassination attempt on Suzanne Vega by means of sniper fire. So the local police were getting their flak jackets out of plastic bags, there were spotters on the mixing desk and around the stage, and immediately after her performance they put her in her bus with several Range Rovers for an escort and rushed her out of the festival. But despite having the best resources the police could offer, they still got to the top of Cockmill Lane, wound down the window and asked one of our stewards, which way now? Fortunately, Suzanne Vega lived to tell the tale.

Ralph Oswick

We've got a hundred scenarios at least, and about four or five of us do roughly nine different pieces over the three days. Arabella always kindly gives us a Portakabin as a dressing room because our style is immaculate and we need a professional changing room. In the early muddy year our van couldn't get to the dressing room so they actually pushed the Portakabin to the van with a JCB.

One we started doing in 1989 is the 'coneheads', where these people with cone-shaped heads from another planet all imitate their leader in unison, whether taking a photograph of the sky or pointing at a bald man's head or worshipping a lamp-post or stealing a baby. They've come on holiday from Mars and they've got the wrong instructions, like ten shilling notes and Kodak box cameras. It nearly always works.

Manning the barriers

Dan Plesch

It sounds a bit macho in retrospect, but tractors were our secret weapon during those difficult years. Nobody could really argue with them. We'd find some people in a van who were obviously thieving and surround them with two tractors and a Land Rover and then hitch up a chain to the front of the van and say: 'Either you start it up and drive out or we'll tow you straight off the site, and probably break your transmission in the process.' The Young Farmers used to love it.

One of my friends from Devon and I would always wear gimmicks. Neither of us cared for the supervisory approach of the male, who generally has a black metal torch three foot long strapped to his thigh, large boots and an attitude to match. We did the job one year wearing silver angel wings, another year we had flashing lights on our heads. I'm a large geezer and if there's a certain situation going on and I arrive, experience taught me that the mere arrival of a 6' 2" male, particularly if covered in walkie talkies, escalates the situation. So if you wear something that looks ridiculous, as well as your proper steward's identification, then some fellow who's about to punch somebody in the face because they're not letting them in for free will come up and say 'What's the wings for, mate?' and you've got a whole different situation.

Nobody got the joke as far as I know, but for many years we ran the East German flag over the main gate, because with all the floodlights and this mass of steel in either direction, earth pounded flat and a barren, ghostly environment, especially at night, it looked a bit like the Berlin Wall.

Warwick Blenkinsop, college teacher, Somerset

In 1989 I was 18 or 19, working with some mates in a caravan factory in Hull when we decided at the very last minute on the Friday that we'd bunk off early and drive down to this Glastonbury Festival that we'd heard so much about. We'd heard about it through the *NME*, although it was nothing like the publicity you get now. We didn't have tickets or anything – we couldn't have afforded them anyway – and we were completely ill-prepared. We just hopped into my knackered old Mark II Escort and headed south. We really didn't know what to expect or what we were going to do, but along the way we picked up this mystical Welsh hitchhiker, who filled us in a bit. I remember him saying in his really strong accent, 'It's a magnet, you see, it draws you back.'

We ended up dumping the car in one of the little lanes, then we crawled through bushes, ditches, following where the noise was. Then when we got to the fence we decided we'd kick a football over, and that's where we'd climb. There were a couple of aborted attempts when we panicked because we heard a noise, but then the three of us managed somehow to scramble over in a hectic rush, and all fell on the other side, pretty much landing on somebody's tent. What I remember most is the sense of elation that we'd got in, because we'd heard all these stories about baton-wielding security guards, and underneath we were petrified.

After that we had a mad weekend. We'd taken our week's wages so we just burned the lot. I'm sure we took some stimulants, largely because we didn't really want to sleep. I remember smoking a joint within the eyeball of a copper, which seemed quite odd, but not very risky because there were so many others doing it. We did have one unfortunate incident with these Jamaican lads, who took the money and then didn't give us anything in return. They were very big lads, it all got a bit sinister so we just legged it.

Then we all had to get back to work first thing the next morning, so we left as Elvis Costello was playing on the Sunday night, but when we found the car again there was a guy asleep in the back seat. So we had to get him out, and then we drove back to Hull. The stink was unbearable – we hadn't had a wash and we'd done nothing but drink cider for two days solid – and we were so tired that we could only stay awake to drive by singing along endlessly to a couple of Neil Diamond tapes.

Green Fields

Steve Chatters, cyto-geneticist, London

When I was a teenager it was my one holiday, my one escape to the country. I used to save up all year for the ticket. One year, 1989 I think, I hitched down with just a quid in my pocket, and outside there were all these guys lining the paths selling drugs, almost like gangsters. It was a really dry, dusty year. But once I was inside and pitched my tent up in the Green Fields I managed to last the whole weekend on the goodwill of people I met – cadging beer, eating food from the Hare Krishna tent – and then hitched back again to the outskirts of London with virtually the same pound I started with. For me it was the legendary free Glastonbury.

Liz Eliot

At that time the Green Fields were run by a collective of green activists, and it was always a bit chaotic. Everyone was invited to the meetings, but it could take three weeks to decide whether to use blue pencils or white. So in 1989 I was asked if I would take over, although I'm not quite sure how I got bounced into doing it.

I'd never done anything like that before, except for a small green gathering I'd organised in Wales. But that was hundreds of pounds, and here we were talking about £100,000. We had our own budget, so we had to buy everything from marquees to nails to food for the crew – about ninety people a day. The only thing we got from the central festival organisation was water and the emergency services.

Booking the Bands

Martin Elborne, music agent and Glastonbury Festival programmer

I was at Bristol University, involved in putting on concerts, and later I set up my own record label there. I was also a co-founder of WOMAD; that was the early days of world music. I knew about Glastonbury but I didn't go to any of the early ones, the original hippie ones. But I do remember Michael [Eavis] being very suspicious about anyone involved with the first WOMAD, because it was at the Bath & West Showground – right on his doorstep! It lost money though, took years to get back on track; he needn't have worried.

Later I became an agent with Rough Trade, towards the end of punk and at the start of the big indie band movement, I suppose you'd call it. I had The Smiths, and they were the first band I sold to Michael. It was the first time really he had had a new young band, for that first CND Festival in 1981, instead of Van Morrison or some old blues band.

Punk just didn't happen at Glastonbury, mostly because there weren't any festivals when it was happening, and this was the next thing: the first really credible, 'new' band the festival had put on. And it really was an event; people stormed the stage and got hurt in the process. There were maybe 30,000 here, a much smaller event, much less variety, but this was the first time the festival was young and exciting and happening and it moved on from there.

Glastonbury became the only place for world music, as it was at the time, and indie. And you've got to give credit to Michael for following that. Suddenly the festival was doing The Smiths, and then, later, New Order, when they were really big. Plus the first wave of world music stuff; King Sunny Ade I remember really well. It was adding a little bit each time. And once it got above 35,000, then 40,000, it was an obvious thing that it was out on its own – there really was no competition.

Melvin Benn

There weren't really many festivals around then, only Glastonbury and Reading. It was a very strange place to come down to, there were so many idiosyncrasies. You basically entered a bartering culture; straight away there was Michael's wheeler-dealing and bartering, and your first impression was that the franchises and security were a nightmare, the organisation was chaotic. It was totally different to the normal structure at a big event.

I still describe it as a terrorist organisation with lots of independent cells. There's a common cause, but they all do their own thing, they're not dependent on a single dictatorial position, except of course for money. So Liz [Eliot], Arabella [Churchill], Tony [Cordy], they'd get their budget and their passes, and then they'd be these little cells operating in their own way. And the politics would be incredible. For a long time Arabella was the most feared lady on site.

On the ground we were a rag, tag and bobtail army who somehow got through. Everything needed fixing all the time. There was a guy called Pete, based up at the old Gate 3, who was just a genius at fixing things. There were years when the festival wouldn't have survived without him. Another famous character was Jed, who ran the fencing crew in the days before Herras fencing even existed. The only hope of getting any security was getting Jed. Of course a very significant currency was beer. You could get anything for a case of beer – quite useful if you were working for the Workers Beer Company.

Richard Abel, site manager

Glastonbury Festival was an annual part of my life for a very long time and provided some of my greatest moments ever, and some of the hardest challenges. I first started as site manager in 1989, straight after Andrew Kerr left.

Because there was really no other festival in the world like Glastonbury – no other regular event has had anything like the same number of people over so many days and so many acres – much of the increasing national and even some international legislation was formed around our experience. I recall one licence condition 'prohibiting the sale to the public of untreated milk' being quoted to festivals all over England and in Ireland, even if there wasn't a dairy cow in sight. I think that was a direct result of Mendip District Council's reaction to Michael's early experiments to find a solution to the problem of the tanker not getting through to collect his milk at festival time!

●●●

1990

On its twentieth anniversary and to reflect its increasing diversity, the festival adopted the title of the Glastonbury Festival for Contemporary Performing Arts. The Happy Mondays and Sinead O'Connor played to a rain-drenched crowd of 65,000. Anarchic French circus troupe Archaos transformed the Pyramid stage, with chainsaw duels, cars hurtling down the sides and performers walking across a high wire from its pinnacle to an oak tree. On the Monday afterwards a brewing confrontation between travellers and the security team ended in a riot and £50,000 worth of damage to property and hired plant. There were 235 arrests. As a result of the disturbances Michael and Jean Eavis decided to take a year off in 1991.

Bands in 1990: Adamski, Aswad, Courtney Pine, De La Soul, Deacon Blue, Del Amitri, Galaxy 500, Green on Red, Hothouse Flowers, James, Jesus Jones, Julian Cope, Ladysmith Black Mambazo, Lush, Mano Negra, Neville Brothers, Nik Turner, Ry Cooder, Sinead O'Connor, The Cure, The Happy Mondays, The Pale Saints, World Party.

Nik Turner

After leaving Hawkwind, I formed a new band called Inner City Unit with Barney Bubbles, who did all the graphics for Hawkwind and Revelation Records. We did a series of gigs for people who'd had their vehicles trashed by the police at the Beanfield. In the Eighties we sometimes went to both Glastonbury and Stonehenge, which was a bit more anarchic. My pyramid became the stage at Stonehenge, right up until the end.

Eventually I formed another band called Nik Turner's Fantastic All Stars, we play jazzy dance music, and I think I was there with the All Stars in 1990 and played with Hawkwind as well in the travellers' field.

Mark Cann

There are those who try to get more than their allocation of passes. The Happy Mondays turned up in a bus in 1990 and we suddenly realised that they'd picked up a lot of fans or whatever along the way. They were all hiding in the belly of the bus. It turned out that someone had been photocopying passes and laminating them all. We weren't too pleased about that.

Martin Elborne

There was a watershed in 1990, the first example I can think of. It was James – the festival definitely broke them. They were on a very early slot, maybe the mid-afternoon, but the reaction they got proved to them what they were capable of, lifted them out of thinking small venues, ordinary tours. That appearance established them as a top band and gave them a nice ten-year career.

Tim Booth, singer, James

My first memory of Glastonbury is of being towed in and out of the festival in one of its quagmire years, towards the end of the 1980s. It was the first gig I ever played wearing wellington boots – not so easy to dance in when weighed down by clumps of mud. That was a casual relationship, an in-and-out job. In those conditions one didn't wanna stick around.

We returned, more triumphantly, to the main stage in 1990. We'd just had the hit 'Sit Down' and the organisers were trying to move us higher up the bill than our modest afternoon slot. Del Amitri refused to be moved, as we would also have refused in their position.

We played one of those special gigs, after which people are suddenly looking at you in a different way. That gig definitely took us to a new level.

When we played 'Sit Down' the audience did. Del Amitri were not happy to follow us. Eclipsing all this, twenty minutes after I came off stage my 11-month-old son, Ben, took his first steps (16 of them, if I remember) across the backstage area into my arms.

Polly Bradford

The best one was The Cure in 1990, which was a really hot year because there were people on the stage cooling the crowd down with hoses.

That was also the year we were given a backstage pass. We found The Cure on their tour bus watching the football and Robert Smith came out, so I asked him for his autograph and he signed my pass. I was very excited and shook a lot.

I remember seeing Julian Cope, he was pretty amazing, he had that funny microphone stand with bits sticking out that he puts his feet on and swings around. They had the circus troupe Archaos, and instead of just being on the stage they were all over the Pyramid and right on the top doing circus tricks. I don't think they had any clothes on either. They had lighting effects and were swinging on trapezes and they had the lasers, which were always amazing.

Vojtech Lindaur, journalist, *Rock and Pop*, Prague

My first Glastonbury was in 1990, when the Iron Curtain was torn down and my friend Andy White, an Irish songwriter, came to Prague, Czechoslovakia. He slept a few days in my flat, then he invited me to enjoy what he called 'the best music festival in the world'. I was a budding music journalist, I had had no passport for more than ten years, so it was the very first chance to come to England. A group of us had also just started a fortnightly music magazine called *Rock and Pop*, trying to be similar to *NME* or *Melody Maker*. And when I got there it was another exciting world for me, so different from the one I had to live in for 33 years. On that Sunday night full of mud slides I fell in love with Glastonbury forever.

•••

1990
TRAVELLERS' TALES

Travellers have been involved in the Glastonbury scene virtually from the beginning. In the 1970s and 1980s, Glastonbury – both town and festival – was part of an annual alternative summer tour whose spiritual focus was Stonehenge in Wiltshire for the June solstice. By the early 1980s the free festivals there were attracting thousands of people who camped round the stones and made their own entertainment. When the authorities clamped down in 1985, making Stonehenge a no-go area, attention immediately switched to the Glastonbury festival, then held over the solstice weekend. So after some of the travellers had made a (usually failed) attempt to get inside the Stonehenge 'exclusion zone' they would come on to Worthy Farm. There they expected things to operate in the same way, especially the fact that entry was free.

For a number of years, Michael Eavis tolerated this, even though it involved delicate negotiations with the police, with the travellers themselves and with other people on the site. In 1990, however, the balancing act tipped over into violence. Although its origins are still a subject of dispute, a major confrontation erupted between travellers and security guards, with the police somewhere in the middle. Over 200 people were arrested. Eavis put the festival on ice for a year whilst he recovered from a bruising encounter.

Richard Abel

Travellers...what can I say! Sometimes they put on a better show than we did, other times they came very close to finishing the festival off. But if our society gives no place to people who can't or won't quite fit into its defined norms, then the more tolerant travelling community and festival scene will always offer a haven. While the more destructive travellers have at times nearly destroyed everything Michael built up over the years, in my experience he has never turned away anyone in need and has always been the first to recognise the amazing range of talents and ideas among them.

Phil Shakesby, traveller

I was what people call a new age traveller, I suppose. We went to Stonehenge in tents for quite a few years before we got a vehicle. Then my mate had the idea of getting a bus, kitting it out and going on the road. I said 'I've got a job, I've got children, I've got responsibilities', but three months later I was travelling. That was 1979.

But then in 1985 the police stopped Stonehenge, they came and bust up a festival at Nostel Priory near Leeds, where 200 of us were arrested, and finally there was the Battle of the Beanfield, where they smashed all our vans and 500 of us were arrested. They'd made it a police state, basically, and we were always at the receiving end. After that there was nowhere to go but Glastonbury.

Then the next year we were at Stoneycross in the New Forest when they impounded all our vehicles and offered us train and bus tickets to go back home. The bulk of us had nowhere to go, because we lived on the road, so we decided we'd walk all the way to Glastonbury.

With the police and the media watching us, several hundred of us marched 25 miles the first day, 18 miles the second and then 15 miles each day after that until we made it. We arrived just before the festival. I actually saw Michael Eavis as I walked on to the site at the head of the column. I don't think he was amused to see us.

Our idea was to put forward our plight to the people there and collect enough funds so we could go back down to the pound in

Hampshire, where all the vehicles were being kept, work on them and get the convoy back on the road. And that's what we did. We collected several thousand pounds. People were quite willing to give, especially having seen what had happened to us on the TV news.

We came every year after that, sometimes in groups. Michael had set aside an area at the back end of the festival where the travellers could go for free. It was like a sanctuary from all the hassle we had outside; once there we were safe. It was like a place to meet up with old friends, because after the Battle of the Beanfield a lot of people went back to living in cities, so you didn't see them except at Glastonbury. So we had our rave tents there, and all that kind of thing. I made my money out of selling pizzas, cheese toasties, home-made beer. That's how I managed to keep fuel in the vehicle and go on from festival to festival.

We got on fine with everybody, except that the youngsters who were with us, Black Luke and people like that, they didn't listen to what we told them. We couldn't deal with them. They'd be swanning around, drunk, with baseball bats, beat people up, rob stallholders. They'd go out nicking batteries from the generators, starting pitched battles with the security. It became a regular thing. Eventually it made all of us exceedingly unwelcome.

Thomas Crimble

We used to have 'traveller alerts' – they used to get bolt croppers and unlock the gates and come in in the middle of the night, before all the site crew was there and everything was manned. So you'd suddenly find 20 trucks camped up which weren't there the day before. So we'd all rush off and there were big confrontations. The trouble was if they smashed the gates in and the council saw that it had happened, there was a danger to the licence. And if the site got full up with travellers even before the festival had started, there'd be no room for people who'd actually paid money. It was heady stuff.

There was one time when the travellers were holding the whole site to ransom, as they often did, and there was a double-decker bus, full of people, which had driven in at one of the gates, so no-one could get on site because they'd blocked the road. There were 20 people in the bus, none of them had any money, they weren't going to buy any tickets, we weren't going to let them on, so they just stayed there for the whole day. The traffic had all backed up, so the police got involved. The way they cleared it apparently was by calling up a Chinook helicopter, which hovered over the bus, and the driver was told if she didn't move the bus it would be picked up and flown away. That broke the blockade.

Robert Kearle

The worst people were often the rich people who thought because they were in a posh car they had the right to come in, no tickets or anything. The best one was a guy in a big red Ferrari who had his dolly bird wife all tarted up in gold, and me and another digger driver got this call to come out. He was just being a complete arsehole – I know so-and-so, reeling off the names of loads of rock stars. We said we don't care, if you haven't got a ticket or a pass you can't come in, and he sort of turned the car and said, that's that, I'm coming in anyway. So we started up the digger and raced towards him, and he soon span out of the gate when he thought his £200,000 Ferrari was going to get crushed.

Nik Turner

I travelled about a bit myself at one stage in a VW camper. I went to Greenham Common and we set the Pyramid stage up there, the whole peace convoy moved there, we were all involved in tearing up the fences. I always said to Michael and Jean that you can't tar everybody with the same brush. I argued for the travellers because a lot of them are my friends. I know there's a splinter group of people, the same ones who were so anarchic at Stonehenge, and the convoy was really a drug-oriented group of people at the bottom of the heap desperate to make a buck, but there's a lot of decent people among them, they're not all like that.

Bill Mackay

The problem we had was what we called the illegal festival, which was set up with a group of 200 or so travellers arriving. The police view was that if you let them on to the site you'll get less aggravation than if you try to keep them off. They were allocated a particular field, but unfortunately they'd set up a rival festival and they would go on all night because they couldn't care less – they weren't subject to the licence.

Sometimes they'd settle wherever they felt they could in the area and then, as too many travellers do, though not all, committed mayhem in the process. They're not averse to uprooting someone's fence to get firewood, for example.

Neil Macdonald, local farmer

I was born and raised in Butleigh, just a few miles from the festival site, and I've been farming in this area for the best part of eighteen years. I'm very interested in conservation, so the countryside and its well-being are very much to the forefront of my interest.

Even when I was a small boy, in 1977, we had a huge problem when three or four hundred travellers were camped up on Hatch Hill with lots of tipis and caravans. It's a Site of Special Scientific Interest and they absolutely devastated it. It took several weeks to get them moved. After that, once the festival really got going, we had groups of them moving in every year just before it, going to the festival and then staying for long periods afterwards.

We got so fed up that we formed a group of local farmers so that if one of us had trouble we'd ring around, form a force and move them off physically within 24 hours, which meant, on several occasions, diggers, tractors…We'd frighten the life out of them basically, although we always told the local bobby beforehand. One year they camped on a drove way which we needed to use, so when they left a lot of their junk to go off to the festival we cleared it all up and burned everything.

Fear and Loathing at Glastonbury

Dan Plesch

One can understand that travelling people can't necessarily afford the full ticket price, and some were happy to make a contribution, but when they've got a camp full of Special Brew and ganja and can't find a fiver … In the end there were just far too many people who took on the mantle of traveller who would have been quite happy in Thatcher's cabinet. Whatever beef they might have had with the rest of society, they didn't lighten up when they came to the festival. There was nothing progressive about them at all.

Andrew Kerr

They used to arrive in huge numbers and park nearby, waiting to invade the site. Michael tried to get them a piece of land somewhere else to have their festival. I don't know how well that worked. But it wasn't only the travellers, it was the dealers as well, and that got very violent. It got to a stage when he [Michael] had to do something about it.

One year it was almost like something out of the movies. The travellers were all parked in a pasture at the bottom of a hill, and this lone figure [Michael Eavis] walks down and starts to parley with them, saying they've got to leave. I don't know what sort of communication he had, but the people behind the crest of the hill were obviously saying we're not moving, it's our festival. And then at some given moment all these JCBs came up over the top of the hill, and Michael said again I think you'd better move, and they all went off in a cloud of red diesel.

Michael Eavis

In 1990 the magistrates said at the licence appeal that we had to give the travellers a field, to bring them on to the site. They had to have somewhere to go. So I put them up in their own field. That was the beginning of the Lost Vagueness area, with the Wango Riley stage. Roy [Gurvitz] probably didn't know that at the time, but the council had said no, the police had said no, and the magistrates had said yes. So that's what I did.

Roy Gurvitz

By 1990 I was quite involved with the festival, working as site crew on the 'build', and also tidying up and dismantling the festival. I had a little four-wheel-drive lorry with a crane, so I ended up working with a crew to take all the fire lane posts out. And it was only a few days before the festival kicked off that Michael came down and said there was this problem, with probably about 500 traveller vehicles that were heading towards the festival.

I remember being woken by Keith one morning saying that the police needed to see me. I went out to Cockmill Lane at the back end of the festival at about 6.30 in the morning and saw this line of vehicles that just went on and up round the corner. They went all the way from there out on to the A37. And the police were saying that they'd arrived last night without them noticing. I was in an awful predicament because the fields which Michael had said to use were now full. So what should we do? It wasn't my authority to just open up the field on the other side of Cockmill Lane, which was outside the festival boundary, but that was obviously what needed to happen.

Then I just remember seeing a JCB coming along, with Michael in a Land Rover behind it. I thought, this seems very confrontational. And the JCB proceeded to just drive through the gate to the field and opened up the hedge, and in went all these vehicles.

After that it was a good year, it was a great festival, the atmosphere was fine. A stage was put up, I think the Wango Riley stage, and I remember bands like The Levellers playing unofficially. That was in the early days before they were a big name. And there were other bands like Hawkwind and The Co-Creators. But there had still been a number of incidents during the festival with security and travellers, as there always will be with people selling drugs or whatever.

It all culminated just after the weekend when some people were driving around in a six-wheel-drive lorry, they were 'tatting' the leftovers from the market area, when suddenly security took it upon themselves to assume they were stealing, and attacked them. Later that day a lot of people in about five or six vehicles decided that they would drive on to the site and retaliate for what had happened earlier. They drove towards the security compound, which was by the farmhouse. By the time they got there the security knew they were coming, the police had already been called, so when they got up to the farmhouse they were astonished to be confronted by a riot squad, not the security. The police were there in riot gear and they were more than ready to participate in the fiasco and theatre that ensued.

Thomas Crimble

It sounds silly this but I'd never smelt fear. There was actually fear in the air. I've never experienced that before or since. We heard this distant jungle drumming, so we went round towards the site office and looked down the hill and we could see burning Portakabins and a crowd of people coming in our direction. They were throwing rocks and bricks and bottles with petrol at the security compound. It was pretty scary. I was with Michael so we went to meet them, we recognised some of them, and they were at pains to tell us that their beef was only with the security guys. Someone was filming it and Jean took them to one side and grabbed the camera, pulled the tape out and then gave the camera back.

After a certain time the police came, and got tooled up with shields and helmets. After about half an hour the travellers backed off and went down the hill again, looting and burning as they went. It was the full force of the law, with helicopters flying around with big spotlights all evening.

Polly Bradford

After the festival, most of the people had packed up their tents and gone. We were about the only ones left in the field when they came round the corner of the Pyramid stage, hundreds of travellers, with big metal bars and stuff. They were running towards us but they went straight past and up to the farmhouse. I heard afterwards that they'd surrounded the farmhouse and there was a lot of trouble because Michael Eavis wouldn't let them in for free. That was probably the only time that I've been frightened at all at Glastonbury.

Stephen Abrahall

The night before the riot I was sleeping in a Portakabin near the farmhouse when I heard these people outside talking about putting an oil drum through the window. Fortunately we had stuck a notice on the door saying 'Mid-Somerset CND – working for a nuclear-weapons-free future and a hassle-free festival' because I then heard them say, 'Oh no, read the notice' and they went away. So it was our salvation. But that year on the Monday following the festival one of our information points did get set on fire.

Michael Eavis

In the end we had a lot of trouble between the drug dealers and the security in 1990. It ended up in a pitched battle, we were all a bit scared.

'Surely that must be it,' Jean said. 'You don't want to do it again…'

•••

MUSIC, MADNESS AND MUD

1991–1999

'Those who find they're touched by madness
Sit down next to me'

James (*Sit Down*)

Glastonbury was getting bigger and bigger – a medium-sized town of tents and markets and secret venues. Innovations continued through the 1990s, including circus performances and, most dramatically, one of the biggest dance music marquees in the country. The festival had finally succumbed to the insatiable demand for repetitive beats, bright flashing lights and the best dance MCs. The Green Fields expanded, eventually encompassing nine different areas. In 1992 a miniature version of Stonehenge was built there, and has since become a focus for early morning crowds to watch the sun rise over the vale of Avalon.

Tens of thousands of people camping for days in a field meant that there was a growing army of mouths to feed as well as money to spend. As the numbers of traders increased a more sophisticated organisation was established. In the early years there had been a klondyke type rush, with traders queuing up early until the site was opened and racing down to grab the best pitches. Now each site was marked out and pre-sold. Campsite cafés were developed in the different camping fields which, apart from being sound trading ventures, proved to be essential in 1997 and 1998 when the miserable weather conditions soaked people through. Other traders had added a new dimension to the variety of entertainment on site by setting up sound systems alongside their stalls. In 1995 there were a record 671 official stalls, but three years later this had increased again to over 750. And behind the markets there was always a touch of madness and mayhem...

1992
THE SACRED SPACE

With the ending of the Cold War people's concerns had shifted away from the possibility of armageddon to concern for the environment, so the Greenpeace campaign became the main new beneficiary of festival support. A large part of the site was now devoted to green and creative activities, with alternative technologies like windmills and solar power, a healing field of therapies and meditation, demonstrations of crafts like stonemasonry and glass blowing, poetry readings, a circle of tipis and a quiet, vehicle-free meadow overlooking the festival. On the main stage, Primal Scream and Tom Jones played to 70,000 people and helped to raise £250,000 for various causes.

Bands in 1992: Billy Bragg, Blur, Carter USM, Curve, James, Joan Armatrading, Kirsty MacColl, Kitchens of Distinction, Lou Reed, PJ Harvey, Primal Scream, Shakespear's Sister, Spiritualised, Television, The Breeders, The Fall, The Levellers, The Shamen, Tom Jones, Van Morrison, Youssou N'Dour.

Michael Eavis

So we took 1991 off. Then we looked at it again and thought we'd try once more in 1992. What was driving me forward? It is exciting, that's why I do it. It's such good fun. It is a challenge, and there's so many people involved. Everyone enjoys working here. I think the reason it's so successful is that it's such good fun.

Festival programme, 1992

This year sees for the first time the creation of a Sacred Space in Kings Meadow. This beautiful and special field has over the years been enjoyed by many as a place to 'be', a space to relax, to lie in the grass, greet the oak tree, walk the labyrinth, and enjoy the spectacular vista. This year we have taken all this a little further and deeper, and, in harmony with the field (and its inhabitants, seen and unseen), created a space where you can come and reconnect with the Earth, with the elements, with the spiritual or sacred aspects of all things Green... Come and experience the pure elements of Earth, Air, Fire and Water in the magical Elemental Gardens. Sit with the stones in the stone circle. Listen to the birds sing, watch the sun rise and the grass growing! Enter the Temple of Night and Day...

Mark Cann

When Tom Jones appeared, his band turned up and looked very, very nervous because this was outside their normal experience – they just wouldn't normally perform in the middle of a field in Somerset. It was almost like they took a deep breath when they got off the bus. But they soon relaxed into it. Most people do have a very good time; some have an exceptionally good time and go AWOL. There's always been the occasional star who disappears and the tour manager is tearing his hair out trying to track them down.

Often you find you break through the airs and graces that are created by the entourage around these people, and they turn out to be an individual just like anybody else. When Lou Reed came, he'd been staying with Peter Gabriel, who brought him down to the festival. But by the time he wanted to leave, all his crew had gone, so a friend of mine, Steph, was deputed to drive him to Castle Cary train station. 'I can take trains,' he said, so Steph had the excitement, outside the normal bubble that surrounds such people, of chauffering her hero and putting him on a train to London packed with festival-goers.

Emily Eavis

When I was about 11 or 12, during the [1992] festival, I wandered off on my own and actually walked around the whole site, without telling anyone. I was on my way back, going through the old Jazz Field, when I heard this announcement on the stage: 'Has anybody seen Emily Eavis, she's completely disappeared and her parents are looking for her', and there'd been one on every stage, though nobody knew who I was…

At festival time people would wander up to the house all day and night, and there would be others staying, if they needed help. I'd be playing rounders at school, and going into a daydream about one girl who stayed when I was about 13. 'I've got to go home and Ann-Marie's there, what's she going to do now?' She put everything in my bedroom in carrier bags, or lined everything up in the hall. She was really sweet, and she recovered, but it was someone like that my mum would definitely take on.

Tony Andrews

There were mystical experiences in the 1980s, many of them, but we needed them en masse and Michael didn't share that view, which I think is a great shame. With Taj Mahal it was close to critical mass, then again with Spirit later…until the sound generator failed. And then with acid house I felt the explosion of something new. No terrible bands, not even any DJs at the beginning. Just the people dancing and enjoying the music, and people being there for each other. I am personally still committed to that. It's nice of other people to say that I had something to do with that at Glastonbury, because it was important.

Eventually I asked if we could do an experiment – by then we'd passed the main stage sound on to Britannia Row – and that led to the setting up of the Experimental Sound Field in 1992, and that to the worst, the scariest, the most dangerous night of my life. They actually put us in the traveller's field, where all the riots had happened the year before, and there was no security, no chance of any security. And we had 8,000 people there, it was all going off, and literally our lives were being threatened. It was Underworld, and, who's that guy from Essex – the DJ? – Darren Emerson's first gig and we were running over but it was way too dangerous to turn it off. We wouldn't have got out alive.

Chris Howes

What I associate most strongly with Glastonbury is not the recollection of specific incidents, but a hard-to-define mixture of excitement, pride, comradeship and fulfilment, which at good moments can add up to something quite extraordinary. A serene English Sunday afternoon in June, standing with the pit crew in front of the main stage looking out at 30,000 people in the arena. In the distance, a policeman on a white horse moving sedately across the hillside, behind me the incomparable Van Morrison singing about 'going down to Avalon'. A butterfly appears in front of me and I lose it altogether, tears flowing. Do I believe in magic? Yes, I think I do.

Angie Watts, festival employee

We live under the Tor now, a magical spot, but I've been in Glastonbury since 1977 – teacher training, evening classes to become an accountant, then the children. I started helping one of Arabella's co-ordinators with the paperwork one year and then a bit more the next. And I'd been up during festival time and they all seemed so pressured. I did all the P45s for the Children's Area. One year Sheelagh [Allen] was snowed under and Michael had rung up asking about me: 'Your friend Angie, what does she do these days?'

I had an accountant's training and I was slowly moving away from the days when every receipt was either verbal or scrawled on the back of a paper bag, which wasn't really enough. Like, it would be quite

△△ Michael Eavis at the first festival
△ There was music on the stage, but everyone made their own entertainment
– the spirit of Glastonbury Fayre in 1971

△△ 'People were so able to express themselves, running around naked
in the mud.' – 1970s model Dee Palmer on the prevailing fashion
△ Arabella Churchill, grand-daughter of Sir Winston Churchill, has been a key
figure in the organisation of the festival from the very beginning

▷ Peace child – author
Crispin Aubrey's daughter
Meg at an early 1980s
festival
▽ 'A wonderful shining
diamond' – the first Pyramid
stage at night

The infamous 'Carhenge' was constructed by the Mutoid Waste Company,
who travelled from festival to festival creating anarchic sculptures

△ 'The travellers
sometimes put on a better
show than we did.' –
Richard Abel, 1980s site
manager
▷ The Wicker Man finally
goes up in flames in 1992

Lightning strikes twice – both 1997 and 1998 were muddy years

△ 'I remember David Bowie because his music was wonderful and, like so many of the boys, he looked like a girl.' Actress Julie Christie recalls watching Bowie at Glastonbury Fayre

△▷ 'It was the most wonderful experience, having that number of people singing my words along with me .' – David Bowie on performing in 2000

△ New meets old – a twenty-first century projection stands before the remains of the fourteenth-century church on top of Glastonbury Tor

Time off – organiser Michael Eavis enjoys the festival from the photographers' pit

helpful to know what this receipt is for and who paid it. We moved to Northload Street in Glastonbury for the winter. Cold was definitely a factor; I always wore a coat and fingerless mittens. Our site office Portakabin started sagging at both ends. We were always having to have bits cut off the door to make it shut properly.

People running the festival definitely did seem more eccentric at the beginning, but it was always changing. When I started I think it was the beginning of the 'Let's get organised phase' that saw the festival through the Nineties…until it got to that kind of inevitable turning point, where it was obvious that a much bigger infrastructure was needed. 1992 was a kind of turning point too; the first year we technically made a profit.

Jean [Eavis] always used to say to me: 'You look so calm, it looks like nothing ever worries you.' But, especially later on, it was stressful and difficult quite a lot of the time. Getting cheques out, paying the bands. Then people would stay on after the festival and become quite disruptive, and that's always the time when there is the most paperwork, that flurry as soon as it's over, and you'd have to carry on, not looking or not listening. I had a knife drawn on me once, by a litter picker who was quite distressed.

Michael Eavis

Up to 1991 the police had not been exactly supportive. But in 1992, they were all on board and it made such a difference for the better.

Thomas Crimble

By the 1990s it felt a lot safer. I was working with Angie Watts and the accountant, and we used to pick the money up from the farmhouse safe and run it round the site to pay people, all the bands on the different stages. People were paid when they'd done their show, so they had to have the money. We were taking round a couple of hundred thousand pounds to half a million quid in cash and cheques – and getting a Land Rover so we could do the job was like getting blood out of a stone.

But the festival still used to rely on people working above and beyond the call of duty – a lot of people worked 24-hour shifts. Working at the farmhouse we'd only get a couple of hours' sleep, it was crazy. I'd say I've experienced more in a few weeks at Glastonbury than some people have experienced in the whole of their life. You get twisted in and out, you've got the highest highs and the lowest lows, you get the ridiculous situations when your radio falls down the bog, bizarre situations that you couldn't possibly dream of. I've never worked with such amazing people before or since, it's been a pleasure and a privilege. You have to be there, that's the magic of it, that's why the guys who have experienced it go back year after year.

Greenpeace

Michael Eavis

What I enjoy is getting people to work, firing them up and keeping them interested in it so that they're going to do more and do it better, the whole thing improves. It's a big thing, you can't just leave it alone. But then fifteen years ago I was a lot younger, I was only 50. I was in the prime of my life and I didn't really want to stop it.

The other thing that happened was that the wall came down in Berlin, there was the demise of the Soviet Union, and I thought maybe, after ten years, we ought to move on to something else than CND. It seemed a bit tunnel vision. We'd been putting loos in for the women at Greenham and so on, but I thought we ought to have something more abrasive. The weapon thing had been done, the Soviet Union had been busted, the threat wasn't quite the same, it wasn't that sort of simmering, smoking gun. I think people found the environmental message a bit more attractive.

So I decided to take a vote on it – should we move to Greenpeace? I put it to the whole crew on the lawn outside the farmhouse, and they all decided to go with it. That was the majority wish. Then later we got involved with Oxfam and WaterAid.

John Sauven

After the 1990 festival, Michael phoned me up and asked if Greenpeace wanted to be involved. I'd moved to work there from CND. There was one director who was concerned about the image of the festival, but Lord Melchett was the head of Greenpeace then and he'd championed festivals in the House of Lords, he'd worked in the Release tent at Glastonbury, and he was very supportive. So in the end it was quite a smooth transition.

At the beginning Greenpeace did all the information points at the gates, we had a huge number of volunteers, although we didn't do the tickets any more, and we promoted the festival to all our supporters. It was the same reciprocal thing as with CND, you were expected to put a lot into the festival to help make it work. We provided a service, whether information points or publicising the festival or running a field – and in return we got a donation.

We developed the whole idea of having a Greenpeace field and in 1992 turned the original structure of the jazz stage into the Rainbow Warrior, rebuilt it in the shape of a ship, with the sails and everything. It became a huge children's climbing frame. Even now, that's one of the few things that's allowed to remain on site when everything else gets cleared away.

Stephen Abrahall

I was quite instrumental in getting Oxfam involved in the festival in 1992. I think it was a chance remark to Michael that maybe they should be one of the main beneficiaries. Then I went along with Jean and Michael to hand over the first cheque at Oxfam's HQ in Oxford. I think it was for £60,000. They showed us round one of their warehouses where they super-compress blankets to be able to send them off economically, and how they erect water containers in emergency situations. We even talked about selling tickets through Oxfam shops, which of course are all in high-street locations, but I'm not sure they could cope with the security issues of having tickets worth several thousand pounds.

The Stone Circle

Ivan McBeth, designer of the Worthy Farm stone circle

I have been passionately interested and inspired by the megalithic culture and structures for as long as I can remember and I've spent a large proportion of my conscious life travelling to these sacred sites. My belief is that the main purposes of stone circles are to provide a network to regulate energy flows between the heavenly bodies and the earth, to create a network of sacred space over the earth and to be guardians of the secrets through which humanity can realise its divinity.

In February 1992 I got the go-ahead to design and build a permanent stone circle at Worthy Farm. Then two weeks before I moved on to the King's Meadow, Michael and I walked around the field searching for the right place. We walked directly to a circular flat area in the middle of the field and he felt sure it was right.

My first vision of the design was hazy and restricted but I was sitting by my fire on the night of the May full moon, pondering the dilemma, when I remembered that many so-called stone circles are in fact egg-shaped. Within a couple of minutes of this realisation came the final piece of the puzzle. The shape would be that of the star constellation Cygnus the Swan. The major stones of the design would correspond with the brightest stars, and if someone looked over the stone representing the belly of the Swan at midsummer sunrise, the sun would rise directly over the Swan's head.

I had originally ordered 19 stones from a quarry near Wellington, but when they arrived they had been badly damaged during transport. Both Michael and I were not impressed. We then heard that there were some much larger, very beautiful stones in the Torr Works, close to Pilton. They were indeed wonderful and I chose 19 of the most suitable. They were delivered to the farm individually, and so suffered minimal damage. As the stones arrived I marked out the circle in relation to the sunrise and the sunset.

During the digging process I became quite negative and had attacks of doubt. After three or four days I prayed for confirmation that what I intended to do was right. That evening I was sitting with my girlfriend by the fire when we heard a strange sound. It was eerie and frightening, a rhythmical whistling like spirits singing. It grew rapidly louder and we were both very frightened. Suddenly seven swans, flying very low in a V-formation, flew over our heads and directly above the stones. We looked at each other in amazement. Any doubts forever faded.

On 21 May we started digging. We dug holes for the direction stones first of all, in order to magically define the space. I was determined to dig all the holes by hand, despite constant pressure from Michael and Keith, the digger driver, who couldn't understand why we wanted to expend such a lot of energy when it 'would be so easy' to use the machines. I don't think they ever totally understood ...

I had put the word around that I wanted crystals from different places both in Britain and around the world to place underneath the stones. Many people gave me such gifts, and they were placed where appropriate. And what a sight the stones were, plonked in their holes before being set firmly into place. Megalithic drunkards, lolling around at all angles; stone beings seeming to defy gravity in a frozen chaotic dance. But after many days of adjusting their positions and returfing the damaged ground, we downed tools and completed our physical work on the Swan Circle at 5pm on Midsummer's Eve, exactly on target.

The Glastonbury Order of Druids performed a delightful ceremony to inaugurate the new stone circle, the sun rose directly over the head of the Swan, and there was much celebration.

Since then the stone circle has been a wonderful temple of harmony, healing and celebration. Many tens of thousands of people have entered its portals and have celebrated their spirituality in their own ways, whatever belief or religion they practise. As a builder of sacred space, I am happy and fulfilled. For I know that whenever anyone enters sacred space, consciously or unconsciously, they will be changed by the properties of the place, at a deep and fundamental level.

Tony Cordy, Children's Field organiser

I was a traveller originally, Stonehenge every year. I was one of the people that coined the phrase 'new age travellers' at Inglestone Common, where we used to hold events. I was part of the Tibetan Ukrainian Mountain Troupe. We did everything – performing, clowning, security, welfare. Our blue and white marquee went up at every free festival in the late Seventies and early Eighties.

I started running the kids field in 1992, mainly because I saw it as the last free festival going. No other festival lets in all these kids for free, and creates an entire space for them to be in. That's how I see it, I run the free festival part of Glastonbury.

The Wicker Man

Arabella Churchill

The big fire shows are always exciting. The wicker man performers were an amazing group, there were about 50 or 60 of them – dancers, high tightrope walkers, people inside huge plastic balls, and then this giant person made of wood, sixty foot high – it was a real act of faith on our part. It was a completely new show and you really didn't know for certain whether it was going to work.

Then there was another unnerving thing because we'd had phone messages saying that the wicker man is a pagan symbol and if it's burned I am going to incinerate myself in it. So I'm up with some friends next to the pigtail security barrier ready to rugby tackle anybody who runs towards it. We really thought somebody might do it – we even searched the wicker man first to make sure there was nobody in there.

We were all ready to go on the Saturday night and word had really got out about this show, so there was a lot of expectation. But then there's a bit of a wind, Haggis thought it's a bit strong and we asked the firemen and they said go, go. But then the first fireworks go off and they start landing on top of the cabaret tent. The guy who runs it, Mike Hearst, was in tears, and Haggis said you've got to stop, and I say the firemen said it's fine. And Haggis phoned Michael and he said we had to stop.

By now we have an enormous crowd all wanting to burn the wicker man. So I get a microphone and say, sorry the wind is all wrong, we're not going to do it tonight, please come back tomorrow. But nobody goes away, and they stand there shouting, burn it, burn it, and even burn the farmhouse and burn Bella. So I had to remain by the wicker man all night, patrolling it, otherwise somebody was going to set it off for certain. I was determined that wasn't going to happen. And then on the Sunday night we did set it off, we had the whole performance again and it was fantastic. Word had really got round about it and that was the biggest audience we've ever had.

●●●

1993
HEATWAVE

Advance tickets were sold out by mid-June, the earliest ever, reflecting the event's growing success and popularity. The Velvet Underground and Rolf Harris headlined one of the best festivals ever. The sun shone gloriously for all three days and another £250,000 went to Greenpeace, Oxfam and many local charities. Attendance reached 80,000, with the festival now including a separate NME music stage as well as circus, cabaret, jazz, cinema and 60 acres of green activities.

Bands in 1993: Alison Moyet, Belly, Dodgy, Donovan, Eddi Reader, Galliano, Hothouse Flowers, Jamiroquai, Lenny Kravitz, Lindisfarne, Midnight Oil, Nanci Griffith, Omar, Ozric Tentacles, Robert Plant, Rolf Harris, Spiritualised, Stereo MCs, Suede, Teenage Fan Club, The Black Crowes, The Blues Band, The Kinks, The Lemonheads, The Orb, The Velvet Underground, The Verve, Transglobal Underground, Urban Species, Van Morrison.

Evan Dando, musician, ex-member of The Lemonheads

I first played Glastonbury in 1993, with The Lemonheads. People love music there, man. It's like nowhere else! A festival like this could never happen in the States. It would be impossible to have a festival like Glastonbury. It would be too violent, because too many people carry guns.

I've always wanted to do a hippie festival and the experience of playing there really inspired me. I've even thought of a name for my festival – Popscapade!

Rolf Harris, entertainer

My first time was in 1993 during an incredibly hot summer. I think they booked me as a bit of a joke. They'd put me on early on the Sunday morning when I think they assumed most people would be asleep. I was all right until I got to Glastonbury in the car and saw the huge crowd and all the tents. I tell you, the nerves started to kick in and by the time I was backstage unloading my kit I was beginning to think it was all a big mistake. But as I lugged my accordion case up the ramp, a huge cockney stagehand slapped me on the back and said, 'You're the only one I'm interested in seeing here today, son.' He really put my mind at ease.

When I eventually walked out onto the stage and saw the audience for the first time it knocked my socks off. They reckon there were 80,000 people there that morning and they'd all got out of bed to see me. The people seemed to stretch to the horizon like a brightly coloured blanket with a million tents behind them. I kicked off with 'Jake the Peg' (with the extra leg), and shouted, 'What about that, Jake the bloody Peg at Glastonbury?' And the crowd went mad! The whole place sang every single word with me. It was the same with 'Tie Me Kangaroo Down, Sport'. And everyone got all the jokes. There were a dozen or so people in the crowd with didgeridoos, holding them up for everyone to see. By the time we played 'Sun Arise' the volume from the audience was so loud I couldn't hear myself or the band. And of course we all sang 'Stairway to Heaven' together which was funny, because Robert Plant was playing that year as well.

Robert Plant, musician

Even before the festivals started a lot us were aware of what Glastonbury represented. It was a natural meeting point for the summer solstice. I used to go to the Tor and watch women walking in backward spiral circles to the top, holding torches and stuff. You felt that Joseph of Arimathea was as likely to turn up to do a set as Janis Joplin. I always wanted to play there but after the demise of Zep, it just wasn't going to happen for a long time.

When I eventually did it felt like one of those old times. I remember with Zeppelin, our manager Peter Grant always used to make sure no matter what point we were on the bill something went wrong with the equipment so that we would always go on just as the sun set. And somehow, by hook or by crook, that's what happened when we played at Glastonbury.

I've been back again and again, and it was my pleasure to come along to christen the brand new Pyramid stage which Michael Eavis commissioned.

We launched it with a bucket of milk...

What To Do About Fence Hoppers?

- Have a double fence system and fill moat with water or cow shit.
- Have motorbike patrols going round fence.
- Put barbed wire on fence (illegal). Electrify it (illegal).
- Smear with grease (any volunteers?).
- Have smaller gates spread round the site so that no part of the fence would be hidden.
- Sell tickets to people who want to pay so they don't have to jump over fence (council licence won't allow it).

Post-festival evaluation, gate and traffic team, 1993

•••

1994
FIRE AND WIND

An accidental fire reduced the Pyramid stage to ashes just days before the festival. A replacement was hastily erected and a giant wind turbine rose like a phoenix beside it. Channel 4 broadcast live for the first time, with four hours' coverage each day. Björk, Elvis Costello and the Manic Street Preachers led the biggest line-up ever with 1,000 acts on 17 stages.

On the Saturday night there was a shooting incident in the market area, although fortunately nobody was badly hurt. There was also the first death in the festival's history, when a young man was found dead from a drugs overdose.

Bands in 1994: The Beastie Boys, Björk, Blur, Chumbawamba, Echobelly, Elvis Costello, Gallagher and Lyle, Galliano, Glenn Tilbrook, Gorky's Zygotic Mynci, Jah Wobble's Invaders of the Heart, James, M People, Mary Black, Nick Cave, Oasis, Orbital, Oyster Band, Paul Weller, Peter Gabriel, Pulp, Radiohead, Rage Against the Machine, Ride, Saint Etienne, Spin Doctors, Spiritualised, The Boo Radleys, The Lemonheads, The Levellers, The Pretenders, The Manic Street Preachers, The Tindersticks, Tom Robinson, Transglobal Underground, World Party.

Emily Eavis

My dad always had a joke that the Pyramid was like my doll's house. It was my world, my playground. I had more attachment than you ever believe you could have to a structure. I'd be on it every weekend, I'd climb to the top and write little messages on it, we just spent so much time on it…and it burning down was just one of the most heart-breaking moments. About four in the morning my sister Sandra ran into my room and told me about the fire, and I thought it was some bad dream. We drove down and just watched it cave in, the firemen couldn't get near. I was devastated.

Mark Cann

I was living in the flat above the farmhouse by then, and I was woken up in the middle of the night by Sandra, who was then working in Goose Hall, to be told that the Pyramid was on fire. It was like being woken from a bad dream, you think you're still in it. To be suddenly presented with a situation as dramatic as that, you think, what's real? You just don't expect that sort of thing to happen.

I got down there just as the fire engines were arriving, but the place was already well ablaze. That meant we had no stage, and ten days to go before the show. So Steve Caulfield from Serious Stages, who already arranged the Other Stage, came down the next day as they were dousing down to see what size alternative we could fit in. Fortunately we had a company on our doorstep that could take that on. They got the new stage up within ten days.

Most people think it was an electrical problem that caused the fire in the first place. There's absolutely no evidence that it was arson.

Elvis Costello, singer-songwriter

If you want to see Glastonbury you ought to be there. You have to get some sun on your head and some mud on your boots. You can't be an armchair hippie…

Roy Gurvitz

The first year of Channel 4's coverage (1994) they asked me if I could help them make their backstage presentation area less sterile – they wanted to interview famous people coming off the stage, and it just didn't look like Glastonbury. It could have been anywhere. So we got a fire going and a couple of buses and put my marquee up. I thought that neither Richard nor Michael Eavis would expect to find me running a bar there. I also drove the Channel 4 presenter Katie Puckrick round the site because I had a Land Rover and they could film her going round looking at all the other stuff apart from the bands. Bill Oddie was in the Green Fields with a bender doing some ecology thing, so we went and visited him. So all the interviews were taking place on the bonnet of my Land Rover, but on the last day, when Michael was being interviewed, he was really shocked to see my whole bar set-up because I'd promised him that I wouldn't do it. I think he realised then that I wasn't going to go away.

Tom Rowlands, The Chemical Brothers

We went along to Glastonbury as punters in 1993 and 1994, and Orbital were playing on the second stage. It was the most amazing night, and it was the first time that a dance band was allowed to finish off the show. Live techno, outdoors, is the most brilliant experience – dancing under the stars with music wafting around the open air. After we'd experienced that, it was a real thrill to be invited to play ourselves.

My worst experience of Glastonbury happened one year when Ed [Simons] and I were there as punters, it was five or six times in all we went, and we were sharing a tent. We hadn't realised how hot it was, and we woke up at 2pm burning hot and with heat stroke. One year Ed got trench foot – that was pretty bad. We stayed on after we'd played, and he was wearing trainers all weekend.

Sally Howell, partner, Croissant-Neuf Circus and Green Roadshow

We've always had the bright yellow, red and white striped Croissant-Neuf Circus tent, which everybody knows. We took that round the festivals and folk fairs for years, doing the music and the circus. But now we've taken over a whole field and made it the Green Roadshow. The circus tent is the hub of it, but there's a whole outside arena with environmental and renewable energy themes, sustainable living, electric vehicles, a solar-powered roundabout. It's to educate people through the medium of entertainment – it's fun, it's exciting, it's hands on. It's like a condensed version of the Green Fields all in one place.

We've always tried to live a green lifestyle ourselves as much as possible and right from the word go the whole thing has been solar- and wind-powered. The solar panels produce enough power for full-on bands for 14 hours over five days. The last time the power cut out was, I think, in 1994 in the middle of a Sunday night when Nik Turner's All Stars were playing. It's the best system around, and we've inspired a lot of people, so nearly every venue up there now is solar-powered. We constantly get sound engineers and lighting engineers coming in to look at the set-up.

Glastonbury Television

Martin Elborne

There were a few bands that didn't work. The Fall goes down as one of the disasters that people still talk about. A bad hair day for Mark E Smith. On a major scale…But even in the 1990s there were less stages, less diversification; a great gig on the Main Stage could make a difference. Shows that make a big, lasting impact have to be on the Pyramid, maybe sometimes the Other Stage. If there is a 'type' of Glastonbury music, it has come out of that whole indie/rock thing: The Happy Mondays were a good example of a band being right for Glastonbury at the right time. And although we had completely missed out on punk, all the major music movements since then we've been ahead of.

We came late in the day to dance, but it was there anyway. Orbital and The Stereo MCs got amazing reactions, before the Dance Tent. And I'm sure the whole Bristol movement, Massive Attack, Portishead, was influenced by Glastonbury. They'd come and been part of it before they played here.

By then the festival was attracting interest from television. Television has made a huge difference. I think Waldemar Januszczak, who was doing Arts at Channel 4 in the 1990s, really does deserve a major credit there. He pushed it, and he made the money available. He proved to people it could be done. He was determined not just to film the bands, but to go out and try to capture the whole atmosphere as well. And, let's face it, Glastonbury is a bloody difficult thing to film! He talked and talked until people got really fed up with him. But he made it happen, his commitment made it happen.

With the TV interest, we were able to trial a business deal, and in 1994 I set up Glastonbury Television, with Ben Challis. We stuck to our guns, and we got a deal whereby we owned the footage of the bands playing at the festival, and that has carried on. Waldemar was very important for starting that off, because really it secured the festival's future.

The Wind Turbine and WaterAid

John Sauven

One of the reasons we worked so hard to get the wind turbine down there was that we wanted to do something that was iconic in terms of promoting renewable energy, and Michael also wanted to do something that was a feature of the festival in terms of its greening, all the environmental issues. Our argument was that nobody had seen a wind turbine unless they happened to live near one; most of the people were coming from cities and they had no idea of the size or scale or beauty of these things.

From a staging point of view it was absolutely brilliant because you had this amazing structure right next to the main stage. It was a real landmark in terms of visibility and presence. It was still quite expensive because we had to dig quite deep foundations to put in a concrete base and you had to hire massive cranes to assemble the thing and then you had to link up all the power – it was a huge undertaking. Because it was a temporary structure you didn't need planning permission and in the first year, the Mendip health and safety people came down and it was there, already up.

Fiona Hance, Oxfam

In 1994, when there was a refugee crisis in Rwanda, we were providing water for over a million people in a week flat. Michael has a couple of our large water tanks on the farm, so there's a bit of cross-fertilisation in technology. We even tested out our refugee camp toilets at Glastonbury because it's the nearest comparable place we have in the UK.

Sharon Brand-Self, press officer, WaterAid

It started in 1993 through the Shepton Mallet Rotary Club, which Michael had a great association with, and so did WaterAid. So we floated the idea that the festival should have African pit latrines.

In 1994 we had just two pit latrines as an experiment. They're basically a hole in the ground, that's the first principle, a nice deep hole so you can't see anything, with a structure round it for privacy, and very simple to construct. They're called VIP latrines at Glastonbury, which isn't a posh term; it actually stands for Ventilated Improved Pit. There's a little funnel at the top which any flies inside head for and then get trapped, stopping them getting outside and spreading diseases, and they're also waterless. In Africa they'd use local materials like ash from fires to throw down and stop any smell, at Glastonbury we used eco-friendly disinfectant, which does mean they don't smell at all. And the great thing is they don't have to be emptied – in Africa they'd wait for everything to rot down and then use it as compost on their crops.

Talking about sanitation isn't easy, people get quite prim about it, but at Glastonbury you don't have to worry. We were walking around dressed as giant turds this year, with a giant feeding fly on top, which would be difficult at a charity flower show. Of course we made sure it wasn't just a gratuitous poo, it was holding up a placard saying that there are 10 million viruses in one gram and lack of toilets is killing people. It engaged people immediately, they wanted to know why, and didn't realise that a third of people in the world don't have toilets.

The Shooting Incident

Ian Japp

By the end of the Eighties ecstasy had made its first widespread appearance, creating an unfulfilled demand for all-night sound systems. That's when you got a lorry arriving that was supposed to be a stall, and it was a sound system, probably not as massive as it seemed at the time, but going all night anyway.

By 1994 we were up to a five kilowatt system, and we had the feeling that the Markets Manager loved us; we had 25 free tickets and a great position. Only it turned out to be the spectacular year of the Glastonbury gunman, who himself turned out to be a guy from Shepherd's Bush. He had been shot at by a guy in a road rage incident in London and obviously decided the best way to defend himself was to get his own gun. In the middle of one of our brilliant parties on the Saturday night, this guy walks in, looks like Devon Malcolm, the cricketer. I want to come backstage, he says. I told him to sling his hook, and as I did I could see him starting to pull what I could see was a handgun from his waistband. Now earlier in the day Bernie and I had heard gunshots, and he already had a plan. Basically to put a pole under a blanket and pretend it was a sawn-off. Bernie's a fearsome looking Maori, a right character, and he said: 'I wouldn't do that if I were you, I'll blow your balls off'. The guy beat a retreat, but only as far as the two towers we had set up. Then he handed something over to someone in the crowd who disappeared.

At that time a lot of the really heavy dealers used to hang round Butt's Bridge; we were one stall away, and there's maybe 3,000 people, pretty ragged by that time. Within seconds, though, the armed response team arrived and tried to grab him. Most people didn't even notice. This Devon Malcolm character, wearing a poncho, was fortunately stopped and arrested. The police found the old bullet wounds, and he was subsequently charged with shooting five people at Joe Bananas' stall earlier that day.

Brian Schofield

I'm sure that for many years weapons have been down there on site. These types of criminals, particularly the drug dealers, regularly carry them. So it wasn't a complete surprise when it happened. I was an Inspector in charge of the support groups on duty at the time, and also an authorised firearms planner and carrier. So once we had the report that there had been a shooting it was a case of trying to look at some sort of plan to contain it, that's always the initial aim. But can you imagine trying to contain a festival of that size, with six or seven exit points and perhaps 200,000 people? It was very difficult. We actually sent somebody who was armed to each of the exit points and contained it from that point of view. We had a brief description of somebody we might have been looking for, but obviously we didn't find anything and after a couple of hours we stood all the firearms guys down. We also tried to sterilise the scene by pushing everybody back from the vicinity, but that was very difficult because we didn't know the exact point.

One of my other roles was organising a search of the crime scene. So the following morning when everybody had disappeared we started a fingertip search of the crime scene, and we actually found the bullet cases, even though they'd been trampled into the ground, and other bits of evidence that were used later on to establish who the individual was. He was eventually arrested in London.

•••

1995
DANCE CULTURE

The twenty-fifth anniversary of the festival saw the return of two performers from the first event – Keith Christmas and Al Stewart. Demand for tickets had never been so intense, and the event sold out completely a month in advance. The Dance Tent was launched, a major success with names like Massive Attack, System 7 and Eat Static. The Stones Roses were forced to pull out a week before, to be replaced magnificently by Pulp. Greenpeace received £200,000 and Oxfam £100,000.

Bands in 1995: Ash, Billy Bragg, Difford and Tilbrook, Dodgy, Elastica, Jamiroquai, Massive Attack, Menswear, Mike Scott, Nick Lowe, Oasis, Orbital, Page & Plant, PJ Harvey, Portishead, Pulp, Shed 7, Simple Minds, Skunk Anansie, Sleeper, Steeleye Span, Supergrass, The Black Crowes, The Charlatans, The Cure, The Lightning Seeds, The Prodigy, The Shamen, The Verve.

Billy Bragg, performer

I've played every year except one since 1992, and a lot of the Eighties as well. In 1995 the tent was so packed that my guitar got broken. I had to abandon the semi-acoustic set I'd played in favour of a full-on punk set.

What makes Glastonbury unique among the major rock festivals is that the site is miles from anywhere. It's not tacked on to a dormitory town or in a purpose-built arena, there's no cosy link with civilisation. The challenge of how to get there is the same for stars and punters alike – narrow back lanes filled with wandering hitchhikers and trucks all searching for the speediest way in. And once you're there, you're there. There's just no point in trying to come and go as you please. How much time and money have bands spent checking into hotels in Shepton Mallet only to waste the day sitting in their coach waiting for the drummer and his girlfriend to get back from the Jazz Field? There are even those who never leave the charmed enclosure behind the Pyramid stage for fear of mingling with the Great Unwashed.

Simon Roiser

The festival had got bigger by the 1990s, but even then there was nothing like today's amount of money involved. Doing the press stuff we were still working out of an old caravan at the back of the wagon shed, usually with only one phone line, and the fax machine was still a walk away in the farmhouse. Michael always had other things to spend the money on. Ridiculous conditions, but it still worked. Michael's brain is always somewhere else, looking down the drive to see the next person coming along. That's how it works, there's nothing else to be said on the subject.

By 1995 you had the feeling that Glastonbury did kind of lead the world, even if you didn't quite know why. The others didn't have our universal appeal.

Jeremy Frankel, television producer

A load of us traipsed up the hill to see Portishead and stood around for ages for them to appear. Everyone was getting restless and pissed off.

Suddenly Evan Dando from The Lemonheads appeared on stage and started an impromptu number. Apparently he'd missed his own slot. He got booed off. It was weird.

Janine Smith, senior producer, Channel 4 Interactive

I've been as often as I can, either in Puntersville or working. But even working, I'm still going as a fan. This year it was three in our group, then another five or six friends out there somewhere, plus four or five more from work. The Other Stage field is my home.

Every year I've been it's been really hot. I've got very pale Scottish skin and by Saturday I've usually got sunburn. It always takes till Saturday to get used to it; to get used to being dirty, and realising everyone else is too. And getting used to carrying a loo roll in your pocket, and finding your way around. Glastonbury is always about co-ordinates and knowing where you are so you can find your friends. We've got plenty of markers. That big bush in the main stage field, that's how we track each other down.

My favourite thing now is going with someone who has never been before. They're always starting by thinking, 'Bunch of crazy hippies, lots and lots of mud', and then by Saturday they're overwhelmed by the size and variety of it all. We always take our 'blanket of love', that's our home base. It's a tatty old thing, I think we nicked it when we went to India, but it's always there, and someone has to be responsible for it. The blanket of love only comes with a group, the last person always has to bring it back.

Janet Convery, former CND worker

I had a bit of a reprieve from working during the 1990s because I was having babies. My children have been every year since they were born. Dylan's the interesting one because he was actually born on 28 June in 1996, when there wasn't a festival. He was in fact conceived in 1995 when we went down for Michael's 60th birthday party. So he always has his birthday at the festival.

The big difference between Glastonbury and any other festival is that people will just come and create. All the sculptures that go on, the gardens that people make, especially up above the crossroads in the Green Fields. They seem to take responsibility for making it happen in their own little way. It's a labour of love, considering it all has to be taken down at the end of the weekend. At other festivals you pay your ticket and just go, at Glastonbury people contribute a lot more.

Liz Eliot

The fence always created a lot of problems up in the Green Fields because it was the first place for extra people to settle in. Most of them were quite anarchic, so they weren't easy to handle. If they wanted to put their tent up somewhere that was it as far as they were concerned. So we had to meet them on their own terms. We missed a fire show one year because I'd felt sorry for people in the mud and allowed them to camp in King's Meadow, and then they wouldn't move the next day.

The first year the fence came down (1995) was very, very frightening. There was no guarantee that there was nobody underneath when it was lifted. I warned people to move away but they were so slow at moving. They were undoing the bolts from the inside, and every time I went up to check they ran away, but I knew what was happening. When it eventually fell, the whole section along the top of King's Meadow collapsed.

Dance Scene

Ian Japp

It was unintended, but with Glastonbury encouragement and our own musical policy, our own little system catering mainly for our friends, part of the stall, simply expanded...then it became almost a crowd control unit, there were thousands and thousands of people out there who wanted something. I remember about midnight on the Saturday in 1995, the whole of Butt's Green was full of people, right back to the stalls at the edges. One of our features has always been a tower. Sometimes with flags, and quite a few times we've used it for projections and visuals, which really come into their own at night. And in the day, there's a tower with a skull and crossbones flying, it really stands out.

The view from up there was amazing. It was rammed, and for an hour and a half I was playing records to 12,000 people and Grant Plant took over from me and kept it going. No matter who has followed in that space, and Radio 1 has had it twice, that's the largest crowd I can remember. Looking back, it was a high point, and we'd like to go back to that space again. We set the pattern after all...

Melvin Benn

I challenge the prevailing view from the straighter side of Glastonbury that dance and rave culture contributed to the overcrowding and the downfall year. It's not true. I saw the emergence of dance as a breath of fresh air – comparable to punk when it first broke through. I saw a very stale early Eighties glam rock and pop scene reaching a natural conclusion – nobody had a clue where music was going. And this new thing was absolutely awesome, and that's from someone who's never even had a cigarette! God, what a movement, I thought. It was more than that, it was an uprising; the establishment wasn't providing what they needed. And I had to respond to it.

I created Tribal Gathering in 1995, against incredible police opposition through the Criminal Justice Act, and that had a significant impact overall. The same year Glastonbury had the Dance Tent for the first time, although there had been signs of it arriving much earlier. If there was a pre-rave reference point I'd have to suggest it had something to do with Tony Andrews, the original designer of the speaker box systems on the main stage, who was nothing less than a sound genius. He was a Glastonbury mainstay for years, and then he had a falling out with Michael and hasn't come back. He was a hippie, no ifs and no buts, but he knew everything about sound. He created the first surround sound system, the best boxes in the world. He created, or certainly helped, the first lot of market people playing ambient music all night, and that became established at the end of the

1980s. He wanted to push the boundaries – and if the boundaries had to be pushed anywhere they had to be pushed at Glastonbury.

Michael Eavis

I got cancer in my stomach in 1994, but I decided that we had to do 1995 because of the 25th anniversary. And I just about felt well enough, because I was getting chemotherapy.

I suppose I did think then about giving up, but I also thought if I'm going to die that's going to be it. But thankfully I didn't die, touch wood. And then in 1996 I took my cancer recovery year off basically, and I really enjoyed that year. It was a lovely year, I was feeling better and we were going back to normal life again.

•••

1997
YEAR OF THE MUD

The 1995 festival had been marred by the perimeter fence being pulled down at the top of the site, aggravating problems of trespass on neighbouring people's land. Again it was decided to give the farm a rest, the cows a chance to stay out all summer long and everybody involved a chance to take a break, so no festival was held in 1996.

Torrential rain in 1997, just before the weekend, resulted in this being the 'year of the mud'. Undeterred, festival-goers boogied in their boots to more live performances than ever before. The first proper Greenpeace area included a reconstructed Rainbow Warrior boat and solar-heated showers. The site expanded to 800 acres, a daily newspaper was published and BBC2 broadcast live. The Prodigy, Radiohead, Ray Davies and Sting played to 90,000 people.

Bands in 1997: Alabama 3, Aphex Twin, Ash, Beck, Beth Orton, Billy Bragg, Cast, Catatonia, Daft Punk, David Byrne, Dodgy, Echo & the Bunnymen, Finlay Quaye, Galliano, Kula Shaker, Mansun, Massive Attack, Nancy Griffith, Neneh Cherry, Ocean Colour Scene, Oysterband, Placebo, Primal Scream, Radiohead, Ray Davies, Reef, Republica, Sheryl Crow, Stereolab, Stevie Winwood, Sting, Super Furry Animals, Supergrass, The Chemical Brothers, The Dharmas, The Divine Comedy, The Levellers, The Orb, The Prodigy, Travis, Van Morrison, Youssou N'Dour.

Crispin Hunt, musician and songwriter, former member of The Longpigs

It's a phenomenal thing, Glastonbury, a tremendously thrilling place to play: the only place that still has that prefabricated Woodstock feeling, and the wildness and anarchy that festivals should have, and everywhere else never does. It's the only one remaining that still does its own thing. I've literally grown up with it, I first went when I was 15, and it's always had that magic combination of being good and scary at the same time. I still remember the massive kick I got just from having a spliff in the open when I was a teenager…like, I'm here and I'm doing it.

We've always known people in Somerset, and I did play a couple of times when I was in my studeny band – you could just turn up in the Circus area and play. Then when I was in The Longpigs, Michael came along to see us at a club in Bath. I think maybe he thought we were a local type band. Later that year he saw us on Top of the Pops and he was like: 'Oh, if only I'd realised, I would have put you on!' But he was as good as his word, and we made it on to the main stage; we played in one of the Battle of the Somme years where everyone soldiered on regardless. Again, it's something you wouldn't endure anywhere else, but you just do at Glastonbury, it's expected, it's part of it, the whole festival just turns on your bullshit spirituality and togetherness, whether you're up there or paying to watch.

Personally, playing the main stage was an enormous thrill. It really is an honour to be a part of it, to get the chance of turning on a very special audience. When you're on the bill at Glastonbury, you're a catalyst for enjoyment, not the reason, which is a welcome change. We'd been in the charts, played a lot live, we had a culty thing going on, and there was this moment in the mud that was like the English and the Germans stopping the war to play football – the crowd and that view out from the main stage going on and on, it's incredible.

If there's a moment when you say, now I'm a rock star, then playing Glastonbury has to be one of the major ticks…you've become part of it. I drive past Stonehenge a lot, and it's nothing, a heap of stones. But the Tor never fails to give me a rush, and even if you don't believe in all the ley lines and stuff there is still something there. Now I'm doing arty records with Howie B, pottering along to the left of centre, and writing songs, hits even, for Emma Bunton and Mark Owen, but I miss playing: it's much better than going as a punter.

Fran Healy, Travis

Glastonbury stands for:

G = Gathering

L = Life

A = Art

S = Smiling

T = Toilet paper (do not leave home without it)

O = The Original

N = Nature

B = Bonfires

U = Umbrellas

R = Rock 'n' Roll

Y = You haven't been to a festival until you do Glastonbury

My own best Glastonbury experience was headlining the Main Stage – it was all such a whirlwind. My abiding memory is of this sea of humanity submerged in a layer of smoke from the many bonfires that dotted the massive area. I will never forget this moment as long as I live. It was truly unique.

And the worst was in 1997 when it rained. I remember trawling through the mud to the acoustic tent and seeing a baby crawling around in the mud and all these folk just walking past it. The parents were nowhere in sight, but I assumed that they must have been. I just thought the child would die of some terrible disease from the germs.

Year of the Mud

Richard Abel

Worthy mud is legendary – but the wet years did seem to produce a calmer, better atmosphere on the site than the really hot ones. I don't know anywhere else that can turn from dust to liquid mud and back again so quickly. I am told it's something to do with the unusual combination of peat underlying the clay. 1997 was the really bad one, with much of the site including the markets sunk under 12 inches of mud. One unforeseen problem from this was that the stakes on several of the big tents were now sitting in a sort of soupy porridge and they all started to pull out of the ground. That was probably the only time I have thought we might have to close the show and tell everyone to go home again – something we had calculated would take at least two days and could lead to massive congestion with cars also coming in to try to pick people up.

However, thanks to the resourcefulness of Yorky (Martin York), two crews spent the whole night going round replacing stakes with railway sleepers pounded into the ground. The extra depth and wider profile offered by a railway sleeper held firm, and the tents were all able to open the next day. I didn't discover where Yorky was getting all these railway sleepers from in the middle of the night until halfway through the next day, when we found Michael wondering where the entire lining of his silage pit had disappeared to overnight.

Mark Cann

In 1997 it was so wet we couldn't bring any vehicles like tour buses down to the backstage area, because the parking area is in a low-lying field. There was no point in even trying. Nothing could move. Plan B was to park all the non-essential backstage vehicles in a field near the main road, which drained very well because it was on high ground, and all the tour buses at the main gate. But then overnight, Thursday into Friday, I said to Michael, we need to create a hard standing base from which we can shuttle people from the main gate to the stages. He must have got on the phone to the quarry because at 4–5 o'clock on Friday morning the first stones started coming in and a large temporary holding area was created for the buses.

Then we commandeered three or four vehicles from Greenpeace, Theatre and the BBC, and two of the guys who normally do the parking spent all their time shuttling the bands to and fro. I remember taking Radiohead back myself in two trips at one o'clock in the morning, the last band to leave on the Saturday night.

We had to cancel the first three or four acts on the Friday because the pit in front of the Other Stage was too wet and muddy for people to work in. The security crew said it was too dangerous and a rumour went round that the whole stage was sinking.

Arabella Churchill

Wet years are difficult, although there's always a high when you can still make it work. But the vast majority of my performers, even the street ones, just go out and do it. The staff behave wonderfully and the audiences respond. It's the trenches spirit.

I remember we were going to do one of our very big fire parades that year (1997 or 1998), and I called a meeting for seven o'clock in the green room and nobody looked like they wanted to do it. I had to stand on a table with a megaphone and make a very Churchillian sort of speech. It was great – they went straight out to rehearse.

It got very, very muddy in the Dance Tent, so muddy that for people dancing it was quite bad. So somebody had the clever thought that the sewage sludge gulper could go in and gulp out all the sludge. But they put it on blowing instead of sucking, and there was a terrible mess.

Liz Eliot

In the mud year everybody suddenly decided to take their clothes off and cover themselves in mud and have mud healing sessions. They got a bit carried away, and several relationships ended at that point unfortunately.

Martin Village, art dealer

The first time I camped on the cattle-tramped sod of Worthy Farm I didn't have to stoop to climb into my tent. I walked in. The thing we had was more modern than any tipi, a confection of plastic tubes and silver spandex that might have been designed by old Buckminster

Fuller himself. It was, literally, a 25-person geodesic dome. The only other one I've seen down there was being used as a backstage bar by EMAP [magazine publishers] and they had about 200 people inside. And a bar and a barbecue. I had it all to myself because my partner in crime was out there in the night, staring at a log fire with a man called Joe Strummer.

I managed to get to sleep but then I felt a presence hovering over my possessions. A burglar, turning us over. I grunted and he got out, taking what he could. The next night it was a new strategy – back-up accommodation in a 1950s Milletts one-person job.

Then the rain started. That downpour of 1997 is, I think, still spoken about with a degree of respect by those who experienced it. And when Michael Eavis drove past in a muddy Land Rover I started to think Old Testament. Here it was, right on cue. Glastonbury, The Flood. Most of the rain seemed to run off in my direction, and a small lake formed. Passers-by laughed. I laughed. The tent had collapsed in the middle but was still standing! In the middle of a muddy pond! So I ended up back in the dome. It had filled up with my children and my friend's children and their mumbling, grunting friends. My space was now a dormitory for stoned, farting teenagers where I had to find what damp space was still left. Maybe putting the little tent inside the big one would have been the best idea in those conditions. I could have defended it against all comers – and the rain.

The Fence

Liz Eliot

For the 1997 festival we had to keep the fence up at all costs. The council had said if the fence came down that would be the end of the festival. But we had a real problem with people collecting outside – because they knew the fence had come down before – and the security people getting very heavy, and people inside trying to take on the security. There was quite a lot of fighting. I got involved, this time in Pennard Hill Ground, which is a camping field, and somehow managed to defuse it. I worked out later that what I'd done is use tai chi movements, telling everybody that everything was alright, I could sort it out.

So I homed in on one of the security guys and said I was going to take control. I said I wanted the people on the outside of the fence to be let in. I decided that was what had to happen to defuse it, and it did.

Polly Bradford

A lot of my friends from the Bridgwater area would jump in. Sometimes you had to pay a security guard £10. The 'urban myth', which I'd heard a few times, was that a few years ago, when you could still jump over the fence, this girl was with her friends, and they threw all their stuff over, everything was fine, they got up to the top, jumped over, and ran straight into the crowd to avoid getting detected. They're so ecstatic that they've made it, start dancing in one of the tents, and then after a few minutes someone comes over and says, what happened to your finger. And she looks down and there's blood dripping out and the end of the finger has come off where her ring was caught on the top of the fence.

I didn't completely believe this story until my friend Catherine met this girl in Glasgow who was missing the end of her finger because of climbing over the fence at Glastonbury. So it was true.

A Few Brownie Points

Rachel Austin

It wasn't so much wanting to work for the festival, it's just I'd finished university, I'd been travelling for 16 months, spent all the funds, and was back in Pilton living with my parents and trying to find work. Having been away, I'd tasted freedom and I just wanted to work for a year.

Then one Sunday, actually in church, Mum was talking to Michael and Jean and I knew she was dropping hints and I was really embarrassed. She was going: 'It must be all right for Emily, with the festival and everything, but poor old Rachel's stuck at home, no car, the bus service is appalling. Even if you did get a job in a neighbouring town there's no way you'd get to work on time, blah blah...' And I stood there thinking: 'Shut up, Mum, this is really embarrassing.' I think I was actually blushing.

Then two weeks later Michael phones up in his usual fashion. 'I hear you're looking for work. We've got something, but it's not very interesting. You could find something more interesting later, but this'll give you a few brownie points.' And I'm like, OK then. I was going to start off helping Angie Watts, who'd been at the site office for many years, trying to get on top of the P60 employment forms for all the casual workers.

So it comes to my first day and I'm really quite nervous in this new world, even though I've lived here all my life, walking down Hitchin Hill, heart pounding and Sheelagh [Allen] drives past and gives me a lift, which kind of broke the ice. Sheelagh's daughter Bev used to babysit for me when I was younger so it was a familiar face. She took me into her little office which she's always had, and it was quite incredible. It's still quite incredible. Paper everywhere, phone numbers everywhere, it's like the whole history of the festival is in that tiny little cubbyhole.

I'd been there a second, taking it in, and in waltzes Michael, literally wearing his underpants and a vest. His kitchen's right next door. 'Oh Rachel, there you are.' No welcome, good to see you, he just launched straight into it. 'Can you drive? Good. I've got someone coming to see me about catering at Goose Hall. She lives in Bath, and she can't drive. We've got a hire car at the moment, take that and go and bring her here, alright.' And Sheelagh just turns round to me and says: 'Welcome to Worthy Farm!' That really sums up how Michael is. You can have such good fun with him, a good laugh. He's got a brilliant sense of humour, and he likes a bit of cheek. Socially we got on really well. But you never have the niceties. If you have an agenda, it's straight into it, get on with it, you can do it, off you go.

It didn't take very long before Michael decided that this person who was a complete novice was going to take over all the vehicle passes for the whole site; they'd never really had one person who co-ordinated them all. My family say that's because I'm always prepared to put in 110 per cent, and they were also aware that I was always supporting Michael. He's always talked about locally, for and against, and as I got to know him more I'd be standing up for him and everything he did.

You'd hear stories, but you'd always just gone to the festival and never really thought about the organisation. It was just there and it was brilliant and it happened. Now I could see exactly what had gone into all this – a phenomenal number of people, so many of them there because they loved the festival, not because of the money.

I didn't ever work there and think: 'What a glamorous job.' It always came part and parcel with hard work and a tremendous amount of stress. You needed to make time to get out of the office, get down there, to see people enjoying themselves and remind yourself that was what it was for. You also needed to understand what people were doing – was what they were doing worthy of what passes they needed? Were they worth it? There's a kind of embedded PC-ness about the festival, which we were lucky enough to have been brought up with as kids as well.

Glastonbury has grown from a family run thing, a real family feeling, and like any family there's a lot of respect and a lot of politics. That spirit added to the end result, where you've got a lot of very professional amateurs who've learned their skills through working there, and then what they achieved became the industry standard. It's one of those amazing things that in the original government Pop Festival Code, the standards were set by what Richard Abel did at Glastonbury.

A Life Less Ordinary

Louise Harding, Green Markets manager

I'm from Cheddar originally. We moved here with the kids when they were young. I'm now living 150 yards from the Festival Office in Glastonbury town, close enough to water the window boxes if Hilary is away. I've been involved in running a music promotion business since the Nineties. Before that it was pretty much a Laura Ashley life. I met the man who later became my husband when I was 14, had two children, ran the playgroup.

I had never been to the festival, and had no interest in it. From where I was from I thought it was the playground for the devil children, a place for people to take drugs and party till they fell over, a terrible place to be, Hades itself. Then I did some stewarding with my children's school, St Dunstan's – volunteering to make money for the school PTA – and, blow me, I thought it was fantastic.

You can't form opinions until you go. So I did car park stewarding for three years. It was great fun. One day there was a naked man in socks and trainers running around the field in a mathematical pattern. I went up to talk to him and he wasn't quite himself, but he wasn't going to hurt himself. People were taking photographs and a crowd was gathering. He had to go for medical attention with sunburn on every part of his body. He was 17, somebody had given him something, he couldn't remember what happened – and he missed the whole show. And I was hooked by that point myself. You can just walk around and hear all these sounds and performances and people just merge into your psyche, or pass through it – it's like watching a movie through a tunnel.

The last four years of my marriage, I was tunnel digging as it were, starting to look at things and see things differently. I began to think, I don't have to listen to someone else's opinion, like my husband's, I can go and find out for myself. One idea generated another idea and so on. The festival fascinated me because it was so huge – our job meant trotting around – so we could walk around to see what was happening. It was mind-blowing, finding out different parts of the site. As far as I was concerned, what was on the main bill was what you could get in HMV, but the other stuff – the smaller stages, the fields – was definitely not.

There were a few mums who had been before, and we found the best way to stay awake on night shift was to go to the Dance Tent for a few hours. We had green tabards with Security printed on the back – and they were much sought after! We had a scuzzy caravan where we could have a cup of tea and operate from, and we were very smug when it was muddy. We worked with school staff, the deputy head as well as mums, and you would sit there on a shift late at night. In school it was fragmented and ghettoised – staff, 'good parents', 'bad parents' – but here we were all together, it was great.

The first year I went back home at night, on a PTA shuttle minibus, but after that I stayed and my kids came with me – and went crowd surfing. They had to hold their trousers to keep their wallets in their pockets. Their main aim was to get on television.

This was definitely a time of transition for me, the festival affected every area of my life. It was a time for me stopping being someone's other half. At the end of my marriage, eventually, when I had moved out and into another house – I felt I could start being the person I had been waiting to become, when I had been someone else's significant other, home builder, child bearer, nest maker. So it was part of the Louise Harding liberation to go to things like that.

There's not many women my age who can say that they've pulled a Zulu, or ended up living with him for three years, some of the time with Jason's family in a mud hut in the bush in Zimbabwe. I first went to a workshop at the Glastonbury Dance Festival, saw some African artists, found it very exciting, went to visit them, watched them performing in a township, and it developed from there. I said I'd have a go at booking them a tour, Zimbabwean singers who had never been out of Africa. I got them over here to do the Globe Theatre. We were doing the tours and the workshops when I got involved with Glastonbury again, almost by accident. I was looking to rent some space in the town when I was offered a job running the Green Market, 'not much money but good fun', they said. I brought some major artists back with me; Imbezo was the first. Twelve handsome Zulus – I couldn't ever have said that in my Laura Ashley life.

I brought them in a minibus and driving down Muddy Lane the first thing they saw was a naked man with two Tesco bags and just a pair of sandals on and they absolutely fell about laughing – white people, they're so funny without their clothes on. The next year I had a witchdoctor as well, staying in a Millets tent in the healing fields. Which is where they found the sauna, which they called the Channel 5 tent. They stood outside and you could see naked people coming and going. 'We never knew they were so many shapes and sizes,' they told me and it kept them occupied all the time they weren't on stage.

•••

1998
ALL NIGHT FUN

Rain again turned parts of the site into a brown quagmire, but resilient campers still enjoyed the evergreen mix of entertainment and all-night fun. Over 1,000 different performances on 17 stages included a new marquee for up and coming bands. The enlarged Dance Tent was as packed as ever. Mud surfing proved popular. There were better loos and a proper bank. American singer Tony Bennett rose above the mud in an immaculate suit and tie. Over £500,000 from the festival's income went to Greenpeace, Oxfam, WaterAid and many local organisations. Acts included Blur, Primal Scream, Robbie Williams, Tori Amos, Pulp, Bob Dylan, Roni Size and The Chemical Brothers. Official attendance 100,000.

Bands in 1998: Alabama 3, Asian Dub Foundation, Audioweb, Babybird, Beth Orton, Blur, Bob Dylan, Catatonia, Cornershop, Dr John, Eddi Reader, Faithless, Fatboy Slim, Finlay Quaye, Foo Fighters, Gomez, Herbie Hancock's Headhunters, Hothouse Flowers, Ian Brown, James, Joe Strummer and Bez, Julian Cope, Mansun, Meredith Brooks, Moby, Morcheeba, Nick Cave and the Bad Seeds, Portishead, Primal Scream, Pulp, Robbie Williams, Rolf Harris, Roni Size & Reprazent, Saint Etienne, Sean Lennon, Sharon Shannon, Sonic Youth, Space, Spiritualised, Squeeze, Steve Earle, Taj Mahal, The Chemical Brothers, The Divine Comedy, The Doves, The Jesus and Mary Chain, The Lightning Seeds, The Stereophonics, Tony Bennett, Tori Amos, Tricky, World Party, Wyclef Jean.

Rolf Harris

I've played four times now, the second time in the infamous 'non-stop rain' year. I remember watching this couple diving into the thick grey mud, skidding along in it, then getting up and doing it all over again. They were having the time of their lives. They had to use a tractor to drag our tour bus up a slight incline. What a year!

Toby Cann, teacher, London

I was working in the backstage area in 1998 when a guy came up looking for a wristband to get into the bands enclosure. He explained that he was a striking docker from Liverpool, he'd hitched all the way down and he'd got all the way to the press tent without a ticket or anything. He told me that everybody always supports the Liverpool dockers and that's how he could get through security.

He wanted somebody performing to wear a T-shirt about the strike, especially Billy Bragg and one of the indie bands on the main stage. It was a mock-up of the Calvin Klein logo, so the word 'docker' had CK in big letters. I thought it was quite clever.

I wanted to help him so I managed to scrounge some wristbands from somewhere, we went inside, met the manager of one of the bands, which happened to be Cast from Liverpool. And when they came on stage, one of the brass section from Cast was wearing one of the T-shirts. And later Billy Bragg did say something about the strike. So it worked.

Ashley Parsons, housing support worker, London

I think it was 1998 when I saw Massive Attack on the Jazz Stage. We'd basically done some mushrooms, I think, and me and a friend went down to the field for the start of their set. It was brilliant, we started dancing away and had a great time, although everyone around us seemed to be looking at us a little bit funny. I turned to the guy near me, the field was now pretty full, and I said to him, it's a brilliant gig, they're wicked aren't they? And he just looked at me and said, there's no-one on stage, mate, there hasn't been anyone on stage for the last hour. But then Massive Attack did come on, and they were brilliant.

John Shearlaw, journalist and researcher

Usually if it's muddy, it's muddy two times in a row, that's what the old timers say and I believe it myself now, but you don't really acknowledge that during the build-up, you just get on with putting the show on. Joe [Strummer] had been working with Bez, hanging out with him a lot, and he'd come up with this idea of doing something at Glastonbury in 1998. He'd been involved with Keith Allen as well, and Keith had made this World Cup record with Alex James from Blur, 'Vindaloo', but that's history.

The plan was to do a DJ set, playing Mexican stuff, something different, but great tunes. He asked me to get a slot at the festival, and Martin Elborne agreed to give them a space on the Other Stage on the Sunday, late on, a kind of low-key thing for virtually no money. And that was it for that year – the whole weekend's preparation and planning was for the campfire, which grew and grew and grew, and the Sunday night thing, which was going to be flags and banners and music and everything Joe stood for.

Joe's camp just got bigger and bigger behind the Other Stage, another four-day party with all sorts of people joining in and becoming involved; all the Manchester contingent who Joe had known for years, bizarre guys in kilts, children. The few people who were there could hardly believe it, this weird and wonderful collection partying away up there, children dancing all over the stage, odd records going on and off, 40-foot flags waving and then, finally, Keith Allen shouting himself hoarse to 'Vindaloo'. And then the curfew, with the sound system turned off unceremoniously. It was anarchic and almost out of control. But it wasn't the performance which was important, it was the rallying, the way Joe stuck at it, and got everyone behind this mad, doomed venture, a whole weekend's worth of show…

Martin Walsh, multimedia computer programmer, Dublin

It was the first time I'd been to the festival, 1998, the last muddy year. I'd headed down with a mate on our motorbikes, but we had no concept of what we were going to get involved in at all. It was the football championships on TV and we'd just come out of the pub in Pilton, planning to pitch our tent, when a guy came up and asked if we wanted somewhere to store the bikes. He was a complete stranger. We were a bit wary initially, but having looked at the festival site, with mud sliding down the hill and tents capsizing, we decided to take up his offer. In the end he not only gave us somewhere to keep the bikes, within walking distance of the site, he gave us a place to sleep in his stable, having booted out the horse. Our host even woke us up in the morning with orange juice and tea. After that we felt nothing could go wrong.

I wasn't sure whether my mate would get into the whole festival thing, he was a bit reserved, but when I got out some ecstasy tablets, his eyes just lit up completely. And over the course of that evening it all became completely manic. I remember walking back from the Dance Tent and suddenly this mud, which had been ridiculously sticky and disgusting before, was transformed into an amazing velvety experience, like chocolate underfoot. After that we spent time walking round in the mud saying, have you felt how good this is?

Then later the same evening, I met this woman, she was a friend of a friend, and there was this almost instant chemistry between us. We were sitting in this darkened tent, drinking wine and smoking pot, and within fifteen minutes we had legs entwined, becoming quite intimate. It was a lovely atmosphere, and it was only when we walked out into the bright lights that I realised that she wasn't as attractive as I'd thought!

We often stayed up all night, following round the sound systems. Even after everything was shutting down we were still keyed up.

•••

1999
IN MEMORY OF JEAN

The sun finally shone on Glastonbury again, bringing a broad smile to the faces of performers and campers alike. £150,000 was still spent on downpour precautions. The widest range of entertainment ever was on offer, with over 300 bands, a kaleidoscope of theatre, comedy and cultural adventures, and more than 250 food stalls – all publicised on a buzzing Glastonbury web site. Orange mobile phones joined a queue of companies wanting to sponsor the event, but all overt branding was banned. Greenpeace, WaterAid and Oxfam again benefited. This year's event was sadly overshadowed by the death of organiser Michael Eavis's wife Jean. A winged wicker sculpture was ceremonially burned in her honour, whilst fireworks erupted into a moonlit sky. Acts included REM, The Manic Street Preachers, Fatboy Slim, Hole, Blondie, Al Green, Skunk Anansie, Lonnie Donegan, Marianne Faithfull and Courtney Pine. Official attendance 100,000.

Bands in 1999: Al Green, Ash, Beautiful South, Beth Orton, Billy Bragg, Blondie, Bush, Cast, Coldplay, Courtney Pine, David Gray, Death in Vegas, Dodgy, Faithless, Fatboy Slim, Feeder, Fun Lovin' Criminals, Gay Dad, Gomez, Groove Armada, Hole, Ian Dury, Joe Strummer, Jurassic 5, Lenny Kravitz, Lonnie Donegan, Marianne Faithfull, Mary Coughlan, Mercury Rev, Merz, Orbital, Patti Smith, Paul Oakenfold, Pavement, Queens of the Stone Age, REM, Skunk Anansie, Super Furry Animals, Suzanne Vega, Texas, The Cardigans, The Chemical Brothers, The Corrs, The Doves, The Manic Street Preachers, Tom Robinson, Travis, Underworld.

Jean passed away on Sunday morning… During the last two months when the seriousness of her illness became apparent I have been with her constantly, and she was exceptionally brave and did not suffer.

I am thankful for more than 30 years I have spent with my beautiful and loving wife. A wonderful mother and a great lover, she became the cornerstone of the festival, offering not only unwavering support, but a determination which has seen the Glastonbury Festival develop into the unique event it is today. I hope those who come to this year's festival will join with me in celebrating a life so well lived and loved. There can be no greater tribute.

Michael Eavis, 17 May 1999

Billy Bragg

My most controversial moment was when I saw this ridiculous notice on some backstage toilets which read, 'These Facilities Are Reserved Exclusively For The Manic Street Preachers'. I saw red, so to speak, and the story even made the national press.

The real Glastonbury experience comes from all of us being in it together. The joy of seeing a favourite performer, the frustration of missing a mate – 'I said three o'clock at the beer tent' – the fun of buying clothes you are never going to wear again, the glory of a Somerset sunrise, the chill of the rain. These are the things that encourage a sense of community at Glastonbury that you seldom find at other festivals.

Mark Cann

Even now, if you compare it with other shows, the backstage facilities are rudimentary, although increasingly the bands bring big tour buses and their own facilities with them. We do the drinks rider, although we ignore some of the more eccentric requests. Lenny Kravitz wanted plants in the dressing room, especially an aloe vera plant, other people have wanted a massage table and a masseuse – that's been very easy, we'd just get somebody down from the healing fields.

Tim Booth

Two great memories stand out for me in the Nineties. Morrissey dropped out at short notice and we hastily filled the gap, by this time deeply in love with the festival and its unique spirit. We arrogantly covered his song 'We Hate It When Our Friends Become Successful'. I say arrogantly, because he had intimated to me that it was about us.

The other recall was playing before a big England World Cup game. The game was being shown on the screens beforehand. We had written two possible set lists, one that would fit the mood of a wake if England lost, the other a huge celebration. We won twice that night.

John Shearlaw

At heart, Joe Strummer was Rebel Wessex, which was the name of the political party he wanted to set up. Once he decided to live down here, he got involved in everything. When Joe came back to Glastonbury, to the festival, he was there for the first time as a 'local', creating his own space, bringing the logs in for that enormous fire from a guy who lives down the road and sells the best dry oak in the Quantocks; it was lovingly planned, with all his friends coming along, and Lucinda organising all the vehicle passes and the logistics for what seemed like, actually was, six months ahead.

The first night he was there, it must have been the Thursday, and the rains had come and deluged the place, Joe went out for his wander with everyone in tow. Moschino jacket, Mexican hat, champagne and tequila and a word for everyone all over the site. He was being greeted as a legend, and he was out there in the Jazz Field, in the mud, really talking to people, the weekend only just beginning.

The energy and enthusiasm lasted right through. It was a battlefield on the Monday after that muddy one, and there was so much stuff either stuck in the mud or abandoned. And Joe was on the phone in the afternoon trying to organise a trailer, a van, perhaps even someone who had an artic…There were fridges going begging, room-sized deep freezes, banners and flags, so much stuff you needed a lorry to get it home, and his enthusiasm was so great you had to get involved. It was bringing Glastonbury back home through the swag, keeping the party going.

A couple of years later, once Joe had gone back on the road with The Mescaleros, one of the Bridgwater carnival floats had a Mexican theme and along with these two great polystyrene cowboys on the cart, standing about eight feet high, there was a local joke going on. One of them was pre-Viagra, the other was post-Viagra, so it had an erection, in polystyrene, a foot high. So we tracked the cowboys down to a barn in Westonzoyland and bought them for a donation, lugged them back up to Joe's at night and tied the bastards to his gatepost, these eight-foot Mexican cowboys. Welcome back, Joe.

Drew Culshaw, festival volunteer

During my second year of uni, I managed to get a job in the Glastonbury press office for a three-month work placement. I was told that I would have to sort myself out with a caravan to stay in at Worthy Farm, and happened to acquire one for £100. I bought a nice bit of red carpet for it, the sort that wine can be wiped off, and some fluorescent purple nets. With a few photos and posters, it looked quite homely. There was a really damp smell to it, but luckily it never leaked.

The year I was there, so-called camp shouts were still prevalent (before the government bill was passed, banning all shouting of random words within a one-mile radius of a tent or open fire). Hearing *bollocks* every night got a bit boring, as well as associated shouts of *dog bollocks* and other testicular ditties. I won't deny that my favourite word is 'seepage'. I only allow myself to say it a maximum of three times a day to prevent wear out. So on the Saturday of the festival, while walking to the loos with seats, I shouted *SEEPAGE* at the top of my voice. By the time I'd started to walk back, everyone was shouting *SEEPAGE, SEEPAGE*. I think I even managed to get the word into the *Guardian* by pretending to be a press spokesperson and giving them a quote.

Sadly, *bollocks* returned for the remainder of the event, but then, everyone might just have been shouting at the Bishop of Bath and Wells or even, straight from Donnington, the Avalonian Free State Choir.

Ashley Parsons

In 1999 I saw Orbital on the Jazz Stage, who just played a blinding greatest hits set. The whole crowd was with them, the field is just the right size so that even at the back you can see the stage. And halfway through it this carnival boat came along the path at the back of the field, with loads of wizards and stuff on it, and there was a moment when the crowd saw this wonderful show in front of them but then someone was tapping them on the shoulder saying, look behind us. There was a sense that everyone was equally excited to be at both gigs.

Matt Jones, company director, London

Musically, I'll never forget The Chemical Brothers in 1999. Right place, right time. I'd had an 'e' and that probably helped everything come together. Another time we were walking past something like a Christian tent and a guy was standing out the front saying, 'Do you want someone to talk to?' It was just the genuine nature of the guy, he just blew me away. I just love the religious tents where you can kip if you've been tent-jacked or you're just too wet or too cold. The support around is extraordinary.

Martin Walsh

I came down on the bus from Bristol with a guy who'd been on an experimental drug binge for weeks, he was quite out of it, and the strange thing was that I ended up helping him get over the fence, even though I had a ticket in my pocket. So we were climbing over fences, dodging holes, all so that he could catch up with his mates.

The Portaloo Saga

Ashley Parsons

It was Sunday night, the end of the 1999 festival. We'd just seen Mogwai, and we were all drunk and stoned and feeling a kind of exhaustion but also the weird excitement of the last night as well. It was rammed that year because the fence hadn't worked properly, so people like us had got in for free, or a fiver on the door or whatever. As soon as the last tune finished there were just hordes of people pushing everywhere, a mass movement. I realised I needed to go to the loo away from the crowds, so my friends waited at the side of the stage whilst I fought my way through to find a Portaloo. I had to go quite a way before I found some, in a little field away from the main drag.

I went into the one at the end, I was a bit pissed and I'd just started to undo my zip, having locked the door, and then realised I was even more pissed than I thought because I started swaying badly, and then in the space of a few very long seconds I realised it wasn't me, it was the entire Portaloo. I fell backwards, let out a cry of surprise, landed on my back as the whole thing came down, and as I heard peals of laughter outside I look up, and to my horror, in slow motion, I look along the now horizontal Portaloo and see a full tank of other people's effluent just emptying out over me. And in a very short space of time I'm shin-deep in it, liquid everywhere, soaking through my clothes, on my face, and I'm trapped, because it's fallen on its door.

The smell was so strong, unforgettable, like ammonia, really acrid. Then, after the shock of being in this poisonous mixture of other people's bodily fluids, I'm immediately screaming, in panic, and yelling, oh my God, what's going on, and then very quickly realising that there are people outside who've pulled me over. It sounds like six or seven young lads, they're Mancs, and they're obviously delighted with what's happened, they love it, it's a brilliant joke. I started appealing to them to let me out. Along with the intense revulsion at what I'm covered in, claustrophobia is kicking in, and I feel I'm under attack. They start laughing and talking to me through the little ventilation grill, which is the only source of light. They say, pass your money out and we'll let you out.

I was suddenly feeling very scared. They'd started to drop in matches and said they were going to burn me by pouring in lighter fluid, and I did think briefly that I might be the bizarre Glastonbury death, good party chat fodder. I thought, they hold all the cards, so the only thing I could think of was the best thing would be to go quiet, play possum. But you can only stay quiet for so long with other people's piss up your nose, so after about a minute I started banging again, making as much noise as I could. Some people came by then and let me out, although it took quite a few of them to roll the cabin over, which sloshed the stuff all over me again.

I got out ready to swing, I just wanted to punch the first person I saw, but I was confronted by this small group of bemused, semi-horrified, half in stitches people who were just looking at me and not wanting to come close, because the stink was immense. The sting in the tail was that the people who let me out also had Manc accents, so for all I knew I was saying thank you to the same people who'd pushed me over.

I then went to wash a bit at the taps nearby – people were looking at me like a leper – and when I went to find my friends again the same crowds I'd had to push through before just parted like the Red Sea. It was like the walk of shame. My friends didn't know whether to laugh or feel sorry, it was a comic-tragic situation, but luckily one of them was working backstage, the security guard on the gate took pity on me and I had the most thorough shower I could possibly have.

It was really horrible at the time, but it's something I look back on with a wry smile now. It's contributed to my respect for the diversity of the festival because it makes it an even more ludicrous collection of strange happenings.

Bob St Barbe, infrastructure manager

I was manager of the concrete works in Wells until 1993, when Michael had cancer and felt he couldn't do it all himself. I said yes immediately. I'd been doing the other job for 20 years and I wanted a change. And it was certainly a big change.

My job involves transforming the site from a dairy farm into a festival site and then back again afterwards. That means getting together all the roads, electricity, water, toilets, sewerage, as well as making sure the fence goes up on time. Michael has always wanted it to look as much like countryside as possible, without permanent structures, which makes the job a lot more demanding. There's lots of things hidden away which people don't really know about – the drainage system under the ground, the excavations for the long drop toilets.

The toilets were quite rudimentary when I started, and people always complained about the smell. We've tried all sorts of different things over the years to alleviate that. The first idea was using a blower to pump the smell of oranges through the air near the loos. Then we put special crystals in the corner of the polyjohns. Probably the best thing we've got now is this stuff called Back to Nature, which is a natural liquid a bit like tea that's normally used to get rid of the smell on pig farms. I poured 45 gallons of that into the sewage lagoon near the farmhouse, stirred it up and the smell was almost gone within two days.

The long drops used to be dug every year, and the toilets erected on top of them. They were just holes in the earth, very unstable, so if it rained people could be sliding down the sides of them, all sorts of things. So we decided to make them permanent by sinking big concrete block and fibreglass tanks into the ground. There are 32 of those tanks now, and each one can take 3,000 gallons of effluent. There's been a big improvement in recent years – more toilets, better quality ones and more in the right places.

It's amazing what you find in the loos. When we clear the long drops out we find all sorts of things people have thrown in – beach balls, washing-up bowls, concrete blocks. Somebody who comes to the festival has even produced a line of special Glastonbury loo stickers with cartoon strips about things like dropping a mobile phone down them. Reading those lightens the day a bit. And we've had the outside doors of some of them painted – with cows or a circus carousel. You've always got to have a sense of humour when you do that job.

Once we'd collected it all from around the site the effluent used to stay in the lagoon at the farm all the summer and then be spread on the fields in the autumn. But it did smell a bit, so we started taking it to the local sewage works. There's so much of it now – about 800,000 gallons – that we try to get rid of it as fast as we can. The only problem is that there's such a high percentage of alcohol that it puts the level of ammonia up, so the sewage plants can't cope with it.

In terms of messiness the worst problem was probably when the slurry tanker was trying to get rid of all the water inside the Dance Tent – and blew instead of sucked. The effluent literally went everywhere, so the tent was closed down until we'd cleared it all up. It was still raining like mad, pouring in through the top of the tent, and even though we had lorryloads of straw coming it still took fifty stewards in a line with scrapers the best part of four or five hours to clear it up.

Jean Eavis: 1939–1999

Arabella Churchill

Jean was quite anti-festival for a long time. So was Emily, until she was old enough to realise that there was quite a bit of kudos attached to being involved. It must have been a bit much for her when she was young, people just taking over where she lived. Sometimes it would be Mendip problems holding us up, but quite often it was Jean, who wasn't sure at all. I think it was the mess and everything, and all the 'lost' stuff that happens up at the farmhouse, the most tripped out ones who go to welfare. But in the end she got really into it, as Emily now seems to have done. Jean was always the human side of Michael really, so if you really had a problem you went to Jean. If you burst into tears with Michael it works as well, although I don't like to do it too often.

Melvin Benn

I met Jean at a very early stage. I thought the world of her, and I wasn't alone in that. To me she epitomised the good, open-minded liberal mother. She was a free thinker, she didn't put people in boxes, she let them express themselves. She had a knack of getting the good to come out of people. Jean didn't have the ideology, the political language, and that was very refreshing. I think it's a very Somerset-based thing. Jean was someone who could gel a lot of things in a stable way. She would sit Michael down and tell him: 'You can't do that.'

From 1991 onwards I was developing festivals along with Vince Power, so for a while I was on the outside looking in. Vince wasn't exactly seen as the angel of the industry, so there was no love lost between Mean Fiddler and Glastonbury, but Michael and Jean always made me welcome. Michael was more guarded, as he was obviously more connected with artists and agents, so it was slightly easier to be friendly with Jean. She maintained until her death that Michael had always said: 'If I die, ring Melvin.' That still gives me a very warm glow.

Michael Conconnanon, festival worker, now marketing executive in Cork

With the true luck of the Irish I landed the best work experience college gig of my life. Glastonbury. Start in May and work right through until July. I was living with Lou, a happy, hippie, smiley, lucky girl. We had her parents' old caravan set up in the back yard, outside the upcoming new site office. Eager-eyed and slightly dumbfounded I wandered around the farm a little and really couldn't believe my luck. The smells, the sight of cows grazing, the sounds of the milking machine. We were told by Sheelagh (who incidentally turned out to be from the same small town in Ireland I am from) that Jean was very ill and to keep it pretty quiet. We did.

The next morning, I stumbled out of the caravan to look for the toilet. On my way back I saw the back of what I thought to be Michael Eavis leaning on the gate, looking out on to where the main stage would be. Cows were grazing and it was a really still morning. I was heading back to the caravan and he turned around. He asked me who I was, and I replied that Angie [Watts] had taken two of us on for work experience and we had just arrived yesterday. He smiled and headed back to the farmhouse.

It was only later I heard that Jean had passed away about three hours before that.

Emily Eavis

When my mother became very ill we'd spent most of the year planning the festival, and it felt a really natural thing to proceed with it. It was almost a saving grace, something to get stuck into, because the festival was so significant in her relationship with Michael: all the taboos they'd faced at the beginning, how much they'd been through. I can't emphasise how important it was. They'd put a real united front together and created this event, which was born of an intense love affair. Continuing after she died was the natural thing; a great mark of respect for what they'd shared over 30 years. And it was the first time I'd really stood back and looked at this incredible... thing. How on earth did they do it? You couldn't write it down or put it in a textbook or anything. It was very simply a sequence of events and a passionate thing going on between two people in the face of all adversity.

That year you could plough a lot of love into the festival. Although it was a difficult time, it was also the result of everything they'd had together. It was one of the best festivals ever for me, as well as being the most painful. And there were so many moments where it struck me just how much it all meant to people, and how much of an impact it had already had on their lives. I saw a sign saying 'God Bless You, Jean' and there were little tributes all over the place, from REM on the stage to the tapestry in the Theatre fields. And when I was running down to the stage for the minute's silence people were already standing quietly in the campsites. I think people were very touched, and really felt the enormity of the festival that year, and of everything it stands for, it was a great feeling of togetherness.

Sheelagh Allen

Jean was very, very supportive, but she was also the one who stopped Michael from running away with himself. She was the sensible one, she made him slow down a bit. I remember the quiet that spread around the site when they had that minute's silence. I went to the top of the hill looking down towards the Pyramid and just stood there. It was absolutely amazing, I've never seen anything like it, and then I turned round and bumped into Chris and Anne Howes. We just had a cuddle and that was that.

Mark Cann

At the 1999 event, we decided to announce a minute's silence from all the dozen or so stages right across the site for 11.00 on the Sunday morning. The London Gospel Choir were on the main stage and we brought everything to a standstill. I said a few words, and then asked everyone to be quiet. Michael got a great response when he came on stage.

Emily Eavis

I spent nearly all my time with my parents; I used to get really worried and I'd take on their worries too. If I saw someone in a state, I'd worry so much. This is our land, I'd think, so I felt responsible. I took that on to another degree after my mum died, but I think that's in the way she would have wanted. I find it hard to go a day without checking in with Michael, seeing how things are going on. I still worry about him, and I still worry about everyone!

I do have a particularly close relationship with my dad, and when my mum died that was reinforced. Patrick and all my sisters had families; husbands, wives and children. When you lose a parent and you have your own family, it's really different. Because I was so much younger, I didn't even have a boyfriend at the time, I became very dependent on my dad, and likewise he with me. I was always in the sitting room, where the phone is, and the phone is always ringing at all times of the day – you answer the phone to anybody, a band's agent, a councillor, a villager, anybody, so I'd just be there answering the phone, doing what he would have been doing. I'd always been dad's little girl, but when Jean died, some of the emotional stuff transferred to dad as well. Other people have speculated on our behalf since then – maybe people just like the family thing. But I think in my heart of hearts that I can't see it happening without him; he is so central to everything.

•••

CRISIS
AND
CATHARSIS

2000-the present

'We've got stars directing our fate
and we're praying it's not too late'

Robbie Williams (*Millennium*)

The year 2000 was crunch time for Glastonbury Festival. Despite numerous attempts to reinvent the five-mile long perimeter fence as impenetrable – with a second barrier, watchtowers with guards on top, more patrols, even a posse of local riders on horseback – it never totally worked. And in the millennium year it collapsed spectacularly. Unofficial estimates are that at least 200,000 people enjoyed a balmy three days in the Worthy Farm valley, many more than the official licence allowed. Among the happiest people were the stallholders, who sold more vegeburgers and chips than they could ever have imagined possible.

With Mendip District Council officials breathing down the festival organisers' necks, and with eight people recently crushed to death at the Roskilde festival in Denmark, this situation could not last. During another year off in 2001, a serious rethink took place. Eventually, Michael Eavis decided to ask Melvin Benn, managing director of the Mean Fiddler music organisation, to take responsibility for the licence application. This would hopefully give Glastonbury Festival a new security, but without losing any of the elements that had made it so unique.

2000
COLLAPSE OF THE FENCE

A spectacular new Pyramid Stage – 100 feet high clad in shimmering steel – rose like a phoenix just in time for the millennium event. It was baptised in Worthy Farm milk by former Led Zeppelin singer Robert Plant. The biggest festival ever, with 1,500 performances on 17 major stages, the site had become a vast cultural melting pot, with everything from aerial circus shows to a fire ceremony to the magical atmosphere of the Green Fields. New features included the Glade outdoor dance music venue, an interactive sound tunnel and traditional ballroom dancing in tuxedos and gowns. £500,000 again went to good causes. Acts included Travis, Basement Jaxx, The Chemical Brothers, Macy Gray, Pet Shop Boys, Willie Nelson, Nitin Sawhney, Suzanne Vega, Moby and David Bowie, magnificently dressed in the same style of flowing coat he had worn for his last performance in 1971. Official attendance 100,000, unofficially up to 200,000.

Bands in 2000: Andy Sheppard, Arthur Brown, Asian Dub Foundation, Badly Drawn Boy, Basement Jaxx, Beta Band, Brand New Heavies, Burt Bacharach, Coldplay, Counting Crowes, Cypress Hill, Dogstar featuring Keanu Reeves, David Bowie, David Gray, Death in Vegas, Elastica, Embrace, Fatboy Slim, Feeder, Groove Armada, Hothouse Flowers, John Martyn, Ladysmith Black Mambazo, Leftfield, Moby, Moloko, Morcheeba, Muse, Nik Turner,

Nine Inch Nails, Ocean Colour Scene, Orbital, Pet Shop Boys, Priory of Brion featuring Robert Plant, Reef, Reprazent, Rolf Harris, Saint Etienne, Suzanne Vega, The Bluetones, The Chemical Brothers, The Dandy Warhols, The Doves, The Flaming Lips, The Happy Mondays, The The, Willie Nelson.

David Bowie

My second showing was in 2000. An altogether different cup of poison from my first in 1971. This time I was headlining and due to the fence situation not being completely secure, over 250,000 saw the show [police estimate]. It was the most wonderful experience having that number of people singing my words along with me to so many of my songs. A magic moment indeed.

Norman Cook, aka Fatboy Slim

Glastonbury was not so much about the bands, it was about being there. And my motto is still: 'Have records, will play', even if there is gallons of mud. It sells out before they even tell you who the bands are…and then there is always this thing about the Sunday night – who's going to be the surprise guest, ha-ha! Thing is, a large proportion of the people who seemed to be going never went to see a band at all.

But for years there was no official dance culture – it was guerrilla tactics. Playing and trying not to drop the records in the mud. I did the NME party, I did 'not playing', I did tents here and there. The first year I actually did the Dance Tent, in 1997, I looked around and said: 'This is where I'm supposed to be at last.'

And by 2000 I'd got up to my fourth year running. Probably more from my insistence than them actually inviting me back! There was trouble the year before that because of everyone trying to get into the tent at once, the height of Norman-mania. It's quite flattering to be remembered as the fire risk.

I'd always try to get the proper one over with on the Friday, then that leaves the rest of the weekend when you can play randomly. Or go out in disguise, even though it never worked. But always go out in the darkness, I say, sleep during the day. I remember, at the height of my fame, trudging up to some faraway field and asking if I could DJ at the 'Miniscule of Sound': capacity, six people, billed as the smallest nightclub in the world. They didn't bat an eyelid and asked me if I had a demo tape.

We bumped into Keith Allen's Karaoke one year, but the real highlight was doing Sunday Best with the Cuban Brothers. It's the time when sleep deprivation is really kicking in, and everyone's really losing it. The Brothers did this naked breakdancing – on grass. I think they must have had the worst carpet burns ever.

My favourite time was when I lost my records just before I went on, and I had to DJ in my wellies. And one year I didn't even get to play. It's never dull, though, is it? Usually we make quite a big weekend of it. Me and Tom and Ed [Chemical Brothers] park our buses next to one another – in a circle, to repel all boarders. We're quite a big gang. It's like going on holiday together.

I started going with Zoe when we got married, but she'd been there before independently. We ended up comparing notes: 'Were you the bloke who was doing that thing with the…?' she'd say, because our paths had crossed a couple of times. Or 'very strange music going on in this or that tent – so that was you!' Now Zoe's got a policy of not working. At one point we were camped right by the Dance Tent, when she was pregnant, and she was saying: 'This is wrong!' She could feel her chest vibrating, from the bass bins. 'My chest's vibrating – the baby's vibrating!' She had to leg it over to Babington House for a rest.

Glastonbury is great for kids, after a certain age. We were debating what age we should start taking him. It's lovely seeing families there, but perhaps not camped right by the Dance Tent. And keep the Cuban Brothers away from them. Or at a safe distance. The same goes for sheep.

I hope to be a fixture at Glastonbury forever. By the time I'm 50, I'll be in a little tent on the outer fringes somewhere. And people will be really nostalgic and say things like: 'Remember when we used to dance to DJs playing records?'

Ed Simons, The Chemical Brothers

The last time we DJ'd at Glastonbury on the Saturday night and the way people reacted, the atmosphere, it was as good as anything else we've ever done. And that's supposedly at this nadir of people not being interested in dance music. The tent was full, people were happy, it was intense. We were playing pretty off-the-hook records that drove people wild.

I've always liked Glastonbury. We met Noel Gallagher there, and it was Noel who really got 'Setting Sun' released. Back then people allowed us to make a pretty demented record that, for a lot of people, was unplayable. Noel was also on 'Let Forever Be'. He's really funny, he told us loads of stories.

Hopefully there are some more good times ahead at Glastonbury, but as it stands finishing off on the Pyramid Stage in 2000 was the best moment of being a Chemical Brother.

It was such a wonderful feeling looking out and seeing that huge crowd of party people enjoying our music. When you're right there you get the sense that it's the very best place in the world to be. Beautiful scenery, beautiful people.

Noel Gallagher, Oasis

It's the only real festival, the best. The rest of them are just rock bands playing in fields...

Robert Kearle

People go to some incredible efforts to have a good time. The best thing I ever saw was when I was walking through a camp site, and this gang of lads, about twelve or so of them, had brought all these sofas to sit on round their camp fire, they'd brought a stereo system and a generator to run it, and they'd brought a big chest freezer which was stacked full of booze. And it was all run off this little portable generator which they obviously shouldn't have had in there in the first place. They must have made some effort to bring all that in.

Liz Eliot

In 2000 Michael and Jools Holland both played on the piano in the Green Fields dugout. And the BBC filmed it, although I was a bit unhappy because they took all the ordinary people out and put in their own invited guests.

Roy Gurvitz

It was technically like a European style sports bar, with lots of televisions behind it – though I'm not into sport at all, I just thought this would be completely incongruous with Glastonbury. I'm keen on bringing things that people aren't expecting. So behind the bar we had a smaller tent and ran this as a casino.

In 2000 we introduced the casino in a bigger way, with a bigger tent and brought loads of costumes for people to change into for proper ballroom dancing. Michael came down in a tuxedo and got into the dressing up thing and opened the festival in the ballroom with Emily. That was really the start of Lost Vagueness.

Lost Vagueness was really a pun on Las Vegas, a theatrical, glitzy town in the middle of a desert just like this was a lost part of the festival in the middle of green fields. It's all quite deep and meaningful, but also vague, like my relationship with Michael has always been quite vague. Las Vegas was also very pioneering as a town, Elvis Presley came out of there, and this is a music festival. It's linked in every possible way you can imagine.

Andrew Kerr

When Robert Plant was christening the new Pyramid stage with milk, I taught Emily (Eavis) how to water divine. And suddenly the twig went off at an angle, and she said: 'It works!' I'd like to think that was the effect of the same forces we'd discovered many years before.

Polly Bradford

The things you enjoy best are like one of those gorgeous hot idyllic nights when you've been up lying in the stone circle all night and then the sun comes up and everyone's drumming. That's why people go to Glastonbury – to have those kind of experiences.

I usually try to stay up until about six in the morning. But what's on offer has changed since the late 1980s when there was a lot going on all night, before they stopped the sound systems. It's livened up a bit now in the mad Green Fields bit and Lost Vagueness.

Michael Conconnanon

Everyone was told to 'wear sunscreen' in 2000. I didn't. I subsequently burned and rippled like a sun-dried buffalo tomato. It must have reached 30°C. Fantastic. Highlights for me that year included taking shelter in the New Bands tent, to see David Gray. I had annoyed the office with my adoration for him, rating him alongside John Martyn and Van Morrison, usually to the sort of look that suggested I'm talking utter bollocks. I and every other Irish person on the site that year sang along to every song, I would imagine to David's resignation, as he must have thought the Irish are feckin' everywhere.

On Saturday at lunchtime the name on everyone's lips was Keanu Reeves, as his band Dogstar played on the Other Stage. With all the hype surrounding *The Matrix*, he was a must see. I got the brilliant job of escorting the photographers into the press pits. I have never seen so many squashed breasts as every girl on the site pushed forward to scream their adoration at him. He and his band were utter rubbish and I laughed as a load of bananas and apples were showered towards him. Fruit!

Bowie played on Saturday night and this has to be my all time favourite Glastonbury moment. The main arena is colossal and no-one has filled it like he did. I was completely blown away by him, he played plenty of classics, but for me 'Under Pressure' was the best. The bass player on backing vocals and the final chorus sent a feeling down my spine that I could only describe as being something like sticking a wet finger into the generator that was powering the stage. The crowd that night was amazing, with everyone down from the stone circle who probably hadn't come down since Bowie played the first festival in

1971. I have been back every year since and intend to come back for every year of the future.

Janine Smith, senior producer, Channel 4 Interactive

In 2000, my best year, the massive year, the 'blanket of love' was back by the Other Stage, my stage, all the time we were working. We had lots of proud plans, they all went tits up, and it got busier and busier but we still had to produce the work. It used to be that in a Glastonbury situation you couldn't rely on anyone. Now strategy has entered the occasion.

Mobile phones have made a big difference, I've really noticed that. Now you actually find people. Society has brought about this change. The vibe isn't to lose yourself anymore – it's to party with the friends you know. It's like you don't have to find your way home now, you ring your dad to come and pick you up. Once you went to lose yourself, now it's a found weekend. Because it's easier to stick with what you know and people aren't so open. The bulk of people have credit cards, phones and their mates.

But it's still beautiful and I'd miss it so much if I couldn't go; I was straight on the phone to buy a ticket this year because I was so disappointed last time, not going.

We've done Reading, probably the biggest live webcast ever, nearly 40 hours on four channels. But it's not beautiful like Glastonbury. When I'm working there, feeling like I've got a purpose, it's the best.

Gavin Ellis, environmental charity worker, London

I've been to every festival since 1999. David Bowie in 2000 was a high – just seeing the man perform a greatest hits set, two hours of incredible music, an undoubted genius. Orbital was the same year, really good. In 2000 it was ludicrously busy, a lot of trouble, a really different atmosphere, a lot more aggressive than in 1999, a lot more hassle just walking through the site. It was quite unpleasant at times. There were gangs of lads who could be quite threatening.

Sharon Brand-Self

In 2000 Michael went to Ghana on a two week joint Oxfam– WaterAid trip and saw projects in some extremely remote rural areas. It was the hottest period, so he had quite a gruelling time. But he loved it, walking into a village and being greeted by people giving him chickens as gifts. They were really hospitable. And he was incredibly interested in looking at the technical side of people's wells and latrines, which meant the men loved talking to him. He also liked having a dance with the women and a bit of a celebration. He really loved it and from what I've heard he still talks about it. After Michael had been to Ghana, we started to get real income from the festival – £35,000 in 2000. For WaterAid that's a lot of money from one event.

The Fence

Emily Eavis

We did eventually run into some serious problems with numbers. 1995 when it was hot was incredibly crowded, then there was 2000…it had become like one of those little tops that keep spinning and spinning and there's only so far it can go. The council put their foot down, and changes were enforced because of tragedies at other events, like Roskilde and Big Day Out in Australia.

Then again, fence jumping had always been such a part of the culture. My dad used to go round the perimeter and pick people up and drive them in, saying it was better for them not to jump and break their ankle. Suddenly we had to revise all that, and we had to fight again to get our message across.

Richard Abel

We had to make up many of the rules ourselves on how to deal with crowds – nowhere else I knew of, then or since, had such large numbers of people on such a manifestly unsuitable site! I think we were the first to develop among other things the idea of 'island pits' at the venues, escape gates at bottlenecks and programming the stages with crowd movements in mind. And despite police estimates of well over 200,000 people in 2000 (which I don't argue with), we never had any of the serious crushing incidents experienced at some other events.

One lesson learned was that people will always take a straight route from A to B. I have worked at other festivals where a road grid has been imposed, but inevitably, by the end of the festival the grid has all but disappeared and a natural Pilton-style network has replaced it. In the early Nineties we used the Bath and West Showground as a car park and people were meant to walk along the lanes to the site. The lanes wind their way around – but the walkers didn't. By Saturday morning there was very nearly a straight line across the map from the Showground towards Worthy Farm, including several swathes cut straight through the middle of some rather distraught farmer's crops. The crowds seem to do amazingly little damage to Worthy Farm. I have seen foxes, deer and about a dozen mink all wandering around the site during the festival. All seemed to survive (although the mink particularly were in grave danger of getting trodden on) and the badgers, while keeping a low profile during the event, soon reappear after everyone has gone.

Ashley Parsons

I've been roughly every year since 1993. I love it. I look forward to it all year without really thinking about it, it's just something I know I'm definitely going to do. I paid the first two years I went and then the next few times I was naughty. We usually paid a fiver to a dodgy security guard to get a re-entry stamp. That was the scam. They'd always do that. In 2000 we just found a gap in the fence.

I'd get out of it in my head by thinking, well, I am skint, I know they've sold out their quota of official tickets, so the money is there to pay for everything. People like me are black market money but we're still contributing to the economy of the place by buying stuff on the stalls, donating money to Greenpeace.

Rachel Austin

The crowds built up over the years. It became a cool thing to have got into Glastonbury for free. Jumping the fence or a blag, some scam or other forgeries…Jean and Michael cared so much about people they were welcoming, but all the extras started to get a little scary. At the 2000 festival there were all these people coming in. I went round with Bob [St Barbe] in the Land Rover and I got quite upset. I started shouting at people: 'What the hell do you think you're doing? If you want to kill the festival this is the best way to do it.'

Then one of our sponsors, who shall remain nameless, announced that the fence is down, get on down there, which led to even more getting on the bandwagon. But it has to be said all the site systems held up. And it didn't feel unsafe because people were looking out for each other. But it was the beginning of the realisation that Pilton, the festival, could no longer support this free culture.

Brian Schofield

If we'd had the 100,000 or whatever the licence was for, it wouldn't have been an issue, but because we got 250,000 in 2000, or whatever the true number was, there were a lot more vehicles down there than the car parks could cope with. Therefore a lot of the local landowners thought, we could make a quick buck here, and set up their unofficial car parks. Many of those weren't a problem because people were parking off the road and the farmers were making a few bob, but there were also a lot of people who didn't want to pay that £5 or whatever and would park on the roadside, and that started clogging up the roads. There were some years when there were literally hundreds of vehicles which had to be towed away and taken to the Bath and West showground, where we had a compound. It's something like £120 now to reclaim your vehicle, plus £20 a day storage.

Melvin Benn

Then I went back to Glastonbury in 2000 with my wife and kids. On the Saturday we were going to walk down to the Other Stage – I think it was still called that – to see David Gray. He hadn't broken through fully by then, but he was being managed by someone who was also involved in the rave side of the music industry and I was interested to see him. We went to walk down from the Acoustic Stage in plenty of time – and we never got there. We couldn't get through the crush. I hated it, I hated it. I passed the Smirnoff dance tent, which had bouncers and a crowd outside, and I remember thinking, this has gone past what it should be. We left. I really believed Glastonbury was finished – it had lost everything it stood for. It had lost its vibe, it was out of control. Driving back to London we heard Fatboy Slim on Radio 1 and there were stories about people nearly dying at the crossroads, and of massive crushing. I genuinely thought that was the end.

•••

2002
NO TICKET, NO SHOW

The large number of people who gatecrashed the 2000 event prompted a thorough review of security arrangements. No festival was held in 2001 whilst these issues were resolved. After lengthy negotiations with Mendip District Council, the festival re-emerged with a new management structure and a £1 million perimeter fence to keep numbers within acceptable limits. The message 'don't turn up without a ticket' was largely successful. Inside, the same eclectic mix of cultural feasts continued to erupt. Innovations included an enlarged dance music area, an even longer list of theatre, circus and cabaret performances, a new Leftfield with speakers like Tony Benn and the Lost Vagueness area, where multiple wedding celebrations in a makeshift chapel jostled with a black tie silver service restaurant. Despite the extra cost of security measures, a record £1 million still went to 'good causes'. Headline acts included Coldplay, The White Stripes, The Stereophonics, Manu Chao, Rod Stewart, Isaac Hayes, Badly Drawn Boy, Roger Waters, Garbage and Richie Havens. Official attendance 100,000.

Bands in 2002: Air, Alabama 3, Ash, Badly Drawn Boy, Belle & Sebastian, Beverly Knight, Black Rebel Motorcycle Club, Bush, Coldplay, Cornershop, Faithless, Garbage, Gorky's Zygotic Mynci, Groove Armada, Ian Brown, Idlewild, Isaac Hayes, Jools Holland,

Kate & Anna McGarrigle, Lisa Fitzgibbon, Mercury Rev, Nelly Furtado, No Doubt, Orbital, Osibisa, Queens of the Stone Age, Richie Havens, Robert Plant and Strange Sensation, Rod Stewart, Roger Waters, Rolf Harris, Sharon Shannon, Spiritualised, The Beta Band, The Charlatans, The Dandy Warhols, The Doves, The Stereophonics, The Vines, The Waterboys, The White Stripes.

Michael Eavis, festival programme, 2002

I am very pleased to welcome you all back and I hope you will experience a weekend you will never forget. We're all really excited now as we begin to build the site for the festival this year – I have to say I'm getting the same buzz about it as I did in 1970. We've had problems before with the licensing but never have we faced the difficulties that we've had this time. As you know, we took a year off to address the overcrowding problems – lots of top-level meetings and 78,000 words to accompany our licence application and finally, by the skin of our teeth, our licence was granted on the 24th of January by a vote of confidence from the council of 10 to 3. It seemed like the whole country rejoiced at the news and all major news channels carried the story that evening.

However even the best things have their limitations, and the festival site can't be practically made any bigger than it is. There is only so much room. In order for the festival to continue we have to keep the numbers within limits that can be shown to be safe. I'm sure you will have heard by now about our new fence. I am quite determined to make sure that there will be no breaking in this time. Its construction and security arrangements will be entirely different to previous years. The fact is, the future of the festival is in jeopardy. The council granted us the licence on the basis that the fence would work properly. And this is the last chance we have to succeed. If we fail, we will, understandably, be denied our licence in future.

Please make sure that a new generation of young people can experience the magical, memorable moments that others have had over the last 30 years. Please respect the festival and all that it stands for. It has become a real part of our culture. You need it; we need it; the charities we all support need it. I'm pleading with you to help me keep it alive. I hope you are able to come to the festival, but please don't come without a ticket.

Chris Martin, singer, Coldplay

The Glastonbury Festival, which everybody knows is the greatest event in the entire world, changed our world immeasurably: from the first time we played there as a new band, when we witnessed the whole event like everybody else does, to the last time we played there headlining the Pyramid stage.

We love it to bits, the whole deal.

The greatest moment was driving in a car with Michael Eavis in late 2001. He turned around and asked us if we'd headline the following year and we thought he was joking for about ten minutes. And then we realised he was serious. That's probably one of the best things that has ever happened to us. Even if we'd never played Glastonbury, we would still think it was the best festival of all time.

Every Glastonbury experience I've had has been amazing. Each time we've played it has been really special, and each time we've been we've seen more and more incredible stuff; from the circus tent and the stone circle to the Pyramid stage and the dance tent, to say nothing of the weird and wonderful people .

It is special because it has so much variety, is run not by a faceless corporation but by an amazing family, and because wearing one of the wristbands makes you cool for a long time afterwards.

Michael Eavis

Coldplay have been great for the festival, one of our big success stories. Good old Chris, he even wrote a letter to the council about the licence application, which was very supportive of him. Emily got me interested before they'd really happened, and we got them to do the Pilton Party in the September. They were flying back from Paris and they changed their flight to go to Bristol. I went and picked up Chris and Johnny and got them back to Pilton with about five minutes to spare. On the way back I asked them: 'How would you feel about headlining next year?' After a gap they said: 'Yes, we'll do it.'

It's one of my favourite stories, because when they were looking back later, Chris was saying how important that decision was. They literally crafted their whole album around that appearance: they threw away songs, they got rid of things, they put new things in. They were saying they had this feeling: 'We've got to be so good now, we've got to be ridiculously good, we're going to be headlining Glastonbury!' Chris wouldn't have written 'Clocks', he wouldn't have done this or that, wouldn't have done Fair Trade…it changed everything.

Norman Cook, aka Fatboy Slim

The festival hasn't really changed, it's kind of refined. It's pretty much the same atmosphere as 1986, though there's probably less people! That's a bizarre thing, the human tide all walking in the same direction, an hour in the same place, that's gone. In 2002 we were looking around and saying: 'There's nobody here!' We can actually walk around, we can do things! It's become civilised, without actually becoming a nanny state. Oh look, we're not actually covered in mud, we're not being robbed and the car getting wrecked. We can go places!

It's a bit like Giuliano cleaning up New York, it hasn't got that edge of danger or collapse any more, but it's still fruity.

I think Michael Eavis getting a gong would be apt. Although I think any self-respecting music person would hand it straight back, like: 'No thanks', but Mr Eavis, yes – a gong is definitely deserved there.

Sally Howell

We sometimes ask ourselves why we go on doing it because it involves more work and time than all our other bookings for the whole season put together. We don't make any money out of it. Michael had to persuade us to carry on in 2002. But we do it because we are a bit of a legend, people always come up and say we can't possibly stop. And it's the only festival of its kind, with all that energy and spirit. You can't replace that feeling of community.

Lisa Fitzgibbon, singer, London

I play what I call 'power folk', contemporary folk music a bit in the philosophical mould of Annie de Franco. I'd rather play gigs, create an audience and a following, and leave the bullies in the bullring. But I'm also independent, I don't have a record label or anything behind me, so we just sent in a CD to the Glastonbury address. Hilary in the office was great, she stuck it on the top of the pile, and when I got a call saying they wanted me to play on the acoustic stage I almost wet myself. They only have two or three unknown artists each year, so we were really lucky.

I played the first set at Friday lunchtime in 2002. I was the only artist on the whole stage, together with my fiddle player. It was brilliant, the tent was full of people, the sound was fantastic and I felt really confident. I sold heaps of albums on the spot, and it definitely opened doors for me. Now when I say that I've played on the acoustic stage at Glastonbury people take notice.

Roy Gurvitz

2002 was the first year I was given a budget. So I convinced the guy running the café to run a sit-down restaurant instead. The whole idea was that you could just turn up, hire a suit or a dress and eat this superb dinner, all vegetarian, but with waiter service, champagne, whatever you wanted, all silver service. You're taken away from the festival completely, and then you come back out – it's playing with people's minds, but without the need for drugs.

The Chapel of Love and Loathe was another brilliant idea. We decided we could do weddings but not make it too religious. So we had a preacher who married lots of couples, then went off on a rant until some crazy dance music kicked in. And a boxing ring for those who weren't getting on. It was extraordinarily popular. I thought people would laugh at it, partake a bit, but I couldn't believe how it became the talking point of the festival.

Sharon Brand-Self

I remember doing karaoke with Keith Allen backstage. That's something you don't forget. The first year I was just sitting in the crowd, totally mesmerised by the fact that Jarvis Cocker had stood up and sung karaoke, but in 2002 I was invited round the camp fire with Joe

Strummer and again Keith Allen had an impromptu karaoke session. I did stand up and sing then, I think it was 'Hotel California', if anyone could recognise it.

Matt Jones

I proposed to my girlfriend at the festival in 2002. We were lying back and watching a couple of fireworks go up over the Pyramid stage and I decided that it just felt really right. She asked me if I was sure, and I said yes. So the founding energy of our marriage was established there.

Glastonbury's a time of real reconnection for us. I absolutely love the whole community feel and how this disparate thing comes together for three extraordinary days. More so than anywhere else that I know of, there's a sense that I can really be myself. There's no performance, no pretence, you just see a whole lot of people being themselves, whether it's the first time and they're really in awe or they're regulars. There seems to be such an acceptance of so much there, there's no pigeon-holing people like you normally get, it's a completely different place from everyday life.

Martin Walsh

We went in 2001 – the year the festival didn't happen – and walked through the site, saw the Pyramid stage with just the framework, saw the dragon up near the stone circle, all the things which are permanent fixtures. It was totally mind-blowing to relive everything we had done. Now it feels like a pilgrimage.

WaterAid and FairTrade

Fiona Hance, Oxfam

We took Emily [Eavis] and Chris Martin from Coldplay to Haiti in 2002, which really started the FairTrade campaign we've been pushing this year.

We also get a free campaigning stand next to the main stage, which is worth thousands of pounds. The youth market is a hard one to crack, so having such a high profile is brilliant. In return, we provide volunteer stewards. There were 500 in 1993, now there are 1,500 doing three eight-hour shifts staffing gates, checking tickets, doing pass-outs. They're a band of incredibly committed individuals who come year after year.

Sharon Brand-Self, press officer, WaterAid

We get famous people to sign toilet seats, which we later auction. Back in 2000 we were trying to find Fran Healy from Travis. We made a big speech bubble saying 'Why does it never rain on them?' for him to hold, and when we found him he was so happy to help us. In 2002 the signed toilet seat was auctioned with an invitation from Michael Eavis to have tea with him, plus a tent, and it went for £3,000.

The Fence

Richard Abel

There were lots of myths about the fence. Up until 2000 it was bolted together with conventional nuts and bolts, which could effectively be undone with any socket set from the back of a car, and it was held up with 18-inch pins – one year a long section actually blew over in the wind. But when put up correctly, it was actually extremely difficult to get over without a ladder, and up until 1999 when the ticket system was changed, probably more people got in on ticket forgeries and other gate scams than actually got in over the fence.

But once 10,000 or more people without tickets had arrived in a small village like Pilton, the fence was really rather irrelevant. Keeping out 10,000 people 24 hours a day for four days involved massive numbers of security staff, and providing a new 'alternative festival' outside the fence, with toilets, water, roads, rubbish collection needing to be installed at the last minute, was both a logistical and a health and safety nightmare. If that many people turned up, expecting to get in for nothing, we could never win,so it was only when the police finally agreed in 2001 to stop non-ticket holders arriving in such large numbers – which they had done for years at football matches – that the problem was finally solved.

Michael Eavis

In the year 2000 we had a lot of problems with overcrowding and the fence coming down. So on the Tuesday after the festival I actually sketched some drawings of the fence that I thought we were looking for. I sent them off to Trackway (fencing company) and said the fence we've got now isn't working, this is what we need in future. So I sketched my impression of what we needed, with a road on the outside, so you couldn't actually dig through, and they phoned back and said we'd better have a meeting. Their engineers and my blokes had a chat about it, and we decided to tweak it here and tweak it there and make some changes from my original drawing, although the principle was the same. When we finally agreed the design, they said they could build it and it was fantastic. But the long and the short of it was that this was the most expensive fence we've ever had. We had to pay £1 million a year for the first two years to cover the cost.

Brian Schofield

I left the police in 2000, which is why Michael rang me up one day and said 'Do you want a job?' I think he'd been fishing around for somebody to look after security. One of my jobs is to ensure that the integrity of the security companies is as high as we can get it. You're going to get bad eggs in any group, especially when you're talking at any one time of 1,000 security people and then 1,000 stewards on top. You're bound to get one or two that aren't as honest as the others. We actually now police the security by going round and tempting them, offering them money. They're told beforehand that this is going to happen, and if anybody takes it not only them but the company may well be out of a job next year. We're very determined.

Have people been able to get in since the new fence was put up? It's a big fence, it's capped in the areas where we think they're going to climb over, so I would say that there were only a handful. We know that a few got over because we found some scaling equipment, rope ladders and that sort of thing, but we know that many others who tried were thwarted because they were stopped, either in the middle of getting over, or managed to get over and were caught by the perimeter patrols inside.

And without it there's no doubt we wouldn't have a festival today. That fence, along with increased security to protect it – foot patrols, putting the roadway outside so we could drive round – was the saving of the festival.

The Mean Fiddler Deal

Melvin Benn

I remember talking to my wife in 2001, discussing the link between Glastonbury Festival and Mean Fiddler for the first time, and she asked me: 'Why do you want to go back? Glastonbury was the only place where someone has threatened to kill you.'

To my mind Glastonbury Festival was very much finished after the 2000 event. There was clearly a huge problem, it was out of control, and from the outside the impression was that there was nobody pulling it together; structurally it had lost its way. And the other problem was that the public authorities were now much more attuned to safety issues, especially after the tragedies of Hillsborough, King's Cross, Roskilde as well. Those changes were affecting everyone involved in events.

There was also a new broom in Avon and Somerset police, a new Assistant Chief Constable who wanted to look at things afresh. He'd been schooled in reaction to disasters and he was saying, this festival is out of control. That began the chain of events which resulted in the 2001 festival not happening. As a result Michael made the initial call to me that year...

Michael Eavis

The point is that I'm very good at the heart and soul stuff, I'm very good at persuading people to work here and persuading people to play. I can fire up the energy because I've got the personal energy that's required to keep this show going. I enjoy it, I live for it, I wake up in the morning thinking about it. I'm getting on with it, I'm in the driving seat, so that people feel kind of safe with me. But I'm a slightly reckless driver, and sometimes I drive on the wrong side of the road and sometimes I go round corners too fast, or I go too fast through a built-up area, all those kind of things. And the council and the police have said, Michael, we know that you're good at what you do, but you're not doing the licensing stuff properly, and we're not going to give you a licence unless you get someone else on board. And it kind of made sense, because I know what I can do, I know what I'm good at, and the licensing, health and safety, is not really my forte.

Mark Cann

A criticism of Michael was that he didn't delegate, that everything had to come from him in terms of decision-making. Up to a point that was true, but he did give a lot of autonomy to area organisers to get on and do it. So what appeared to be the case wasn't quite like that in practice. It was also a mistake to think that Glastonbury wasn't professionally run before, including over health and safety standards. Although we appeared to some to be cavalier, actually beneath the surface there was some sound practice that in fact formed the basis of the Home Office official advice, the 'pop code' as it's called. A lot of that was written by people with Glastonbury experience. The fact that the fence comes down and you've got 200,000 people, that's a hell of a strain on any system, so it's quite remarkable that it held together. But if you have to document it, it certainly wouldn't follow the conventional management structure for an event of this sort.

Michael Eavis

So I thought, because Melvin worked here in the Eighties, I'll try him and see if he'll do it for me. He had a good name and a good reputation and he'd got experience, and he had the Glastonbury experience as well. So I phoned him and he said he would actually do it, but he'd have to speak to Vince [Power] first, because Vince was boss. But the thing was I had to know by Friday because the application was coming back to the police, and they wanted answers to these questions. And this was Tuesday.

So I said to Melvin, can you get to Portishead police station by Friday at 9.30 in the morning, because they're going to write the recommendation in the afternoon, and we need to spend a morning with John Buckley [the police chief]. He said, yes he would be there. That's the sort of bloke he is, he's very thorough and he gets stuck in at the deep end. So he scotched everything else, I got there and met him, introduced him to John Buckley, and John Buckley said: 'How do I know he's here to stay? You might just wheel him on for the report and then you'd take him off again in a couple of weeks' time.' So I said you'll have to believe me, John, because I've actually made him a director of the company that's running the licence. He's got a special responsibility. He said, you really have? I said yes, so we had to make him [Melvin] feel like he was well and truly on board, and he wasn't being brought in just to perch there for the event and then fly away again.

That one stroke was what persuaded John that I really meant it. He wrote it down in his notes. Then they went off and had a little meeting on their own [Melvin and John] and they got on really well and John believed that Melvin could actually do what was missing.

Melvin getting involved obviously involved the Mean Fiddler, because he was a Mean Fiddler director as well, so the eventual deal was actually with the Mean Fiddler Music Group. They get a percentage of the net profit after all the charities have been paid. It eventually goes up to a 40 per cent share, but it's not a lot of money really, considering what Melvin has done for the event. Without all this it wouldn't have happened again. It was saved by that meeting in Portishead that morning. If he'd been there at two o'clock it would have been too late.

After that the police simply couldn't recommend refusal at the licensing board meeting because they knew that Melvin had a really good record. Legally it would have been very difficult, with all that weight of experience he brought and all that I'm doing down here.

Looking back I think that the deal with Melvin was one of the best things I've ever done for the festival. But we're still putting the show on, let there be no doubt about that, we're still doing all that we've ever done, and more, and Melvin's doing all the stuff that I was quite frankly not very good at.

Emily Eavis

Melvin was closer to the festival's history than many people knew, he really understood how the festival worked. All the elements were there, in a lot of ways he was the natural person to come on board.

There was a tiny moment of doubt. I remember it really raining in London, and I was sheltering outside a café when I answered the phone to Michael. I was shouting: 'You want to do WHAT?' and he was pressing me: What did I seriously think? He knew in his heart of hearts, I'm sure, that he wanted the festival to continue; but he wanted to challenge the people around him, closest to him, to be really sure. And I did think, perhaps for a microsecond, maybe it had had its day, maybe this is the end. But then suddenly it was: 'No! We've got to do it. We've got to carry on. We've got to do this!' The kickback was quite instant.

Yes, you might be aware of what people will think about you, but the fact is it didn't matter how it was going to be perceived. The simple truth is we wanted to continue with Glastonbury Festival and we still wanted to put it on for as many years as possible. That huge audience who make it, too, they all think it's theirs, they feel they know it so well; yes they may say 'oh no', they may voice strong opinions. But this was the only way. No, it'll never be the same, but it can't ever be the same – every year it changes. We're still about the same things we started with, all that spirit is still there. How we organise the nuts and bolts doesn't affect the integrity of the event…that's the important thing.

Mark Cann

That was a marathon meeting. The police gave us a very tough time, especially about our ability to make it work. There were growing concerns about the management of crowds outdoors, new standards were being developed all the time, and we had to show that we were matching those. The main issue was could we keep the people out, would the fence work, and would the strategy also work to persuade people to not even turn up in the area? It was all very well if the fence worked, but the thought of thousands of people marauding outside the fence, and into the village, were very real problems. We said no, we believe if we get the message across, and if the tickets were sold out relatively quickly and there were no tickets available, you would not get people without a ticket.

Melvin Benn

Both before and after the deal there was a lot of single-direction mud slinging. A lot of people at Glastonbury were horrified that Michael was willing to do a deal with the devil, the devil being myself/Mean Fiddler. But the real issue was that the superfence wasn't the answer in itself. The strategy was absolutely all about management. I've said before that Glastonbury was made up of the classic cell structure, which was fantastic, but without a reasonable amount of central policy and co-ordination it would just go off at tangents. My biggest task was to break down the monstrous distrust between all of those cell leaders and myself.

When I and Harmony, who was the Licence Co-ordinator, arrived at Worthy Farm we became the public face of Mean Fiddler. It was a constant battle, and incredibly difficult for her, resulting in the worst weekend of my life during the 2002 festival. Harmony is the most extraordinarily bright person, but the reality was that she was put through hell having to represent me. She was there in the trenches.

Looking back there were really only one or two people I got support from. Arabella [Churchill] grilled me more than anybody. She took it upon herself to sit me down and find out what my intentions for the festival were. She flipped out a couple of times. I have a huge admiration for Arabella and I'd like to think I changed her mind. Later there were one or two words of comfort from her.

Arabella Churchill

I was very upset at the time. My worry was about the Mean Fiddler reputation, which wasn't good. The festival had proved, probably more through luck than management, to have an incredibly good name, and I just thought it gross that they should take us over. I actually resigned, and I was badgered by everybody, including Michael and Melvin and Mark Cann, and in the end I gave in. And I'm glad I did stay, because it hasn't been as bad as I expected.

I still hate the fact that we're allied with the Mean Fiddler, and that they're making money out of it, but at least they're easier to work with than I thought. It is organised now in a way where you can get hold of people when you want to, and get an answer, which you couldn't before. I think it's good that some of Michael's responsibilities have been removed. The systems all work much better now, so from that point of view it's been very good.

The fact that large amounts go to charity from the festival is very important. If Glastonbury became truly commercial I think a lot of us wouldn't want to do it any more. It's still a very special thing.

•••

2003
BIGGER AND BETTER

Tickets sold out in a record two days, but the festival finally proved it could keep out gatecrashers, stop the neighbouring village of Pilton being invaded and still retain a spirit of surprise and adventure. Crime levels plummeted. Punters were successfully encouraged not to 'piss away the festival' by peeing in hedges and streams. The Lost Vagueness area at the top of the site, now with a mass of offbeat entertainment, was jammed to bursting point. The Archers radio serial recorded episodes in an organic burger stall. Rain clouds only scattered a few showers on the final day. Michael Eavis told the traditional Sunday morning press conference that it was the first year he didn't get a single call in the middle of the night from an irate local. Headline acts included Radiohead, REM, The Manic Street Preachers, Jimmy Cliff, The Flaming Lips, The Polyphonic Spree, Moby, Primal Scream, Julian Cope, John Cale, The Streets, Moloko, Buena Vista Social Club. Attendance 112,000. Tickets: £105 including programme.

Bands in 2003: Alison Moyet, Arthur Brown, Asian Dub Foundation, Beth Orton, Buena Vista Social Club, Damien Rice, Dave Gahan, David Gray, De La Soul, Death in Vegas, Echo and the Bunnymen, Fatboy Slim, Feeder, Goldfrapp, Grandaddy, Idlewild, Inspiral Carpets, Jimmy Cliff, John Cale, Julian Cope, Junior Senior, Kanda Bongo Man, Linda Lewis, Los Lobos, Love with Arthur Lee, Macy

Gray, Moby, Mogwai, Moloko, Morcheeba, Primal Scream, Radiohead, REM, Richard Thompson, Suede, Super Furry Animals, Supergrass, The Burn, The Chemical Brothers, The Coral, The Damned, The Darkness, The Doves, The Flaming Lips, The Gathering, The Kings of Leon, The Manic Street Preachers, The Polyphonic Spree, The Rapture, The Raveonettes, The Streets, The Sugababes, The Waterboys, Tricky, Turin Brakes.

Har Mar Superstar, entertainer, introducing Electric Six on the Other Stage

Something to do before you die…lose your mind at Glastonbury. Drop all your conventions and personal taboos and let your freak flag fly. Why? Because everyone else is, and we're loving it. I entered the summer of 2003 a festival hater, and ate my words when I found myself sitting with Bez and completely understanding the Stone Circle. Yikes! Your experience will be heightened if you get to watch Primal Scream from the stage at sunset while you're peaking. Love will be in the air.

Nik Turner

There was a time when the All Stars played about ten gigs at Glastonbury in one festival. We played on nearly every stage because I was friendly with people who were organising them. We played on the Jazz Stage, the Green Futures Stage, we played in the Croissant-Neuf, other stages in the green area that Sam Hermitage was running. Sometimes it was all night gigs, somebody had a PA set up and we just ended up playing all night, with loads of different people playing with us.

Emily Eavis

This year I was back on the main stage for the second time, though nobody I know even saw me. We did a 'Don't pee in the stream' message from the Pyramid, just before Jimmy Cliff went on. It was completely out of the blue. I'd been backstage and got collared and then we were tumbling onstage, a bit of a whirlwind of excitement; but no bonfires or anything in the distance, none of that stuff, because it was blazing hot and in the middle of the afternoon. It was me and Sarah Cox and Norman [Cook]. I don't know if it was me or Norman who was most nervous, I think we were hiding behind each other, but Sarah was brilliant, she got it organised. She carried it off. Sometimes the best things at Glastonbury aren't even noticed.

Moby, musician, New York

I think it is different, in a way that things happen here that maybe don't happen anywhere else. I was ambushed by a guy dressed as a fairy, a complete outfit. He was trying to get on stage with me, asking and asking. I had to deal with him on my own; I don't know how he got there. I was giving him these lame excuses, like 'health and safety has already been worked out' and 'I'm really sorry, we can't have anyone else on stage…' And still no-one really knew where he appeared from.

It was so good to be back at Glastonbury again, and I felt I was really privileged to headline on the Sunday. I'd decided to play some of my older stuff, my more upbeat stuff, to get a party thing going. It's such a great atmosphere, a great experience. It's really spiritual, a gathering of the people together. I had a really great time the first time I played here, and I wasn't even headlining on the main stage, it was really quite a small crowd compared to what I'm used to now. To be asked to come back, and headlining, I felt really honoured. I never thought I'd ever do anything as big, playing in front of so many people.

Hannah Rossmorris, events organiser, London

The festival has a really special place in my heart. I'd just love to be able to say I've been going since I was seven, or I was conceived there, that would be brilliant, but I actually only went twice before I started working there – and one of those times I jumped the fence. I was a student and I was skint. I'd arranged to meet various people, and didn't meet up with anyone at all.

We started courting Glastonbury as soon as I set up a company to do with sponsorship with my boyfriend, but we were coming at it from a very commercial point of view – looking back we were probably kind of ruthless, trying to introduce them to sponsors. We were going: 'Let's get Lynx down to wash people's hair,' which must have scared them a bit. And my boyfriend knew the festival backwards, lived in Somerset, he'd been brought up with it, and his dad [Mark Fisher] was old Labour, a local MP. His dad was the first cabinet minister ever to get up on the Pyramid with Michael Eavis, which I think was in 1997.

I had this image of it being the ultimate festival and I just knew I really wanted to work there; there was some sort of inner turmoil going on with me. I thought the set-up was ace, just fucking brilliant, there was the hanging baskets outside the office in Glastonbury town, Dick Vernon with his broad Edinburgh accent, Hilary [White] making cups of tea, and all these hippie-type people wandering around. Hilary's great, she's been there as long as anybody, running the town office, and she was the one who helped me understand how the whole thing worked, how much it is all based on community. Later I went to stay with her for a while.

It felt very comfortable and very homely, it just reminded me of family in a way, like meeting a kindly relative. It took two years to work out what was the right approach – Glastonbury helped reawaken all my anti-capitalist feelings. I absolutely turned my back on sponsorship. Walked away. I also had to get out of London at that time. The politics of the festival was the big draw – I just thought that was the way they should be run; the community feeling, the spirit. And Somerset as well, it's that whole fat, plump, rosy-cheeked, cider-drinking thing, those wonderful characters you meet as soon as you get off the bus.

My persistence paid off eventually and I turned up to work one day with nowhere to stay. After two weeks I was in a thatched cottage, which was lovely, and meeting Ben Eavis (Michael's nephew), who was also working in Markets that year, probably kept me sane. It's an amazing, magical place, it was almost like the Holy Grail for me, it kind of saved me, it was all I wanted to do. My expectations of the festival were entirely fulfilled, and for my parents, who'd brought me up in Youth CND, it was the best thing I'd ever done. My mother thinks it's the dog's bollocks, she loves it. In her wild past, she was John Lennon's PA in London for two years. For the festival she came down to work as a steward.

Glastonbury will always exert that pull on me, wherever I work in future. The whole thing's made to happen because it's all grown from what's been put together by hedonists, and expanded organically from there. In that sense it's about the truest reflection of culture, young culture, youth culture, going… Over the last ten years it's become this huge youth movement, a rite of passage, something you have to go to. Things happen there and then get accepted as the norm everywhere else – and they always happen because they're good things to do, not just to sell tickets.

Sheelagh Allen

It gets pretty busy as the festival get closer. When I first started I'd be working till one or two in the morning. Now the hours are shorter but I still coordinate all the festival tickets – and the VAT. This year I lost my voice when there was a mix-up about issuing the tickets for camper vans. The phones didn't stop ringing. There's no switchboard operator here, so we take them all, and everybody thinks their enquiry is unique. Our phone numbers are in the book, which is what Michael wants. He wants people to know we're accessible.

I work at the farmhouse right through the festival, although I do get to watch the bands I really want to see. This year it was REM. And while it's happening we get a few lost stars wandering in – Evan Dando from The Lemonheads I can remember asking how to get backstage, and this year Thom Yorke, who was camping in a tipi near here, closely followed by Michael Stipe. He's an absolute hero of mine.

After the festival we get lovely personal letters and cards saying thank you. I'd say it runs into three figures each year. And just a few complaints. And there are always people who stay behind on the site afterwards that we have to deal with. We made the mistake of having somebody in the house one year, and we couldn't get rid of her. All the year round we get people turning up asking to look at the site. I think often they can't quite comprehend that for the rest of the time it's a working farm. Michael never turns anybody away, just tells them to shut the gates behind them.

It's massive, massive fun. I consider myself to be very lucky. Michael's the most amazing person to work for – and infuriating because he's got so many balls up in the air, and he expects somebody to be there in case he drops one. But I'm happy to be that person.

Arabella Churchill

A few people have bombed in the Cabaret tent, especially women. Less so now, but it used to be a really chauvinistic drongo crowd. Cabaret used to be dreadful for really low-quality heckling. We've really noticed the difference the last two years now that they've gone.

We try not to have too many male stand-up comics, and balance them out with variety acts. But this year (2003) Bill Bailey had a stunning audience, it was absolutely squashed in the cabaret marquee, and ten deep outside, and he was hysterically funny. And he played for free, just some tickets for his friends.

Bill Bailey, comedian

I'm from Keynsham, which is a little place between Bath and Bristol, where the Co-op closes at nine. At Glastonbury, in the Comedy Tent, I had five thousand people in front of me with their arms up, and I had a brief flash of myself as some pagan, God-like figure. It was blood-boilingly, heart-stoppingly, soul-drenchingly exhilarating. I didn't like it at all.

Ralph Oswick

The team actually thought that this year was going to be more tame, but they said it was brilliant. They were able to do some of their best performances because the audience was so receptive. They were at one of the busy market crossroads dressed as pimps trying to sell their leopard-skin suited 'razzled old tart' girlfriends, and people were actually coming up and trying to buy them.

We also performed our *Children of the Damned* scenario. Based on *The Midwich Cuckoos*, the team dress as identical, blond-haired school children in sensible macs, mouthing such threatening phrases as 'We hate you' or 'We know where you live', while staring implacably through weird blank contact lenses. We've never dared to do it at Glastonbury before, for fear of reprisals from someone on a bad trip!

I think our most popular one is the 'kissing coppers' – a couple dressed in absolutely authentic police uniforms who then start holding hands and kissing. It seemed to fit perfectly at Glastonbury when the police were trying to say they had a new soft image and were there to support the thing. I think the first time they weren't just kissing, they were giving away dope. And sometimes they do more than hold hands, they get down to it, a bit of really heavy petting. It's really rude if you see a policeman and a policewoman seriously snogging. One of the first times they were taken off to a caravan by the real police and asked what the pair of them thought the hell they were doing. So Dan said, 'it's my job, I get paid to do it', but they still told them both to take their jackets off, which didn't really make much difference.

There's always an edge at Glastonbury because it's a bit freaky, so these days we send the younger actors because they all want to go. We don't have to push them. And it's bound to be better than some shopping centre in Basingstoke. There's a different kind of edge to the festival now because you still get nutters, but more amusing nutters.

Arabella Churchill

The parades have been one of the most exciting things – we've done three or four – although they need a lot of organisation. I've had to have meetings with all the health and safety people and so on at six o'clock in the morning, which was the only time we'd have any time to do it.

La Companie Malabar from France produced one of the best outside performances. The show itself was very, very good but the thing that really hit it was the parade. They had this huge white ghost-like boat, and the boat was pulled by fantastic leaping and bouncing stilt dancers, everybody dressed in white. We paraded it in a great arc from

Glebeland through the circus field, out through East Holts into the jazz field and then up the main drag and round by Goose Hall and back again. It completely stopped the crowd in the jazz field, everybody just turned round and stared in amazement, and then it went over one of the bridges with a half inch clearance. It was wonderful.

Roy Gurvitz, founder

In 2003 we had an outdoor stage, the Wango Riley stage in fact, and an extra field called the Lost Field, with more music. We had a freak show with automotrons, robotic freaks, very much in the style of the Victorian freak show but with mechanical things made out of mutilated Barbie dolls and teddy bears. Then there was the tree sculpture – that was Joe Rush from the Mutoid Waste Company – made out of exhausts and other car scrap. So there was the chapel and in front of it was the village green and there were the spreading branches of this metallic tree. With the strange mechanical horses we had – a 16-foot-high Trojan horse which you can drive around and a wicker horse covered in latex with lights inside – it was all very dreamy. It was beautiful at night when they were all lit up.

At midnight on Saturday there were tens of thousands of people in and around the Lost area. On Sunday night I had to take a decision to close it for safety reasons. The truth is that out of the 120,000 or so people who come to the festival about 50,000 stay up all night, and they want to be entertained. Now they all want to come to Lost Vagueness.

Mark Ellen, music journalist

The idea that you can go to a psychedelic ballroom with a strange little ska band at two in the morning, dancing underneath these plastic chandeliers, with a Fifties teashop next door, and girls dressed up in Fifties clothes, was almost like a bizarre dream. And the fact that this was all happening in the middle of what is effectively a piece of agricultural land that was going to be populated by cows the following week. It arrives and then it's gone again. That's the magical side.

Michael Eavis

A lot of the people who used to get in somehow we now have working for us. We employ a lot of hippies in the crews, and they're very artistic and creative, and then with the Lost Vagueness thing, it used to be Roy on the outside, with the convoy, and now we've got Roy on the inside with the convoy. I think the police were a bit worried about me saying that, but I don't think they quite understood what I was driving at. But that was my aim, to bring them inside so they weren't going round the outside causing mayhem. And they're very good at it. All the broadsheet posh papers think it's absolutely brilliant. They love it to bits. It wasn't really designed for those people but they do seem to like it.

Jeff Dexter

I was back again in 2003 and it was much easier, even though there were so many 'areas' I was losing count. I couldn't believe how far I'd walked at the end of it. Avalon was the place where I hooked up with really old friends from way back, which wasn't really a surprise, nor was the fact that a lot of them were still doing ecstasy.

Gavin Ellis, environmental charity worker, London

This year and last year have been the best years. I don't agree that it's lost its edge but it's a safer, whiter, more middle-class audience.

Radiohead did an absolutely fantastic gig in 2003, with three encores. The second encore was 'Karma Police', with the refrain at the end, 'for a minute there I lost myself'. The rest of the band went off and Thom Yorke stayed on stage, and just sang acapella, over and over again, 'for a minute there I lost myself', and then he walked off and it went quiet. And me and the people I was with started singing it back, and within about 10 or 15 seconds it had spread through the whole crowd, which was tens of thousands of people. And the whole crowd was singing it back, 'for a minute there I lost myself', until he came on stage again to sing the final song. It was completely spontaneous, a wonderful moment.

Rachel Austin

This year I was back as a punter in a big group of 30 people, camping up at Hitchin Hill ground, which was always our favourite, although the cider bus is the place to bump into all the people we went to school with. We'd taken time off work, really prepared for it, and the return was a terrific sense of excitement, of really looking forward to something. I'd been a small part of it for five years, and I'd been quite proud of that. Now I wanted to do and see everything. And see everyone, instead of skulking about in disguise, in case anyone was going to ask me to sort something!

We had our flashing Moonwalk bras that we did a charity walk in, and I was offered £120 for mine. I was quite impressed with that. But really the best fun is out in the front where all the action is, with your mates, having a wicked time. Then after that there was one of Michael's greatest ever inventions – those painted concrete seats. It's great to have somewhere to sit and just watch it all happen.

Jonathan Tait, student, Somerset

There were about 20 of us altogether, camping, hanging around, strolling around. We were at the field at the top of the Glade, the other side of the railway. Eight or nine to begin with, then a few more and a few more.

I went last year for the first time when I was 16, this year we wanted to be there for the whole duration. We got there on Wednesday and stayed right through until the Monday lunchtime. I don't mind paying, it's got to be worth saving up for. One of my mates worked on security, but I wouldn't do that, having to turn up for shifts, then being out of sync for the rest of the time. It's better to pay and enjoy yourself. I've never been with my parents, though after we got back this year they're talking about going some time, maybe next year. I wouldn't mind, it's not like we would go together.

Some of my friends had already been with their parents when they were younger, or like my mate's older brother, Joe, had been with other people's families, but they got to walk around on their own and they know their way around now.

We strolled around quite a bit, that's what you do. The Glade, the Stone Circle, other people's tents. You're there to witness the atmosphere, so that's what you do…just walking around. Or chilling. We've got a word for it. 'Monging'. We did see a couple of bands, like REM, when we were passing, but that's not what it's all about really. It's the atmosphere, the tradition is more important than the bands.

We did make a point of seeing Bill Bailey though. We knew when he was on, and there was nothing else happening at the same time. I've seen a couple of videos and he's got some classic jokes. He did them, he was brilliant. Later on I was joking, saying to someone, you missed the best thing at Glastonbury, ever. Bill Bailey. In the Comedy Tent. Winding them up a bit.

I wouldn't enjoy Reading in comparison to Pilton. You might get the bands, but you don't get the atmosphere, and I've been to all the skate fests and it's the same, nothing like as good as Glastonbury.

Jack Fieldhouse, beekeeper and artist, Somerset

I have a large brown envelope with 'Glastonbury Sketches' printed on the front. They came about because I was invited along to be an artist at the festival, to paint a picture. I was taken there, given lunch and released, and for the next seven hours I wandered about looking for interesting people and situations. A series of sketches encapsulating the essence of the festival – the plan was vague and the 'instances' had to direct my thinking.

One generously pregnant lady was relaxed – sunbathing in a G string and brassiere; the unhatched within was enjoying the Glastonbury sun unglazed. The Wing and a Prayer ladies had a tent full of exotic garments inviting customers to dress up. The centrepiece was to be a huge paper dove, its wings vibrating in the breeze. It fretted, it had only hours to live. The Beaker people were making a bread oven from mud – brought in sacks. Water sprinkling was the bit where the children of the oven makers decided to slither onto the scene and within seconds they were earth-coloured. Mud, gauze and flowers, so many outfits were prompted by nature.

In fact so much of the festival was earth oriented, and rightly so. Two moderately healthy Chinese were playing a board game called Carrom and I was told it was a healthy game, refreshingly different from our Western drug wizardry. Decidedly not on the Internet!

There were flags fluttering and huge wooden mushrooms springing up from odd corners, and everywhere refreshment bars. Here was a festival of joy, and the people I met were delightful; the whole scene wonderfully organised, subtly policed and with an army of dedicated people who collected rubbish and ensured your smooth passage through the toilets. A triumph for the owner of the land, Michael Eavis, and his daughter Emily.

My picture is now complete. It involves friendship, a belief in fairies, wearing outlandish clothes (or little or no clothes at all), and all in an atmosphere of pure enjoyment. A few mad days of fantasy…with the hope that the whole shebang will happen again next year.

Melvin Benn

There were two or three hiccups, and then one significant breakage, and the breakage was at a meeting to patch up the hiccups. I'd thought about the hostility and threats of violence and decided these were really just acts of loyalty to Michael. Clearly everyone could see I'd performed the will of Mendip and Avon and Somerset and excluded Michael from every significant decision – the threats were as a result of that, which perhaps showed great loyalty to Michael and the festival, but I felt they weren't adequately dealt with at the time.

We had a meeting at Browns on Kew Green – Michael and Bob St Barbe [festival site manager] and Workers Beer. I cycled up there, sat down to what was meant to be an enjoyable bit of lunch, and I lost it, I'm afraid. I wasn't physically violent but I had to say what I had to say. Bob was deeply upset, deeply offended – and rightly so. But I felt I'd expressed what I needed to express. There's no way we would have got to this point had that not happened.

I have no idea how we subsequently patched it up, although we did. But we did overcome it, long before the 2003 festival, and certainly during. There's still an issue – but to a much lesser extent. An issue in a sense that it doesn't anger me, but it disappoints me, and there's a fairly significant difference.

Bill Mackay, Mendip District Councillor

As events turned out, by unanimous acclaim, the 2003 festival was the most successful that there has ever been – successful in terms of the event itself and successful in terms of avoiding any of the problems that had appeared previously. There were still minor issues, still some thefts and one or two cases of assault, but compared to the past they were minor. So I think we can probably say that we now have a professional organisation running it and therefore most people feel far more confident.

Janet Convery, former CND worker

This year it did change dramatically in terms of the people who came, probably just because of the nature of the way the tickets were sold. The kids were more polite, to start with, and I was quite happy to let my 11-year-old son go off on his own. He knows the site so well now, because he's been going since he was seven months, but I don't think I would have let him do that at some of the earlier festivals.

Mathew Bucknall, art student, Bridgwater

It was my first time and I didn't even bother to find my way around. I just went for a walk to see what people were doing and that was a whole day and a whole night really. Sitting in the Stone Circle, people-watching, seeing the lights and the haze and the atmosphere floating up from the valley. I was slightly worried that I might get lost and confused and end up on the bad side of town, like 'don't cross the tracks!' But everywhere you went, you felt welcome, there was always something to experience. And you don't ever feel you've done everything – you don't go back to your tent and fall into sleep feeling contented. You fight the tiredness, you take something, you just carry on.

Zak Sauven, 11, London

I've been to Glastonbury since I was zero. I used to spend time playing in the kids field, I would spend whole days there. Then when I was about nine, I would go off other places with my friends, round the stalls. Then I'd climb the trees right at the very top (of the site), that's the field where I think Michael Eavis's wife is buried.

This year I bought this T-shirt that says Skint, and my friend Manu bought one that says Macshit, like instead of Macdonalds.

There's a lot less people since they put up the new fence. It's still crowded, but before you just couldn't walk, you had to stop all the time. Before, if you didn't get to music early you just wouldn't be able to watch it because there were so many people crowded round the stage. When I went and saw Fatboy Slim, we couldn't really see him, it was so crowded we had to stand outside the tent.

I saw some people fighting once, I've seen a lot of people offering people drugs and stuff, but I've never really been scared. I've been to other music festivals, but this is probably the best.

Green Fields

Liz Eliot

If you walk around the Green Fields it's not a hugely well-known fact that above the old railway line we don't allow anything other than solar or wind or other alternative sources of power. So you can have your batteries which are charged up, but it must be by wind or solar. The Croissant-Neuf stage is completely lit, and a powerful sound system, by a solar power tracking system. There are no noisy generators up there, so it's quiet.

With the crafts field, the whole idea is that you can be in control of your own life, and therefore anything that you need to know how to do you can learn there. So we have weaving, stonemasons, bodging on home-made lathes, brass foundries, smithying, slate cutting, hurdle making – all those basic things, and other more artistic, creative things like glass blowing, pottery, bread making in clay ovens. The whole ethos is about sharing skills and learning how to do it yourself.

The healing field is the spiritual side to the festival, where you can come and really check your whole self out. We're great believers in the four elements, which the whole planet is made up from, and they're represented in the healing field through fire, being the energy of things like tai chi, the water zone, which is for saunas and massage type places, the air zone, which is for sounds, and the earth, which is for pagany, ritualistic type things, the tree spirits. But that also includes volley ball, so it's not all esoteric. There's also divination, card reading, tarot, palmistry, crystals. Loads of very skilful people, all professionals, now come every year from all over the country.

That whole culture has now spun off into the mainstream, although it all originated from that new age alternative green ideology. People's understanding of those things has increased hugely, and it's definitely been helped by things like the Green Fields.

We've had fire shows every year recently – the first year she came, Serena de la Hey, a Somerset artist, made five willow sculptures running up the hill. There were giant fireworks inside them so that as they were lit the next one went off, so the whole lot turned into a wonderful flowing movement. We've had elemental dragons, representing earth, fire, water and air. The water dragon is still there, lurking in the undergrowth. Ray Brooks, who built them, also made the angel sculpture on the edge of King's Meadow, at the entrance to a memorial garden for Jean [Eavis]. And the tipis are there as an example of alternative lifestyles. This year the Rainbow Circle came back and did Norse mythological ceremonies; most of them are lived in by people who live in tipis the whole year. There were getting on for 100 last year, 25 for people to hire.

We used to have lots of weird people writing in saying things like they wanted to bury themselves for the weekend of the festival and just have their heads appearing over the top. Or else they wanted to be pinned out naked on the ground in some ritualistic fashion. All these crazy people. The burial did happen, in fact, although not for the whole weekend.

Then there was the group who came originally with the idea of showing how ancient people would have lived underground in a dugout, with little steps going down and earth seats along the side, with the turf put back on top, and a little stove at the far end. The next time they decided to make it into the smallest stage at Glastonbury. So they had their little dugout as normal, but they put a beam across the top and a piano on it. So you could sit round on the little seats underground and look up at the piano. That was so delightful, it's amazing the talent that's around. Loads of musicians came by and played all sorts of music. I like all that stuff that's slightly off the wall and not meant to be there.

Tony Cordy, Children's Field organiser

I've twisted Michael's arm each year to get more there for the kids. We've always had the big colourful helter-skelter, and the climbing castle, but the main thing is for all the kids to take home something they've made. That's really important. So they see a show, learn a skill and just interact. There's a huge range of amazing people there. It's paradise for kids.

The number of people coming with kids has definitely increased. I've got people on my crew who came to the first festival when they were fifteen or sixteen, dancing around in front of the main stage tripped out on acid. Now they're coming with their grandchildren.

Litter Picking

Robert Kearle

I'm Pilton born and bred and I've been involved in the festival for 20 years, ever since Michael bought the farm next door, Cockmill Farm. I came over at weekends to milk Michael's cows and got more involved. You get roped in.

I'm in charge of litter now. There's about 1,000 people involved during the festival – from Cleanaway, the rubbish collection company, the Network Recycling crew and 600 volunteers who do it in exchange for their tickets. It's all split up into zones based around the various performance areas; the volunteers pick the rubbish and the dustbin carts go out and pick up the bags. We had 7,000 oil drums this year and 110 skips. And I manage it all, when I'm not eating pizza.

The biggest year was 2000, when there were all those people in here who weren't supposed to be. There was about 1,000 tonnes of rubbish that year, that was the record. Now we're down to about 650–680 tonnes, including over 60 tonnes which was recycled – a third increase on the year before. Every punter gets a green and a black bag now as they come through the gate – green for recycling – and we had 1,000 can banks for the first time in 2003. The security take glass bottles off people at the gate, so that and all the bars produces quite a lot.

The litter pickers get paid the minimum wage and three meals a day at Goose Hall. Most of them think it's amazing that they're getting good-quality healthy food, especially the foreign students, who can't believe it. About half of them are travellers, the other half are students. There was a guy who came from the roughest part of Moss Side, Manchester, he'd come down for the festival and stayed on afterwards. We gave him a special job on a tractor, and I found him laughing one day, so I asked him why. He said, it's beautiful sunshine, I'm working, you're actually paying me and feeding me and I get to be here in this beautiful place instead of Manchester, where people get shot every day. He couldn't believe that anyone would moan about the work.

Doctor in the House

Chris Howes

In 1981 we ran the first aid centre from some rooms in the farmhouse. As the event got bigger, we had to expand. The original team was about 50, now it's over 500, including doctors, nurses and ambulance crews. There's a network of medical centres, first aid points, teams at all the main stages and mobile paramedics. And in terms of a major incident, we're about as ready for it as we could be.

When we started it was mostly minor cuts and bruises and stings, asthma attacks, diabetics who'd gone astray. Now there's a bigger range, including unpleasant burns from fires and gas cylinders. We treat up to 3,000 people over the weekend. Several babies were born at the festival in the early days, sometimes in tents. I remember one baby born in a gypsy caravan on a cold, misty morning in a silence that was almost unreal. A couple of girls have turned up at the medical centre not knowing they were pregnant at all, and a few moments later they had had a baby. We'd probably take them to hospital now.

Drugs have never been as large a cause of problems as people think. Alcohol's always been the most frequent. We watched it shift from acid and amphetamines in the Eighties, people with bad trips, convinced that the world was chasing them, through the cocktails involving ecstasy in the early 1990s, with people with quite severe paranoid reactions, and then the heavier stuff, like heroin. But even in the busiest years, you could count the number of serious heroin overdoses on one hand. We've had a psychiatric team on hand almost from the start.

A really important thing is having medical teams in front of the main stages. We now have almost a mini intensive care unit in a tent there ready to deal with people who've got crushed or distressed. It's not unusual for kids to be brought over the barrier unconscious, but the vast majority come round very quickly. Sometimes it's because they've stayed there all day waiting for their favourite band, got dehydrated, very hyped up, and when the band does come on they promptly keel over. There have been one or two we've very nearly lost and then all the resources we've put there have justified themselves.

One vivid memory is of a teenage girl, crushed in the Pyramid stage crowd, who suffered a cardiac arrest and needed full resuscitation in the pit as The Cure played a few feet above our heads. The helicopter to take her away landed precisely in a hole cleared in the crowd. The next day her boyfriend brought along some chocolates for the security guy who spotted her in distress.

When people were jumping the fence we got more fractured ankles and wrists, cuts to hands, and before the police came on site we got more injuries from incidents related to drug dealing. One year we got a lot of cases from 'steaming' – people running through the camp sites stealing things as they go. After the new fence went up in 2002 we noticed a dramatic drop all round, especially in the number of people injured in assaults.

There are occasional emergencies, like the people with gunshot wounds when there was a shooting, or someone who went mad with a pair of scissors and cut himself up really badly. He lost a lot of blood. But our priority is to stabilise them and get them shipped out to hospital as soon as possible. The helicopter can land on the village playing fields if we need it.

We have lots of highly qualified people involved now. The fellow who runs the main stage medical unit, for instance, is a senior consultant from the Radcliffe Hospital in Oxford. They don't get paid – just a ticket – but they love the festival and the work.

Fiona Hance, Oxfam

Oxfam has received over £900,000 from the festival since 1993. The good thing about the Glastonbury money is that Michael has always agreed that it goes into our general fund, which means we have reserves sitting there ready to spend when an emergency happens. That's incredibly useful for us.

Keep it safe

Stephen Abrahall

Some things we hand out on the stalls are more contentious than others. Local opponents used to say that if condoms were readily available then free sex was being encouraged and it proved their point about irresponsibility. But I think people now see distribution of condoms as just being a very sensible practice. We seem to have condoms by the bucketload these days – we had about 50,000 this year, much to the amusement of my neighbours, because they all got delivered to my house – and lots of sun cream and maps and plastic bags to give away. Plastic bags are brilliant, because they can easily be turned into macs if it rains.

Another contentious point has been the needle exchange. The fact that it's available on site is very low key but you can't just ignore the problem. If people are going to inject themselves you're not going to stop them by not having needles available – they'll just use dirty ones.

I think my best moment was at one of the early festivals, when Michael's face wasn't so well known, and I used to wear a similar beard, and a pair of lads came up, about 18 or 19, and said, 'How can we make sure this festival continues – would these two £5 notes help?' I found that truly moving because people do come along having had their lives transformed.

Marriage is a regular request. We've had handfasting ceremonies conducted by a local druid – it's a Celtic thing where you make a commitment to each other for a year, a bit like an engagement. So it's something that either party can break off, and they're meant to return a year later and confirm their commitment. And we've had birds being fed afterbirth from people who've given birth at the festival. All human life is there in a way.

Death always saddens me, especially hearing of somebody who's died in a tent. That has happened a few times in the history of the festival. But in a way you could put a positive spin on it and think what a nice place to die, when you're enjoying yourself at the peak of your happiness.

Births, Marriages and Deaths

Sally Powell, Somerset, gave birth to Kaly in 1987

My baby wasn't due until the first week in July, but I told my midwife I was going to the festival and she said she could arrange emergency cover if I needed it. We run trampolines in the Children's Field so we always go a bit early. On the Monday before the festival I was walking back from visiting some friends when I noticed the first signs of labour. By early the next morning I was in our caravan, it had progressed quite a lot, we called the midwife and amazingly they arrived just before the baby was born. It was a wonderful birth, it still makes me smile.

It soon got round that this had happened and the security guys who worked on the second stage picked a whole bunch of hedgerow flowers and brought them up. My partner managed to get completely drunk, running round the site telling everybody 'it's a girl', and about nine o'clock that evening he collapsed in a heap.

She's called Kaly Sapphire Daisy. The second name came from the security guys, the third one is like a gypsy tradition, because she came up in a field. Kaly wasn't certain at first, but she's now very proud of it, to have been born at the biggest party in Europe. Every year now when we arrive we go and sit under the tree where she was born and stand there for a few moments. It's like our homage to mother earth, giving our respects and love for such an easy passage.

Steve Chatters, cyto-geneticist, London

It was pretty much a spur of the moment thing, really. I was wandering through the Lost Vagueness area with my girlfriend Claire on the Friday about midnight, full of the joys of the festival, when we saw a big sign saying 'Get Married Here'. We just looked at each other and said, that'd be a bit of a laugh.

We were actually staying with some friends in a nearby farmhouse, a guy there turned out to be a wedding dress designer by chance, so he went through a bag of old clothes from the attic and produced this amazing Fifties-style dress, with a gauze flared skirt, a veil, jewels sewn on and even a home-made tiara. I borrowed someone's jacket and we were ready to go.

On the Sunday I bought a wedding ring for £8 from a stall on the way up, although when we got there the ceremony was delayed because the 'priest' was a bit the worse for wear. There were a few other couples waiting outside this makeshift chapel to tie the knot at the same time. Then we went inside to find a kinky nun and this sweating preacher, who proceeded to whip up the crowd with a sort of mid-American rant and a few twisted versions of the Book of Common Prayer. It was all very anarchic, he pronounced us all men and wives and then all the couples got into this boxing ring and started dancing to 'Groove Is in the Heart' by Dee-lite.

When we came outside into the sunshine someone had even produced a wedding cake and some fizzy wine. It was all a bit of a whirlwind. People said to me afterwards, so you're going to have to get married properly now. I said no, this was it. For me, having been to Glastonbury for so many years, to get married on the site was just magic.

Robert Kearle

Lots of people ask for their ashes to be scattered. We get a few every year. It tends to be people who used to come regularly. There's a couple of people who've tragically died here, or just afterwards or going home. There's been a few people from bands, where a member of the band or their family has died. I've had to plant quite a few oak trees in people's memory. It's almost a green burial site now – we could get a good premium if we charged!

It's certainly something that will probably grow as the people who've been involved get older and older. I know quite a lot of people who have definitely said they want to be buried here or have their ashes scattered here when they die – great stalwarts of the festival.

The Power of Glastonbury

Martin Elborne

The Darkness, who opened the festival in 2003, were a good example of a band springing into the limelight through Glastonbury. I booked them really late, very low fee, but knew they were a really good live band. That first slot on the Friday is very important, I either like to start with something wacky – the year before it was the Japanese orchestra – or something that will work…and The Darkness really worked. You just had to look at what happened afterwards.

Shows that make a big impact have to be on the Pyramid. There is definitely a 'Glastonbury factor' there, but it's not something I can quantify. The record companies do, I know they do. I know agents and record companies want their artists to be there. I've quite often seen 'appearance at Glastonbury Festival' in the tour schedule of someone or other long before I've even heard anything, or thought about booking them. And sometimes it's just them wanting it to happen.

It's still a tradition after each festival for us to have arguments about the credits. With Michael, with Emily…big, friendly arguments about whose idea it was to have what. Michael, I will say, and have said before, is extremely good at talent spotting, and he's very loyal. The extraordinary success of Lost Vagueness is down to him, getting back something of the original festival, and that really taking off. And Emily's enthusiasm is very valuable, especially as the age difference means I am maybe less keen on going out to small clubs every night of the week. Kings of Leon, in 2003, who were one of hers, were probably the hottest new act at the festival and went on to add a Glastonbury factor, and they weren't even on the Pyramid or on TV.

With David Gray, it seemed like one great appearance and then suddenly he'd sold a million albums; it helped the breakthrough although he'd been building for a while. And Damien Rice in 2003 didn't even play at the festival – he was filmed by the BBC backstage. And his album sales went up, what, a thousand per cent the next week. That's the power of TV again, but really it's a combination – the festival, the size of it, the history, TV coverage.

But we're independent in what we book, we have to be. The TV people take what they get. And we get what we do, working within our limits, as I've explained before. When you look at it, Reading and the 'V' festivals can afford a million for a headlining act, we can't. But play a great set at 'V' and it means nothing. And there are bands, Radiohead for instance, who would never play Reading or 'V', even though they are effectively 'losing' a great deal of money by doing us instead.

We ask The Rolling Stones every time, but effectively it comes down to money. And U2, who have never played, are always really polite, but that hasn't happened either. Of the other British bands, we've probably had them all. Paul McCartney contacted me personally, which I appreciated. We do want people at Glastonbury who actually want to be here.

I do have my regrets about Neil Young though. I must have booked Neil Young about four times, but he's always pulled out. Bob Dylan we had to have, and we succeeded in 1998. There is the sense of 'let's try to get some of these great ones before they die', it's become an ongoing mission. Probably more of a mission as the years go on, as we're chasing age and ill health. The American artists are mostly very keen to come over, Andy Williams I know is keen. But in terms of legends, John Prine playing, to me, would be very important, and I just hope we will be able to get him.

The Future

Arabella Churchill

Michael's quite difficult to work with sometimes. You send faxes and get no response for yonks. I have to keep all my troops happy and pat heads constantly, and I think we area organisers could all do with a bit more head patting from Michael – we all do a lot of work.

Why do I continue to do it? Because I love the festival. Even though it's far more commercial now than it was, it is still extremely pure. People do it for good and right reasons – for charity and to make it all as wonderful as possible for our punters. It's also working with the same people each year – people you like, respect, admire and who you know are good at their job. I love that weekend in June before the festival when all my stage managers and different crews arrive and we all look at each other and say, 'Here we go again – let's make it even better!'

Of course Michael's the only person who could do it. He keeps the village happy, he keeps a grip on the finances and he's the figurehead, he's become incredibly famous, it's extraordinary, this Methodist farmer … And I suppose he's hoping that Emily will take it on.

Nik Turner

My problem is that I think festivals like Glastonbury are too big, it's hard work getting from one place to another, it takes a long time, it's dusty, I just get a bit bored with traipsing around for miles carrying a musical instrument.

I have rather mixed feelings about the Mean Fiddler involvement. I've met Vince Power and got on really well with him. But the way it's been done at Glastonbury I think is pretty horrible. That great big fence round the place is really quite fascist.

But love it or hate it, for better or for worse, for all its faults, it's a much more acceptable festival than any other commercial event. I've played at Reading, and you get people in the front row pissing in these great beer containers and throwing them at the people on stage. That's not about entertainment, it's about damaged people who've got a lot of baggage they're carrying around. Those sort of festivals are crap, they're totally soulless … So Glastonbury does have quite a lot going for it, and while Michael Eavis is involved it will probably still have those principles. I shudder to think what it would be like if Michael stopped.

Melvin Benn

Do Michael and I share a vision about the future of Glastonbury? At the end of the day it's Michael's show, there aren't really any ifs or buts about that. The greater challenge is actually Michael handing over to Emily. That's the greatest challenge, that's where the next significant phase of this festival will be played out. The relationship and the understanding between us is sufficiently strong and secure to work. But he has to do that next bit, it's not appropriate for me to talk to Emily, to have that conversation, although I would give her a very significant amount of support. There is an assumption that she may want to do it – or let it fade away when Michael wants it. Glastonbury has no God-given right to survive.

Michael Eavis

How long will I carry on for? I've got no idea really. I once said I'd retire when I was 70, but I hate to tell you I was 68 three days ago. I've got no plans to stop, but of course there's a lot of people coming on behind, a lot of people in training. Things are looking really well at the moment and the kids are all keen.

There are five elements to make it work, I suppose. There's the farm, there's me and there's the workers who actually make it happen. After that come the performers and the people who buy the tickets. And the most important element is the willingness of the people who actually run the areas to put in all that time and all that energy, all that skill and all that devotion to making it happen, and to doing it well. They're the most important part of the equation. As long as people keep liking it, still wanting to get involved with the work, still wanting to come and watch, still wanting to play, I'll carry on.

Emily Eavis

It's only really in the last year that I've been thinking about my role; everyone else has made decisions before we have as a family. The festival I still see as a year-by-year thing, and who knows what will happen after the next one? With Michael being such an integral figure, it's near impossible to get anywhere near those shoes. That's why I am cagey. The festival works because of the history and maybe nobody can do it quite like him. But there are a lot of bubbling issues, things will definitely unfold...

Meanwhile I work in London, in partnership with two friends, highlighting issues for Oxfam and Shelter, among others. I'm really trying to prove to myself at the moment that I can work off my own back, establishing myself in my own right is important. Everything I do now is because of Glastonbury; it's happened using almost the same principles: involving charities with the music industry, getting people to lead campaigns, as we did with Fair Trade. I think really what it is, it's getting people excited about charity again. It can make a difference, as it has before with Live Aid, with people of my generation involved in music and charity.

I have a sense that young people have strong feelings about politics again. They are getting more fired up, look at the reaction against Bush and Blair, and trying to channel that energy into things and make it positive. I did an Oxfam anti-war concert, three weeks before the war, and it was the hardest thing I've ever done; I had to touch on those fighting back instincts I've seen with my parents for my whole life. That never giving up attitude is really important. Coming up with the most ridiculous thing and saying: 'Why not?' People laugh at new ideas, and that makes me more determined than anything else. I pull in all the battle instincts I've inherited. I must have emailed Michael Moore's people a hundred times to get help for the concert; and then on the day of the gig there was this Fedex parcel for me, a brilliant video message from him that I didn't even know was coming. Elton John sent one too.

We asked Michael Moore to do Glastonbury as well, it's just his type of event. It would be great to have him speak. Politics are very importantly tied into the festival. I can still hear E.P. Thompson when he made that address from the main stage – 'these young people I see in front of me now…' It was a defining moment. He was saying, really, it's all down to us. It's you who are going to change things. Because in one view there's Glastonbury, the fantasy land, Hedonism Central. But the other view is it's also possessed by this amazing positivity; there's so many people together, and you really have this sense of 'we can change the world'. Whenever do you have that many people, in one space, that have such similar feelings and politics? No other place in the world has that.

•••

2004

Millions of calls jammed phone and internet lines as a stampede of enthusiasm saw nearly all 115,000 festival tickets sold within 24 hours. Undiluted disappointment registered among those who failed, despite sitting up all night at their computer screens. Many still managed to attend by working their pass as stewards, litter pickers or even first-time performers – over 2,000 entries to the first Glastonbury Unsigned Bands Competition were eventually whittled down to a lucky six who performed over the weekend.

Festival novelties included a 70-foot-high sculpture celebrating the global struggle for social justice, the full orchestra and chorus from English National Opera's Ride of the Valkyries (Sunday morning on the Pyramid Stage) and Paul McCartney, the first Beatle ever to appear, whose finale version of 'Hey Jude' was mostly sung by the audience. An estimated 80,000 watched the England football team drop out of Euro 2004, then got back to the serious business of partying. As always, it was anarchic sideshows – from boxing nuns to the Laundromat of Love to a giant parading praying mantis – that gave spice to an event now covered by media outlets from Iceland to Indonesia.

Starting sunny, the weekend still produced enough rain and mud for boots and tailored plastic bags to be compulsory fashion items. In the festival's 'war on waste', recycling efforts, encouraged by a squad of Green Police, saw 110 tonnes of food leftovers turned into organic compost. Afterwards, whilst enthusing that 'it just keeps getting better', Michael Eavis announced that he would take a year off in 2006. Headline acts included Muse, Morrissey, Oasis, Scissor Sisters, Franz Ferdinand, Sister Sledge, Chemical Brothers, Snow Patrol, Suzanne Vega, Toots and Maytals, Bonnie Raitt and Joss Stone. Attendance: 112,500. Tickets: £112 including programme.

Last Words

Michael Eavis

How do I decide which bands to book? I've got Martin Elborne, who does a lot of the booking, and Emily, who also helps now. But the last word on the headliners rests with me. I do consult quite a bit, but the trouble is that I'm not really a very good listener, so I ask questions but I don't listen to the answers. So I decide in the end.

Usually they phone in now for the headlining slots, I don't have to chase them. Just two days after the last festival I had a call from one of the bands saying they were interested in a headlining slot on the Pyramid stage for the next one. So I said, I am interested, but since I've got three or four headliners lined up, or I'm thinking of asking, I'll have to wait to decide.

We've had a lot of them already before, we don't usually do any repeat headliners, although we did with REM and we have done with Radiohead. And I would do that again, certainly for Radiohead.

We don't pay them much because they understand it's a privilege to play. They enjoy playing, they love the event and they're keen on everything it stands for. They charge me about 10 per cent of the normal fee, which is a lot less. And they'll do that partly because they enjoy doing it but also because they know I'm not running off with all the money. I'm not making a fortune, and the bands actually believe that.

Which bands have I enjoyed most? I don't like to pick favourites or slag anybody off. There were The Smiths in 1984. And then there've been Van Morrison gigs which have been absolutely brilliant. Radiohead are obviously the very best, and then there's Oasis, who always pull it off, and even Robbie Williams. When he played five or six years ago, that was his first really successful gig. When he came off the stage I remember him saying, 'I done it! I done it!' and he knew at that point that he was a star. We provided him with the venue and the audience and the sense of occasion that made it work for him. And he did a great job for us as well.

All the way through there've been different kinds of music and whoever they are or wherever they've played there have been a hell of a lot of experiences. Some people have been unforgettable.

Emily Eavis

There's one great thing about the festival…once everyone arrives there's nothing you can do. You've been planning all year, there's incredible excitement – then suddenly it's all down to 100,000 or more people to make it work, which is an amazing feeling.

I think Michael started to give my opinion some real credit when I started to know about bands. It was being in the kitchen again, because that's the nerve centre of the farm, of everything. People would be in meetings and you'd just make a cup of tea and just chip in [laughs]…and I got a few things right.

I do remember playing 'Yellow' by Coldplay, right at the start, before it had really happened. And it is so hard to sit Michael down; he'll think of something and then run off. His brain goes off on tangents, here there and everywhere, he's got so many things going on. I said: 'Just sit there for five minutes' and turned it up really loud. And after about one of those minutes, he said: 'Oh yes, I like this, but hang on, there's something I've got to do…' I had to grab him and pull him back, and play it three times.

But there's always been lots of talk about bands around the kitchen table with me, my brother, Dad. When I was 14, for me it was Jesus Jones, Ozric Tentacles, Ned's Atomic Dustbin, all very different to now, but I had really strong opinions. And I was so into The Stone Roses; it was such a heartbreaking thing when they couldn't do it. The band debates still continue round the table, every day there's one idea or another to this day. The one thing we don't debate, though, is the future of the festival. But there might be a bit of a battle for the credit. That was mine! Like Oasis…getting them when we did was probably quite a joint one. And Robbie Williams.

Now I get really excited about new bands, and as I'm in London I'm seeing maybe two or three new bands every week, so getting them on is great. We'll have a three-way discussion: Michael and Martin

Elborne, who books the bands and has been involved at Glastonbury for so long, he's a good link to the industry. We have a great dynamic and work really well together. It's the contrast as well; I'll say: 'Let's get Outkast opposite Paul McCartney,' try something different. We put bands and artists in positions where they can change the direction of their career. We can say: 'OK, you can go in there' and show it worked out in the past with Coldplay, with Robbie Williams, with Oasis, and with so many others.

I didn't appreciate how hard it was to get bands to do anything until I was working in the industry myself, it really put it in perspective. Because people are extremely loyal to Glastonbury. I'd grown up with that and almost become complacent about it, perhaps not realising how the industry actually works outside of the festival. We can count on goodwill which isn't just financial, it extends to doing things to help; supporting our messages and talking to the media. Chris Martin wrote a letter to the council supporting the licence application, and Norman Cook was very supportive with the BBC.

People are incredibly positive about us. But the festival is so much bigger than us, me and my dad. Glastonbury is its own force, and it is down to all the people who make it work. Individual people are important but ultimately it is everybody coming together which actually makes it work. When bands are loyal to the festival, it's an amazing thing, but it's not down to one, it's everybody who makes it what it is.

Then again, my dad would be the first person to say it was all a fluke – it was just a matter of following his instincts. He has a deep down feeling there is a sense of destiny about it…that it can't fail.

John Peel, Radio 1 DJ

I came to the very first one in 1970 with Marc Bolan, who was on the bill, and since then I've been for the last ten years working for Radio 1. I just like pottering about and looking at all the little stalls and stuff, all the weird things going on – and of course hearing the odd good bit of music. These days that's rarely on the main stage though. The last main stage band I really enjoyed was Pulp. I prefer the World Stage and the odd little bands you see on the bandstand and in various tea tents.

My best memory is of talking to Lonnie Donegan backstage after his gig. I have a picture of him sitting next to me, pissing himself laughing over something I've said. I have no idea what it was, but I'm enormously proud of it. My worst memory is just the mud really. It was such a ghastly experience, and there were two years of it. You couldn't do anything, go anywhere or sit down anywhere.

Sheila never wanted to come to Glastonbury, so it was my time on my own with the children. When they were younger we camped – well, me in a trailer and William, Danda, Tom and Flossie and some of their mates in tents around me. Trailers were always wobbly, if I got up in the night to have a piss the caravan would tip and I'd find myself flung against the far side of the wall. There was a hose running down from the sink through the floor, and once when I got up in the night to relieve myself – I'm afraid to say I headed for the sink – for some reason the kids had removed the hose, and I ended up standing in the trailer at four in the morning in a puddle of my own piss...

The best bands at Glastonbury? Pulp headlining the main stage, Tom Jones, Tony Bennett, Kando Bongo Man this year, Oasis on the small stage before they were famous (when I was compering it), Dreadzone, The Orb, Hole, and lots of bands not on the main stage I can't remember the names of.

Mark Ellen

I've always worked for music magazines – *NME, Q, Select, Mojo*, I'm now the editor of *The Word*, and I've always been very responsive to festivals because I think that any mass gathering of young people has got to be taken seriously. Originally, reporting festivals was just about going from one band performance to another, writing 200 words on each, but I remember we sent down Chris Heath from *Q* in about 1987 and he wrote this brilliant piece about the whole experience. He came back with an image of people covered in woad, people baking bread, the whole children's area, something that appeared to have been transposed from another world. I think I was just envious of people going down and having this blinding experience for three or four days in this beautiful place with a view of Glastonbury Tor, not some horrible windswept disused aerodrome but a tented city with its own hospitals and cinemas and restaurants and even its own suburbs. And the idea that all this was just constructed for three days and then taken down again was extraordinary. So I started going myself from the early 1990s.

On a mainstream level I think Glastonbury is immensely influential on the image you have of bands who appear there. You can go and see people well down the bill, like Ozric Tentacles or whatever, and your image is of a group playing to maybe 45,000 people, and on the television that spectacle is even more enlarged. Even the lowly bands come over as globe-conquering.

And on the other side, the underground side, I can think of two particular experiences. I was driving down by myself and I picked up various hitch-hikers. One of them was clearly having a really bad experience on mushrooms or something, grimacing horribly in the back seat. I asked them who they were going to see and they said they didn't even know who was on. Without sounding too pretentious that was a major cultural moment for me because as a kid I'd always been to rock festivals to see certain bands. So the idea that people were going to Glastonbury and had no idea what was on any bill on any stage was an extraordinary revelation.

It turned out in fact they were going to see Spiral Tribe, which was a fascinating new area of dance music that was coming out of the cracks between the industry, out of the Castlemorton free festival and so on. There were no record companies putting out Spiral Tribe's music, but they had their own generator and they were charging round the countryside causing all manner of havoc, setting up their truck and then having their own festival in the corner of Glastonbury.

The other one was a rave called Sugar Lump in 1992. This was one of those rare moments where you went into something and actually thought you were seeing a very clear vision of the future. I remember it vividly, they'd been building this venue all day long, they drove this army truck inside, built a scaffold round the hood and put two decks on it. Compared with my memory of the Seventies festivals, where you had Atomic Rooster playing 45-minute keyboard solos, this was something else. Now we're used to walking into a tent and finding two and half thousand people with rave whistles punching the air. But at that time, this machine-generated sound was completely new. And although a lot of people now claim to have been there, I was, standing at the back with a couple of mates in our terrible old jerseys and gumboots and clutching our cans of warm Fosters. We simply couldn't believe how thrilling, and slightly scary, it was.

In fact Michael should take the credit because he allowed Sugar Lump to take place, even though the authorities were trying to close down all the raves that were happening after 12 o'clock. I think he'd seen it happening up in the woods and was equally thrilled. That was such an amazing decision on his part.

Big moments? I remember Radiohead in 1997 was one of the most extraordinary performances I've ever seen in my life, and anyone who was there would tell you that. And, although I'm not really an admirer, to see Robbie Williams play on this appallingly drizzly weekend was quite something, especially because at the precise moment that he walked on stage a shaft of sunlight, like something out of a William Blake illustration, opened up and poured down. He went away with a spring in his step. But I remember best seeing bands like The Egg from Bristol, who I watched in the Bread and Roses beer tent in 1994, playing in their full-on jump suits.

The classic Glastonbury experience was probably when John Peel said to me, 'I know this little drinker, let's go', and when we got there it was right in the heart of the tented city. He said you just had to knock in this strange masonic way on this wooden door. So he knocked, a curtain went back, a face appeared, and Peel made a series of evidently recognised hand gestures. When we got inside there was a little shebeen going on, a private drinking club with only about six or seven people, bales of straw to sit on and a ceiling with massive wooden beams, and a series of optics in the corner. We sat there till about three o'clock in the morning telling stories about odd festival moments and being waited on by this fantastic earth mother figure wandering around offering us fine old whisky.

Caitlin Moran, music journalist, *The Times*

I've come nearly every year since 1992, mostly writing for *The Times*, although I think the first year it was for the *Mail*, who wanted a lot of stuff about how everybody was walking around naked taking drugs. I remember having to file my copy from Michael Eavis's house, because my modem had broken, and being so worried that he'd walk in and hear all this 'sensationalism' going out.

I remember PJ Harvey being incredible in 1995, looking slightly anorexic in a pink stretched cat-suit, and thinking that every woman in the audience would want to go off and form a band. That was one of the heaviest rock sets I've ever seen any band perform. She was rocking four or five times harder than the Stones, who I also saw around the same time.

Then the same year it was Pulp, who came in at the last moment to replace The Stone Roses, because John Squire had broken his collar bone. That is definitely one of the gigs that has stayed in my mind. They premiered 'Sorted For Es and Whizz', and they'd got about three songs into the set and everybody just turned around and said, we will remember this. They were so awesome, so much energy, it absolutely made their career. You just got the feeling that that was all that Jarvis Cocker had ever wanted, to stand in a field and have 70,000 people worshipping him.

The really big media interest in Glastonbury seemed to start in about 1997. Before that it was more about bands performing and influencing other musicians. But after that, with the big Britpop publicity explosion and 'it' girls turning up and a lot of it on telly, it really started to influence record sales. With both Travis and Coldplay, the first years they played, the music industry poured out to see them en masse from the backstage area because they had the feeling that they were both going to be massive. And they were. This year people were saying four or five weeks beforehand that Radiohead were going to do the gig of the year.

The media's attitude towards Glastonbury has changed completely. It's a huge story in *The Times* now. Glastonbury's become a British institution, people are proud of it, almost like an annual soap opera – what's the big story, who's going to go crazy this year? But the irony is that although it's often portrayed as youth culture in action, kids taking their tops off, the people really getting into it are the much older freaks dressed as ballerinas or pretending to be dogs. That's what makes it such a surprise.

Within the music business itself it's seen as everybody's holiday, like a weekend in the country, the only fresh air that anybody in Soho sees all year. It's a chance to see the bands they'd never get to watch otherwise. But on the other hand when the line-up's released a lot of people in the business often say, it's rubbish this year, there's nothing worth watching. For me those are the good years because I don't have to stick around the main stages waiting to see what Primal Scream are going to do. I can go off and find something ridiculous, like the weird bloke we found this year dressed as a caterpillar playing this really odd mixture of Celtic soul and zydeco up in the Green Fields at three o'clock in the morning. He was magical but he wouldn't tell us his name.

Vojtech Lindaur, journalist, *Rock and Pop*, Prague

Every year now I drive in my Toyota Corolla all the way from the Czech Republic, that's 1,712 kilometres, with four of us, three journalists and a photographer, crammed in the car. For most Czech people, of course, Glastonbury is very expensive – the price of one ticket is nearly half the average monthly wage.

Why do I enjoy the festival so much? To start with it was my 'super antibiotic', to heal my soul from the communism I had to live in for 33 years. Then in 1992 I really noticed the free spirit of the festival and I was amazed at the large variety of the music. It was opening doors and giving me new hope – as a little bit tired middle-aged rock journalist – for the excitement of modern music. And the spirit of Glastonbury, the spirit of common sharing and feeling, makes me feel part of the bunch of people there. This is the only festival that is more important in itself over those three days than any star on the stage. Has the festival changed since I first came? Yes, I think it's more and more open for creative minds every year. And new generations love it, that's great. I don't mind the higher and higher fence, it's not an iron curtain – and I know very well what I'm talking about.

Tom Rowlands, The Chemical Brothers

What I love about Glastonbury is wandering around and seeing all the strange people. It's a wonderful place, a great feeling. There's something about it that makes it peculiarly British – it attracts a real cross-section, from the cool London music types in their flashy Winnebagos to the people who bunk over the fence – except they don't any more! – and sleep in a hedge. People go for different reasons: to see the comedy, or the bands, or just to hang out. There are new-ager parents with their children having an enlightening weekend by the acoustic world music tent; the odd scrumpy lout.

I love the fact that Glastonbury is not at all organised, so you'll see loads of impromptu sound systems that have just sprung up out of nowhere, or you'll see someone just dancing in front of a hot-dog stand or a rug seller – did I say rug seller? Outside the main festival area, you come across even more eccentric people.

One year, a friend of ours, Nick, who's a drummer in a band, wandered out to a stone circle where a group of new-agers were sitting around in a kind of trance, beating out polyrhythmic patterns on their drums. He asked if he could join in, and they lent him a drum. After a while, they stopped for a break, and Nick asked them, 'Do you recognise this?', and started beating out the theme tune of Only Fools and Horses. There was a look of complete incomprehension on everyone's faces – they'd obviously not been out into mainstream society for a while. Then, suddenly, a girl recognised it; she'd remembered it from the days before she'd opted out. They'd clearly been out of the loop for quite some time.

Glastonbury…there's something different about it; it's not sanitised. It's not like the bands are just wheeled on and wheeled off again. A good festival is not just about buying in a load of acts that you think will go together. With Glastonbury, you get the feeling that there are minds at work behind it. There's an idea, and the line-up is always very varied, which is down to the organiser, Michael Eavis. It's diverse. I love the fact that Glastonbury just keeps going all night, whereas at some festivals the site has to be cleared at midnight. And the location is brilliant…so beautiful, with all those rolling hills – it feels wilder, somehow. We've played lots of festivals, and the nearest in spirit is the Fuji Festival in Japan – the scale of it, the different kinds of bands playing, and the amazing location. I think it matters where you are, that you're outside your normal existence, and living a different experience for a few days. It's the perfect festival, a thrill to play, and always a good crowd.

George McKay, chair, Counter Culture Studies, University of Central Lancashire

One of the things I kept seeing was young men getting out of cars in the traffic jam and pissing in the hedges, and I guess if you're a local and you live round here one of the things you see is an invasion of people, and lots of them want to jump out and piss in the hedges. It reminds me of that C.J. Stone story in his book, *The Last of the Hippies*, about one of Michael Eavis's neighbours, insisting that he would only support his application for a licence if Eavis himself went round and picked all the human turds out of the hedge on his land, where people, festival-goers, had dumped them.

At the gate the security guy, who looked like a regional stereotype of a scally in deepest Somerset, did tell me that I wouldn't believe some of the things people tried to bring in. Not just bottles and knives but one guy had a chainsaw he thought might be useful. He looked in my boot and told me about the knife fight there'd been on Wednesday night outside a beer tent. It's amazing that security guys always have stories you don't hear anywhere else; I'm sure a lot of rumours start with them.

It's a ginormous event, fields, fields, fields, different gates, the lot, it's huge…all the things I was thinking about Glastonbury before I got there – communing with nature, celebrating the solstice, the Arthurian past thing, all that – it's like forget it, man. It's just a massive, massive, mass event. But it's casual too, in the middle of a field, under the sky. And when you look around you see all the fantastic silhouetted trees, you look up in the sky and there's a gorgeous moon, and all around on both sides is the valley, stretching into the distance. And it's also full of contradictions. At one edge of the site you see a big white cross, erected by one of Eavis's neighbours a few years ago, a dedicated Christian, who sees this event as a kind of pagan or satanic thing. So at one side there's this big white cross and at the other side of the site, the valley, there's a stone circle, a fake henge, erected by some of the people at the festival probably only a few years ago. So you've got Christianity at one end and paganism at the other, they're competing narratives underlining it all.

Jane Cady, Street, Somerset

I came to the very first one with my friend Di. We were living in Bristol then and we used to drive around in her van with a plume of pampas grass on the aerial. The only tape we had was Love's *Forever Changes*, and we always sang along to the trumpet parts. Seeing Arthur Lee and Love this year really brought back memories. We'd dyed our hair blue – because you couldn't get hold of proper dyes we had to use old ladies' blue rinse. I think that's why we had our photos taken for the local paper, the *Bristol Evening Post*, which duly printed them with the names we gave the photographer – Janis Joplin and Grace Slick. It was brilliant.

We came again in 1971, when they had the Pyramid. That was fantastic. It was free food, free dope, everyone was into peace and love and having a wonderful time. In fact I lost my job at George's bookshop in Bristol because I took time off for the festival. Then in 1979, when money first raised its ugly head, and you had to buy tickets, it just didn't seem right. There weren't tickets in fact, just paper stickers which you stuck on your jumper.

I've been to nearly every one since then, usually involved in the crew in some way, although the details tend to merge. Has it changed? The early ones were completely different to what it is now. I'm not happy about all the corporate sponsorship and the people who are just there to make money. It's grown out of all proportion to the people who put their hearts into it because they just enjoyed doing things. It's a shame to see it going that way. But having said that I still think it's an incredibly good deal, all the entertainment you get for your ticket, and fair play to Michael for keeping it going.

Michael Eavis

We're still producing 10,000 litres of milk every day. It's a real farm and our herdsmen won an award a few weeks ago for being the best herdsmen in the country. They're a husband and wife team and they're really good at it. We went off to the Royal Showground at Leamington Spa and they were presented with this great certificate saying that they're considered to be the best in the business. So we do run a proper farm, and we've got incredibly comfortable arrangements for the cows to live in when they're kept inside. They lie on thick mattresses. That's why we call the cow shed the 'mootel'.

But then right across the farm there's a water system and electric and roads, all ready for the festival. The roads are quite useful in winter for the slurry tankers, so a lot of that has a dual use. The cows have got more water troughs than they used to, for instance, so they haven't got to walk quite so far.

Just before the festival we mow all the grass, so all the grass comes in to the silage clamps and gets preserved for the following winter, when the cows come inside. After that, the farm looks like it's a newly laid carpet, as if it's all been rolled out. We call it the Cyril Lawn. Do you remember Cyril Lawn?! Then the people come and do their thing for the festival, and then they go away again. And hopefully it rains after the event, and it all sprouts up like rhubarb and the cows go out to grass again. So the farm fits into it really well.

The festival has done a lot in the village. People can actually go now and see the new village hall, the tithe barn, they can see what we're doing with the money. Master carpenter Peter McCurdy did a fantastic job for us. He says it's the best he has ever done. I would have to say this is one of the things I have done in my life for the village that I am most proud of. The barn belongs to the village and it is very satisfying to know that the festival has put something back into Pilton. The village is getting a lot out of it now. There are a lot of benefits, apart from their getting free tickets, which they have for a long time. And the fence has worked to such an extent that people don't even turn up and try to get over it any more. So you don't get those marauding tribes going round the village trying to get in. They've all gone away.

Kate Smith, part-time accountant, Bridgwater, Somerset
I never thought about going to Glastonbury until this year, not at all. I'm a mother of three, married for 18 years, born and brought up in Bridgwater, and I've worked in Boots for 12 years. The only concert I'd ever been to was Madonna at Wembley. None of my close friends went, but I met my friend Charlotte ten years ago, we used to call her Hippie Chick at antenatal classes, and we've stayed friends since. Her brother Jim has been to every Glastonbury.

Charlotte suggested we go so I said, OK, I'll see if I can get the time off. 'Just for the day?' I asked her. 'No, for the whole festival.' My friend I work with said, 'What d'you want to go there for? It's all hippies and stuff!' My husband said the same, but in the end he said, 'You do what you want.' So I decided to go, see what it's like.

We were like Thelma and Louise. We'd got away, this was our trip. I loved the excitement of being away, having a bit of freedom, a bit of a break, something new and different. When we got there it was total excitement – all caravans and tents. We got the little tag on our wrists. I couldn't get over the vastness of it all. My God! The miles we walked was incredible. I wanted to do everything, see everything, but Charlotte was the guide. By Friday night we were well into it. There's an unwinding you have to do from being with the children and home life, it's such a lovely feeling. I didn't see any problems, no trouble, I just thought it was wonderful.

One day we went for a wander, into a tent, and we heard Cajun music. A few people milling around, it was raining. We thought we'd sit there, have a fag, chill out, but the tent filled up, it was stomping – and it was a fantastic atmosphere. I was sat down trying to roll a joint, and this guy came by and said have a bit of that – I said oh that's nice, thank you, so I passed it on; I didn't know him from Adam, but we were all just dancing away, we didn't know who they were, it didn't matter, it was lovely. I wanted to stay in that tent for ages.

Nothing really juicy or exciting happened, it was just us enjoying ourselves, nice to be there, just to get away, escaping. The total atmosphere of it all. Your mindset changes completely. Our body clocks changed also. We'd go to sleep and not wake up until 11 at night – and then go out again. Even if you go on holiday you are still in the mould. Doing what's expected. But there's no expectations, you just do what you want.

I wasn't fussed about seeing lots of bands. We did see Macy Gray, but we didn't think, must see this or it'll be a waste of the ticket. We went up to the Sacred Space, to the stones, and stayed there all night and watched the sun come up. We bought some Pilton clothes, which we knew we could never wear in Bridgwater, trousers with flares. People were asking where I bought them, so I felt I must have arrived. The kids think I'm a total whacko anyway.

We went on the Thursday and didn't come back until the Monday morning. It was another world. We didn't want to come home, except for the children. I've still got my ticket in the drawer. I'd be really disappointed if I missed it again.

I think coming back from there I thought – no, this is me, I'm not so, well, dependable for others as I used to be. You can be yourself, it doesn't matter, people have to take you as you are. That's what it's given me, more confidence. I was there, that was me, Bridgwater could have been another world, it wouldn't have mattered.

I had to make a big decision at that time in my life, but I waited till after the festival. Now I know where I want to go. Glastonbury changed my life – helped me find what I wanted.

Michael Eavis

There are cynics around who invent all sorts of things about what we're supposed to be doing, but the bottom line is that most of the money is given away. We gave away about a million and a quarter this year, including £500,000 to the three main good causes – £200,000 each to Greenpeace and Oxfam and £100,000 to WaterAid – which is a lot more than we ever did before. Over and above that there's a very small profit. And what profit there is will be re-invested either in the village or in the farm or in the festival – upgrading the roads or the plumbing or the electrics. So anything that's left over goes into all that, it doesn't go into a Swiss bank account. That's really important for people to know.

In fact I've still got a million-pound overdraft on the farm. That's because every time I bought some more land for the festival, I had to borrow the money for it. So I haven't even paid off the farm borrowing yet. But having said that, I have a great life. I get a wage for running the festival – £60,000 a year – and the farm gets a rent to cope with the interest on the borrowing. Compared with other farmers I'm doing very nicely, thank you very much!

John 'Boogie' Tiberi, former Sex Pistols tour manager

Why haven't I been to Glastonbury before? I know I've got a photograph at home of Arabella Churchill sitting by a campfire. It was one of those solstice things, somewhere off the edge of the planet, maybe even Glastonbury. It's hazy, it was the early Seventies. Wiltshire first, those stones, then Somerset.

There were quite a lot of festivals going on, generally, but if you smoke a lot of dope you usually can't leave anywhere until it's too late to get there in time anyway. Travelling out of town? We just didn't do it normally. Arabella was kind of pretty, loads of energy, and she was hanging out with all these bearded weirdos like Sid Rawle, the original King of the Hippies. When I was managing The 101ers I persuaded Arabella to lend us a hundred quid to get a PA for a charity concert we were doing under the Westway. Joe Strummer remembered that, and once he got established going to Glastonbury in the 1990s he paid Arabella back, I think with interest. We should never have been sold the stuff anyway, as it was Led Zeppelin's rehearsal equipment.

Then there were all the intervening years where there were too many other things going on, and it was partly, what's CND got do with Somerset? But it's always been talked about as the place you go to connect to the spiritual part of the music business – and possibly the political side too. I was interested to see that, but the thing that got me back was Arthur Lee. That got me down there on a blazing hot Saturday, in time to see Jimmy Cliff.

And it seemed you had this kind of jukebox going on. You switched the selections through the decades, there were no barriers of age, it was like all the generation barriers had been removed. All the self-imposed blinkers. All I could think of was the music and the position it was in – not the variety, because you get different stuff at Womad or even the Festival Hall and that's not really different. But the political position: open, fresh, stimulating, innovative. And capturing lots of different imaginations. Kids could see The Damned as I saw them back then, in their heyday. As a cynical old bastard that affected me. The openness obviously affects the musicians as well, which is why they want to play there.

I camped, though I was very reluctant to do it, and crossed a few generation gaps myself. And I was struck by how I couldn't understand how it all works, such a huge event, how you couldn't see the infrastructure. There's obviously a lot of goodwill holding it together.

1999

25–27 June. Sun shone again but event overshadowed by death of Jean Eavis. Winged wicker sculpture ceremonially burned in her honour, minute's silence during festival

Entry: £82
Attendance: 100,000
Performers: Al Green, Blondie, Courtney Pine, Hole, Jurassic Five, Lonnie Donegan, Marianne Faithfull, REM, The Manic Street Preachers

2000

23–25 June. New pyramid stage built, baptised with Worthy Farm milk by Robert Plant. Second dance music area opened in the Glade. Major breach of perimeter fence led to overcrowding. £500,000 given to good causes

Entry: £87
Attendance: 100,000
Performers: Basement Jaxx, David Bowie, Macy Gray, Moby, Nitin Sawhney, Pet Shop Boys, Suzanne Vega, The Chemical Brothers, Travis, Willie Nelson

2001

No festival. Major rethink on security and organisation

2002

28–30 June. New management structure, £1 million fence and involvement of Mean Fiddler persuade local council to grant licence after lengthy negotiations. Few gatecrashers as festival-goers respond to message not to come without a ticket. New Leftfield marquee for political performers like Tony Benn. Lost Vagueness area enlarged. £1 million given to good causes

Entry: £97
Attendance: 100,000
Performers: Badly Drawn Boy, Coldplay, Fatboy Slim, Garbage, Isaac Hayes, Manu Chao, Richie Havens, Rod Stewart, Roger Waters, Stereophonics, The White Stripes

2003

27–29 June. Tickets sold out in 18 hours, but virtually no gatecrashers. Peaceful, benign atmosphere engulfs the 1,000 acre site. Stone erected in memory of Joe Strummer. Radio 4's The Archers records episodes. £1.25 million raised for good causes

Entry: £105
Attendance: 112,500
Performers: Buena Vista Social Club, Jimmy Cliff, John Cale, Julian Cope, Manic Street Preachers, Moby, Moloko, Primal Scream, Radiohead, REM, The Flaming Lips, The Polyphonic Spree, The Streets

2004

25–27 June. Tickets sold out in 24 hours
Entry: £112
Attendance: 112,500
Performers: Muse, Morrissey, Oasis, Scissor Sisters, Franz Ferdinand, Sister Sledge, Chemical Brothers, Snow Patrol, Suzanne Vega, Toots and the Maytals, Bonnie Raitt, Joss Stone

2005

24–26 June. Tickets sold out in three hours after 2006 announced as a 'fallow' year for Worthy Farm.
Entry: £125
Attendance: 112,500
Performers (booked):

Kylie Minogue, The White Stripes, Coldplay, The Killers, Brian Wilson, New Order, Elvis Costello, Razorlight, The Undertones, Nigel Kennedy, Tori Amos, Ian Brown, Rufus Wainwright, Roots Manuva

Note: Attendance figures are for weekend ticket sales only, and do not include children under 13, who get in free, performers, workers or, especially in the 1990s, large numbers of gatecrashers

SEMINAL SOUNDTRACKS

1970s

'Flying Saucers/Purple Spaceships Over Yatton', Stackridge
Local band, local song. As rough hewn as Bristol was back then

'It's All Over Now', The Valentinos
1958 hit played by compère Mad Mick at the first festival

'Feel Like I'm Fixin' To Die Rag', Al Stewart
Stewart, Keith Christmas, Ian Anderson cover Country Joe's iconic tune in 1970, having driven straight from the Troubadour

'Ride A White Swan', T Rex
Marc Bolan with John Peel in attendance, together at the beginning

'Fire', Arthur Brown
Showily reprised on Avalon in 2003, those at the Fayre said it was 'like entering the gates of Hell'

'Dark Star', Grateful Dead
The exclusive tapes shipped over for Glastonbury Fayre were the nearest the Dead ever got to playing the Festival

'Hole In My Shoe', Traffic
Classic hippy daze from the original Berkshire Downs' commune dwellers

'Space Oddity', David Bowie
Down to earth for the dawn chorus in 1971

'Solsbury Hill' Peter Gabriel
Like a favourite hymn, it has been played for ever afterwards

'Silver Machine', Hawkwind
First point of entry for the space cowboys

1980s

'Moondance' and 'Summertime In England', Van Morrison
Famously grumpy Belfast Cowboy, yet popular year after year. He played as long as Michael Eavis picked him up from his hotel

'Mushroom Valley', Roy Harper
Hymn from the fringes, ingenuously dedicated to Worthy Farm

'Boys Don't Cry' The Cure
High point from the days when you had to pack make-up along with a sleeping bag

'Oliver's Army', Elvis Costello
The Glastonbury audience appreciated the power of his lyrics and Costello enjoyed the open-air life on the farm

'Heaven Knows I'm Miserable Now', The Smiths
Did we love them? Yes we did. Probably the very first main stage sensation, they headlined in 1983

'Glastonbury Song' and 'Bang On The Ear', The Waterboys
Mike Scott adds his footnote to festival history, before returning as a solo artist in 2003

'Levi Stubbs' Tears', Billy Bragg
Everyone sang along to every word, especially 'When the world falls apart, Some things stay in place.'

'International Thief Thief', Fela Kuti
African sounds from the 1980s

'Sweet Gene Vincent', Ian Dury and the Blockheads
Still played and much missed

'Dead Skunk In The Middle of the Road', Loudon Wainwright III
Just one of a string of great American performances

'Avalon', Roxy Music
Wafting across the vale from the Main Stage, a sound-system favourite

'Shut 'Em Down', Gil Scott Heron
Vibrant American anti-nuke protest in 1987

1990s

'Sit Down', James
… and everybody did. Played first in 1990, the year they became huge

'Thrills, Pills And Bellyaches', Happy Mondays
1990 was their greatest show

'Release The Pressure', Leftfield
Experimental Sound Stage madness from 1992 – literally a riot

'Battle of the Beanfield', The Levellers
Topical jump up, also from 1992

'Little Fluffy Clouds', The Orb
From the market sound systems via Anjuna, Goa, to the main stage. Not to be confused with…

'Chime', Orbital
The apotheosis of electronica and climax of Ed Chemical's favourite Glastonbury gig of all time, on the Second Stage in 1994

'Grey Cell Green', Ned's Atomic Dustbin
Authentic UK grunge, almost made up for not getting The Stone Roses

'Roll With It', Oasis
The gallagher brothers' first appearance, also from the Second Stage in 1994

'Unfinished Sympathy', Massive Attack
Arguably the Bristol posse's finest hour, or twelve hours really, as they launch the Dance Tent

'Right Here Right Now', Fatboy Slim
Remix heaven

'White Ladder', David Gray
Were you one of only a couple of hundred who saw him the first time round?

'Common People', Pulp
A last-minute replacement triumph sees Jarvis Cocker sorted…somewhere in a field in Somerset

'Two Little Boys', Rolf Harris
The start of Rolf's ascent towards Glastonbury's most credible 'oldie' (an honour shared with Tony Bennett)

'Angels', Robbie Williams
From backstage boozefest to Main Stage triumph; a career-changing moment

'Changing of the Guard', Bob Dylan
Because he honoured us with his presence

'Decks, EFX and 909', Plastikman
From the killer set in 1998 that made everyone in the Dance Tent forget the mud and the slime

'C'mon Everbody', Dogstar
A pre-*Matrix* Keanu Reeves visits the farm with his garage band – and gets booed

2000s

'Cock/Ver10', The Aphex Twin
Rocking the Glade and turning it (and him)
into a crossover legend at last

'Life on Mars', David Bowie
Full moon, full bowl and full potential in
2000. His best live performance ever?

'No Surprises', Radiohead.
The quiet one that sets the mood.

'Clocks', Coldplay
From Pilton party to the main stage, we
couldn't have done without them

'Everybody Hurts', REM
Pick of the hits in 2003, it brought a tearful
Michael Stipe down into the crowd

'Morning Lemon', Chemical Brothers
Played on the main stage with the ultimate
light show in 2000, and reprised in the
Dance Tent; awesome

**'Glastonbury 2003 Live Mix', Scratch
Perverts**
Triple-deck funtime on a Dance tent
Sunday evening, with Mike 'The Streets'
Skinner following; a real happy hour

'I Can See Clearly', Jimmy Cliff
Brilliant greatest hits on the Pyramid from
the reggae legend

**'Yalla Song', Joe Strummer and the
Mescaleros**
In memory of those great camp fires

**'Give Praise', Siain Super Crew
featuring K'yai Marley**
Stunning Marseilles hip hop. Where do we
find them?

'Da Funk', Daft Punk
At the Dance tent and the Primal Scream
party

'Swastika Eyes', Primal Scream
From 2003's greatest hits set, stronger
than ever

'Molly Chambers' Kings of Leon
Stars of the New Tent in 2003, where the
word first got out about them

'Gay Bar', Electric Six
Introduced by Har Mar Superstar, and the
slogan of the year in 2003

INDEX

ACKNOWLEDGMENTS

The publishers would like to thank the following for the use of their pictures:
Brian Walker, Paul Misso, Crispin Aubrey, Alan Lodge, Clive Farndon, Martin Godwin, Jason Bryant, Angela Lubrano, Gapi Pape.

The publishers would like to thank the following for the use of their song lyrics:
Words and music by Bob Dylan. Reproduced by kind permission of Sony Music Publishing.
'The Whole Of The Moon'. Words and music by Michael Scott. Copyright © 1985 Dizzy Heights Music Publishing Ltd, Warner/Chappell Music Publishing Ltd, London W6 8BS. Lyrics reproduced by permission of IMP Ltd. All Rights Reserved.
Lyrics by Tim Booth from the song 'Sit Down', written and recorded by James.
'Millennium', Words and music by Robert Williams, John Barry, Leslie Bricusse and Guy Chambers © 1998. Reproduced by permission of EMI Virgin Music Ltd, London WC2H 0EA.

All reasonable efforts have been made to trace the relevant copyright holders of the images contained in this book. Any errors that may have occurred are inadvertent and anyone who for any reason has not been contacted is invited to write to the publishers so that a full acknowledgement can be made in future editions of this work.